Working with the Dying and Bereaved

D0223026

Working with the Dying and Bereaved

Systemic approaches to therapeutic work

Edited by

Pauline Sutcliffe
Guinevere Tufnell
and
Ursula Cornish

Routledge
New York

Selection and editorial matter © Pauline Sutcliffe, Guinevere Tufnell, and
Ursula Cornish 1998
Foreword © Marianne Walters 1998
Individual chapters (in order) © Froma Walsh, Monica McGoldrick,
Pauline Sutcliffe, Guinevere Tufnell, Ursula Cornish, K. Eia Asen,
Lawrence Levner, Alison Roper-Hall 1998

Published in 1998 by
ROUTLEDGE
29 West 35th Street
New York City, NY 10001

ISBN 0–415–91993–2 hardcover
ISBN 0–415–91994–0 paperback

Library of Congress Cataloging-in-Publication Data
Working with the dying and bereaved : systemic approaches to
therapeutic work / edited by Pauline Sutcliffe, Guinevere Tufnell, and
Ursula Cornish.
p.   cm.
Includes bibliographical references and index.
ISBN 0–415–91993–2 (hardcover : alk. paper). — ISBN 0–415–91994–0
(pbk. : alk. paper)
1. Grief therapy.   2. Bereavement—Psychological aspects.
I. Sutcliffe, Pauline.   II. Tufnell, Guinevere.   III. Cornish, Ursula.
RC455.4.L67W69 1998
155.9'37—dc21   97–24236
                                                              CIP

*To our partners, our families and to the bereaved
families who inspired us to write this book.*

Contents

Foreword

Marianne Walters

Getting it Right

At first you stay on task, you clutch at whatever task presents itself – stroke it, repeat it, focus on it. It is the ballast that keeps you from being overwhelmed by the sadness that threatens to engulf you. You cry, but avoid the gaze of others; contact can threaten the wall that protects you from succumbing to the grief. You can accept comfort, but it seems more important to be able to give it; to build on what strengths you feel are intact. It gives you a place to be... other than sad. It is a task. You search for what to do. Anything that will make you feel less helpless. You're not used to feeling helpless. Without a task you fear being swept up in the debilitating emotions of grief.

The stories and clinical vignettes in this book chronicle the multi-level processes of how a family copes with death and dying. The response to loss that is unexpected, sudden, devastating, or loss that is out of sync with normal developmental expectations; loss that does not compute; loss that you hadn't figured on; loss that is sudden, without context; loss that lacks reference.

In our current culture sudden death has become an everyday, almost banal occurrence. It's on the big screen, in the darkened theatre, where we experience a scary thrill as another 'bad' guy, or innocent dupe, gets blown away. It's on the small screen, in our own living room, where it becomes more personal, more immediate, but even more unreal; an obvious make believe viewed from the safe corner of our favorite couch. It's in the fear of being out alone at night; fear of the 'streets', of the random violence that has come to be a part of our daily lives.

Personal stories of loss and grief, violence and tragedy, are grist for the mills of popular culture: the talk shows, TV magazines, print journalism, the tabloids. We have become acutely aware of how grief is handled by strangers. And we are made privy to follow-up stories of personal devastation: a year later, five years later, ten years. Where are they now? How have they come to terms with the trauma? How has it shaped their lives? What are the lasting effects? It is this very sense of violence, loss and death as commonplace – another story on the 6 o'clock news, another item in the morning paper that has, in fact, made the particular, idiosyncratic experience, more complex.

A culture of bereavement exists. There are rules for being sad, and for how to express your sadness. There are rules for being a friend of the bereaved; a close or a distant family member; a colleague. Some of the rules are explicit in the form of 'etiquette' for engaging (or disengaging) with one who is facing the death of a loved one. Mental health experts advise 'be involved in their rituals' but don't say 'call if you need me' or 'it was for the best'. 'Avoid talking about your own problems or experiences with loss.' 'Don't offer advice; don't judge or assume things based on your own experience'; 'don't try to distract the person grieving.' In fact, most of the 'etiquette' is expressed in what not to do – particularly in the injunction not to intrude, not to 'do' unless asked (Peterson, 1996).

Loss and the process of mourning has been codified and objectified (for example, by such authors as Kübler-Ross and Vanick Volcan), so that now we pretty well know what to expect, and can identify the stage we are in at a given time. And as therapists we have an array of interventions to fit the stage of grief in which we encounter our client. What was once a private experience surrounded by personal, ethnic or religious rituals, is now a psychological event to be measured by criteria based on what is deemed to be functional or dysfunctional. Is she crying enough? Is he expressing his feelings? Is he in touch with his anger? Is she becoming too dependent? Too withdrawn? Is his recovery too fast? Too slow? Is she in denial? Is he unable to accept help?

Measuring a private, deeply personal experience through the yardstick of social, cultural and even psychological expectations can both exacerbate the feelings of powerlessness and loss and skew the 'natural' behaviours of the bereaved. The interaction of the bereaved with others becomes reactive not just to the event, or to each other, but to the internalised cultural injunctions for 'doing it right'.

The authors in this book are keenly aware of the social/cultural context within which people experience loss and grief. Each chapter deals not only with an individual and his or her relation to the death of a significant other, but with the process by which the event gets transmitted throughout the systems where both were engaged. The ripple effect of a traumatic experience is indeed complex, as these authors describe and explicate. Clearly, the effect of a death is not confined to a dyadic relationship – nor can the dyadic relationship be removed from the systems in which it is embedded – most particularly the family system. The experience of loss and grief is as interpersonal as any other experience. The process of grieving is organised not only around one's own connection or attachment to the person who died, but the relation of others to that person and, in turn, to ourselves.

In each chapter there is a micro-analysis of the systemic fallout of a traumatic death, particularly as that fallout is represented in family relationships. The way people matter to one another in the family is at once intensified and threatened by bereavement. For one family member the loss may not be so much of the person but of that which is familiar. For another, the loss may incur feelings of guilt; for another, of rejection and for another, unimagined sorrow. Each must experience their reactivity within the structures and patterns of the family system(s) in which they have resided.

Moving within and between the concentric circles of the socio/cultural, familial and individual, the inter- and intra-personal, is the challenge presented by the therapists who offer their thinking and their work to the reader. 'Doing it right' may mean having few expectations for how grief is experienced and how it is transmitted. And helping the bereaved may ultimately require the therapist to become an anthropologist, exploring and revealing the threads that weave the intricate patterns of our interpersonal interactions.

References

Peterson, J. (1996) Facing Death. *Washington Post,* 24 September, p. D5.
Kübler-Ross, E. (1969) *On Death and Dying.* New York: Macmillan.

Preface

This book grew primarily from our therapeutic work in different settings with families facing dying and bereavement, and from our later collaboration as a team attempting to develop a coherent systemic approach to our work with bereaved families. In the early days of our collaboration we had used what has become known as the 'structural' model (for example Minuchin, 1974; Minuchin and Fishman, 1981) as the theoretical basis of our systemic work. However, when a family which included three small children was referred to us following the suicide of the mother, we found ourselves wondering if our structural approach would be appropriate. How, for example, within a structural approach, would we be able to address the mourning process which is so central to the individual's recovery from loss? Given the different needs of the bereaved children, the father and the extended family, would it be possible to address these simultaneously, and if not, how might they be prioritised? We also wondered how, in view of the complexity of the situation, might we go about structuring our work in an organised and systematic way? Our search for guidance on these questions led us to discover that much of the published research in this field is based on attachment theory and the impact of bereavement on individuals, rather than on the family as a whole

In *Living Beyond Loss: Death in the Family* (Walsh and McGoldrick, 1991) Walsh notes the lack of attention paid to the effects of bereavement on the family system, and describes this as 'an important and neglected topic in our field'. The book includes a collection of papers which provide a useful introduction to the broad theoretical issues. It does not, however, set out to describe in detail how the systemic perspective can be applied in therapeutic work. This has been attempted by a number of authors whose pioneering case studies of their work with bereaved families has been described in journal articles and by Shapiro (1994) in her scholarly work *Grief as a Family Process*. However, these studies often do not make clear the theoretical basis of the work, the model or models used to organise the therapy, or the reasons behind the therapist's decision to make a particular intervention at a particular time. At a theoretical level, therefore, it is often difficult to understand the rationale for the therapist's actions at a particular stage of the therapy. For practitioners who wish to develop their own practice, this is problematic. When the model that provides the framework for the therapist's approach is not stated, the guiding principles which lie behind particular interventions may be obscure and therefore difficult to understand. In addition, the scope for applying a similar approach in other circumstances becomes limited. In the absence of a comprehensive systemic model, general principles tend to be drawn instead from the now well-established models that inform therapeutic work with individuals. These models, based primarily on theories of attachment or stress (for example Frude, 1990), conceptualise loss in terms of its impact on the individual's emotional state and coping abilities, and adopt a linear perspective. For example, the process of mourning is conceptualised as a normal, universal individual response to loss, consisting of a number of distinct phases, each of which will need to be worked through in order for the individual's mourning process to be resolved. For therapists who use this model in their work with bereaved individuals, the patient's expression of grief is likely to be taken as an indication that the mourning process is not yet resolved. However, for the systemic therapist, the tearfulness of an individual may also need to be understood as serving a number of additional functions. For example, from a systemic perspective, such an expression of feeling can also be regarded as a communication which may have a powerful controlling effect upon patterns of interaction between family members.

The chapters in this book explore these issues from a number of different angles, sketching the potential range of the systemic approach and encompassing a variety of situations involving death and dying. Each chapter illustrates how a systemic approach has been applied by the therapist to work within a particular systemic model, each with its characteristic techniques. The therapist's role and interventions are described in the context of this, with an attempt being made to knit theory and practice together, showing how and why particular interventions are made. Whilst recognising the importance of the emotional effects of bereavement on individuals, we have endeavoured to move beyond the constraints of mourning theory towards an approach which looks at the individual in a broader, more holistic context.

A brief word is needed here about the way in which the word 'systemic' is used in this book. The term originates from general systems theory (Bertalanffy, 1968), which was used by Bateson (1972) and by Watzlawick et al. (1967) in the context of communication theory and cybernetics. The word 'systemic' has been used within the field of psychotherapy to refer to the way in which social organisations, such as the family, function as a unit or 'system' (Frude, 1990). Therapists who use a systemic approach regard the family as a self-regulating communication system, made up of individuals whose relationships are expressed in terms of recursive patterns of behaviour, linked in a circular fashion. These recursive patterns of behaviour are governed by rules and regulated by feedback systems that tend to keep the organisation stable. The family system has two apparently contradictory functions: a) to maintain equilibrium; and b) to have the ability to adapt to developmental change. The behaviour of an individual family member influences all the others within the family system. Each action thus becomes an act of communication that fulfils a particular communicative function. Thus it is impossible not to communicate. A number of schools of systemic therapy have evolved from these basic ideas, each with its own model of what constitutes a family system and each with its own characteristic armamentarium of therapeutic techniques (Fraser, 1986). Therapists using these different models tend to use the word 'systemic' to refer to attributes that are specific to the model within which they are working, and the word will therefore have subtly different meanings, depending upon the context in which it is used. This diversity of usage is reflected in the chapters in this book, which display a number of different models and therapeutic approaches, whilst remaining within a broad systemic framework.

From a systemic point of view, adjustment after loss involves much more than simply an emotional adjustment within the individual or individuals who are affected. The impact on the family system as a whole is likely to be substantial, and the effects of loss may be prolonged. What are the factors that determine the effects of loss on the family and is there a systemic equivalent to the mourning process in individuals? In Chapter 1, 'A family systems perspective on loss, recovery and resilience' , Walsh and McGoldrick provide a theoretical overview which addresses these questions. They review the complex effects of loss on the extended family network, using a multigenerational, developmental perspective. It is clear that the family facing loss is confronted with a major developmental crisis which involves processes of structural alteration and organisational adjustment as well as changes in familiar relationships and patterns of behaviour. The relevance of life cycle stages, social and economic factors and issues of gender and ethnicity in mediating the impact of loss on the family are also discussed.

The impact of a death may also extend beyond the immediate family. The loss of a child, for example, may affect the community and the school of which the child was a part. The effect of the death of a pupil on a school is discussed by Cornish in Chapter 4, 'Death of a pupil in school'. Using a structural model to guide her work, Cornish shows how the schools were affected by the murder of a 10-year-old boy and the accidental suicide of a 12-year-old girl, and describes the different types of intervention that were required from the therapist. If a death attracts public attention, wider social systems, including the media, may be affected. In Chapter 2, 'The relevance of tears: reconstructing the mourning process from a systemic perspective', Sutcliffe and Tufnell show how the death of Stuart Sutcliffe, a founder member of the Beatles group, set in motion a process of action and reaction in which the family and the media have been caught up for more than three decades. This chapter focuses particularly on the effects of homeostasis within the system, how these are manifested and how the therapist who uses a structural model can help the family to move on.

The systemic therapist who is asked to participate in the process of adjustment in the face of loss enters an often dauntingly complex situation in which a large group of people may be involved, each with their own individual needs, and with a number of agendas that may appear divergent. In such circumstances, it would be surprising if the therapist did not sometimes feel perplexed about how best to undertake the work: how to define the client group, how to agree a focus for the work, and how to prioritise the therapeutic tasks. The chapters in this book describe the strategies used by therapists to work with these issues, and how they have used their own particular systemic approach in a range of different situations. For example, in Chapter 3, 'Death of a parent in a family with young children: working with the aftermath', Tufnell, Sutcliffe and Cornish provide a detailed description of how they tackled these issues. In this case, the therapy team used a structural model to organise their work with the family. How to adapt this approach in order to be able to work system- ically with the father on his own became a major focus for the team.

In using a systemic approach rather than one focused on individual emotional experience, the therapist becomes aware that difficulties of adjustment may arise at any level of the system or systems involved, rather than simply within the individual. Mourning theory, with its emphasis on the universality of the feelings experienced by the bereaved individual, also describes the difficulties that occur when the normal process of mourning does not take place. It is commonly held, for example, that a bereaved person who has not expressed grief is likely to become depressed, or to develop one of the other pathologies associated with unresolved mourning. The systemic approach, by contrast, allows the therapist to seek less pathologising explanations for the difficulties that impede the process of adjustment (see Levner, Chapter 6). In Chapter 5, 'On the brink – managing suicidal teenagers', Eia Asen describes the systemic context of attempted suicide in young people, shows how the therapist intervenes at the level of the individual, the family and the social context, and how the focus of the work shifts between these levels. His approach seeks to identify the strengths as well as the weaknesses within the family system and to enable parents and teenagers to communicate more effectively about the issues and feelings relevant to the attempted suicide. The importance of taking account of the wider systemic context is also illustrated. In Chapter 7, 'Working systemically with older people and their families who have "come to grief"', Roper-Hall describes the way in which she works with elderly people who have been bereaved, and shows how a multigenerational approach is able to transcend the limitations of mourning theory, expanding and enriching this within a systemic perspective.

It is also important for the systemic therapist to remember that attitudes and beliefs about loss are embedded in society, not simply in the family system. The importance of social context, and its effect on the therapeutic system is explored from a structural perspective by Sutcliffe and Tufnell in Chapter 2, and from a contrasting point of view by Levner in Chapter 6, 'A "dysfunctional triangle" or love in all the right places: social context in the therapy of a family living with AIDS'. Levner demonstrates ways in which social norms can contribute to a family's difficulties in coping with the process of dying from AIDS. Levner shows that the therapist must be able to understand the way in which social norms and values concerning gender, race and class pervade the family's reality if s/he is to prevent them from jeopardising adaptive change. Levner prefers to redefine social norms of this kind as beliefs or themes, thus reframing them in ways that create greater therapeutic flexibility. The therapist needs to be able to deconstruct such beliefs in order to create the therapeutic opportunities that promote constructive change.

What are the factors that bring about constructive change? The chapters in this book suggest a number of different answers to this question. It seems clear that the answer will depend upon which systemic model the therapist employs and the theory of change upon which this model is based. Detailed discussion of how theories of change differ between the different systemic models is beyond the scope of this book and has been discussed in detail elsewhere (for example Watzlawick *et al.*, 1974; Fraser, 1986). However, all the work described in this book is based on an approach to change which involves individuals as an integral part of a social context, as adapting to new structures, and as elaborating new patterns of behaviour and beliefs within that environment. The family system as a whole also undergoes a 'second-order change' in the sense that there are 'changes in the body of rules governing [its] structure or internal order' (Watzlawick *et al.*, 1974). Not all the authors of the following chapters are explicit about the theory of change which they utilise, but all describe the processes that have been involved in order to achieve this.

Levner sees problems as embedded in the context of social norms, not least society's prejudices against minority groups. He abandons the idea of 'treating dysfunction', preferring to see his role as challenging the belief systems and interactions that create difficulties, reframing them as adaptive (rather than pathological) whilst offering positive alternatives for change. Change occurs, according to Levner, when new patterns of interaction are linked to new belief systems as a result of understanding the presenting problems in terms of their social context. The experience of self-worth and empowerment is a key element in the therapeutic process.

Roper-Hall creates a different perspective, showing how ageism can stigmatise elderly bereaved people, preventing change and diminishing access to therapeutic help. Her work shows how change occurs when the bereaved person develops a narrative to describe their experience of loss which allows a different perception of events and relationships.

For Eia Asen, change takes place when dysfunctional hierarchies within the family system become more responsive to the needs of individual family members. He achieves this by making interventions at the individual, family and sociocultural levels simultaneously.

Tufnell, Sutcliffe and Cornish show how, using a structural model, change entails the realignment of boundaries between subsystems as a result of redefining rules which govern interactions, and how homeostasis acts to prevent change. Similarly Sutcliffe and Tufnell, looking at family process in the context of wider social systems, suggest that homeostasis acts not only within the family system but also at the interface between the family and wider systems.

Cornish demonstrates the way in which a structural approach can be applied within a school system, creating change by redefining rules and boundaries, and thus transforming beliefs and attitudes.

What can be concluded from the diversity of the approaches described in these chapters? Certainly there is no single application of the systemic approach to therapeutic work with families facing loss. Effective results can, indeed, be achieved using a range of different systemic models. However, because each model employs its own concepts and techniques, each defines family 'problems' and the goals of therapy in keeping with these concepts and techniques. This, in turn, has implications for the focus of the therapist's interventions. For example, when using the structural model, the therapist looks for the homeostasis which prevents change in the interactions within and between systems, whilst models that conceptualise systems in terms of beliefs are more focused on changes in meaning or in belief systems. What does, however, seem important – and sometimes difficult to maintain, as a number of our contributors illustrate – is the principle of the therapist being able to retain a systemic perspective, to construct this in terms which are consistent with the model they are using, and to be able to find appropriate ways to link from this into the more individually focused theories of mourning and stress-coping when necessary. If this perspective is lost it is all too easy for the work to lose its direction, become confused or become overwhelmed by the sheer complexity of the task. The support of a therapy team can do much to help the therapist avoid these difficulties.

References

Bateson, G. (1972) *Steps to an Ecology of Mind.* New York: Ballantyne Books.

Bertalanffy, L. von (1968) *General Systems Theory.* London: Allen Lane/Penguin.

Fraser, J.S. (1986) Integrating system-based therapies: similarities, differences, and some critical questions. In Efron, D.E. (ed.) *Journeys: Expansion of the Strategic-Systemic Therapies.*

Frude, N. (1990) *Understanding Family Problems.* Chapter 10 Bereavement. Chichester: John Wiley & Sons.

Minuchin, S. (1974) *Families and Family Therapy.* London: Tavistock.

Minuchin, S. and Fishman H.C. (1981) *Family Therapy Techniques.* London: Harvard University Press

Shapiro, E.R. (1994) *Grief as a Family Process.* London: Guilford Press.

Walsh, F. and McGoldrick, M. (eds) (1991) *Living Beyond Loss: Death in the Family.* New York: W.W. Norton.

Watzlawick, P., Beavin, J.H. and Jackson, D.D. (1967). *The Pragmatics of Human Communication: a Study of Interactional Patterns, Pathologies and Paradoxes.* New York: W.W. Norton.

Watzlawick, P., Weakland, H.H. and Fisch, R. (1974) *Change: Principles of Problem Formation and Problem Resolution.* London: W.W. Norton.

Acknowledgements

We would like to thank all those who have helped us in the preparation of this book. Special thanks are due to the Institute of Family Therapy, London, who supported the project which gave rise to this book, to the Elizabeth Raven Memorial Trust which funded the work described in Chapter 3 of the book, and to Dora Black who referred the family to us. We are particularly grateful for the support and encouragement of Marianne Walters, Eia Asen, Daisy Berger and John Morton. Without the expert editorial advice and practical help of Frances Arnold and Houri Alavi, this book would not have been born. Finally, we would like to thank the many families with whom we have worked over the years, and from whom we have learned so much.

Notes on Contributors

K. Eia Asen studied medicine in Berlin and subsequently trained as a psychiatrist at the Maudsley Hospital, London, UK, in the mid-1970s. He now works as a consultant child psychiatrist at the Marlborough Family Service and the Parkside Clinic (both in north London) and as a consultant adult psychotherapist at the Maudsley Hospital. He has written many papers and three books, the latest in 1995 entitled *Family Therapy for Everyone* (BBC).

Ursula Cornish is a member of the Institute of Family Therapy, London, UK. She works as an educational psychologist and family therapist, especially with children and their families in pre-school and school environments. She has worked extensively with loss in families and with trauma and stress-related problems in schools. She has a wide range of experience with emotionally vulnerable children, including children with learning difficulties and autism.

Lawrence Levner is the Clinical Director of the Family Therapy Practice Center in Washington DC, USA. He is an approved supervisor of the American Association for Marriage and Family Therapy and has a private practice in clinical social work.

Monica McGoldrick is Director of the Family Institute of New Jersey, USA. She also hold a faculty position at the University of Medicine and Dentistry in New Jersey.

Alison Roper-Hall is a clinical psychologist and systemic psychotherapist, developing her systemic practice with people over 65. She is now Head of Psychology in the Primary Care and Family Services section of the South Birmingham Psychology Service, Birmingham, UK.

Pauline Sutcliffe is a member of the Institute of Family Therapy, London, UK, and the Tavistock Institute of Psychotherapists. She is a training consultant to family therapy training institutes in Milan, Italy and Washington DC, USA. She works as a systemic therapist in a team which offers therapy to families who have suffered trauma and bereavement. She also maintains a part-time private practice in London. She worked in the public sector services for 20 years, ultimately as an assistant director of Social Services in central London. She is interested in the arts and is a patron of a university-based postgraduate fellowship award, and co-owner of an art gallery.

Guinevere Tufnell is a member of the Institute of Family Therapy, London, UK. She is a child and adolescent psychiatrist, who has worked for many years in a busy child and family mental health clinic in east London. She also works as a systemic therapist in a team which offers therapy to families who have suffered trauma and bereavement. She is an associate editor of the journal *Child Psychology and Psychiatry Review*. Her most recent publications have been on developing services related to child protection and on giving expert evidence in court.

Marianne Walters is founder and Director of the Family Therapy Practice Center in Washington DC, USA. Ms Walters conducts family therapy training in a wide range of settings, both in the USA and abroad. During and since her tenure as Executive Director of the Training Center at the Philadelphia Child Guidance Clinic she has held faculty positions at several schools of social work and departments of psychiatry.

Froma Walsh is Co-Director of the Center for Family Health in Chicago, Illinois, USA, and a professor at the University of Chicago. She is editor of the *Journal of Marital and Family Therapy*.

CHAPTER 1

A Family Systems Perspective on Loss, Recovery and Resilience

Froma Walsh and Monica McGoldrick

While most attention to death and mourning has tended to focus on individual bereavement, a systemic perspective is required to understand how the loss of a family member reverberates throughout the family system with immediate and long-term consequences for family functioning and for all members and their subsequent relationships. This overview chapter presents a systemic framework to guide assessment and intervention. How the family faces death and deals with loss are crucial for healing; some are shattered while others are able to rebound. Discussion addresses family adaptational challenges, factors that pose complications and risk of dysfunction, and key interactional processes that encourage recovery and resilience.

> Sorrow felt alone leaves a deep crater in the soul;
> sorrow shared yields new life.
> (Ladysmith Black Mambazo in *Nomethemba)*

Coming to terms with death and loss is the most difficult challenge a family must confront in life. From a family systems perspective, loss can be viewed as a transactional process involving the dying and deceased with the survivors in a shared life cycle that acknowledges both the finality of death and the continuity of life. This overview chapter will present a conceptual framework for systemic assessment and intervention with loss. This systemic approach considers the impact of the death of a family member on the family as a functional unit, with immediate and long-term reverberations for every member and all other relationships. We will identify major family challenges and interactional processes that promote resilience and healing in the aftermath of loss. This involves coming to terms with loss and moving forward with life individually and together, strengthened as a family unit. We will also examine crucial variables that can complicate loss processes and contribute to immediate or long-term dysfunction. The importance of a developmental perspective will be discussed, considering loss processes over time and across the family life cycle.

Socio-historical perspective

Throughout history and in every culture, mourning beliefs, practices, and rituals have facilitated both the integration of death and the transformations of survivors. Each culture, in its own ways, offers assistance to the community of survivors in moving forward with life (McGoldrick *et al.*, 1991). Yet, in whatever different forms and circumstances, mourning must be experienced. While recognizing the considerable diversity in individual, family, and cultural modes of dealing with death and loss, family processes are crucial determinants of healthy or dysfunctional adaptation to loss.

Contrary to the nostalgic myth of the traditional family as intact, stable, and secure (Walsh, 1993), families over the ages have had to cope with the precariousness of life and the disruptions wrought by death. As is still prevalent in impoverished communities throughout the world, death struck young and old alike, with high rates of mortality for infants, children, and women in childbirth. With a life expectancy under 50 years, (a period now considered midlife), parental death often disrupted family units, shifting members into varied and complex networks of full, half, and step relationships, and vast extended kinship systems.

Before the advent of hospital and institutional care, people died at home where all family members, including children, were involved in the preparation for and immediacy of death. In modern technological societies, we have come to deny death and distance from grief processes, making adaptation to loss all the more difficult. In contrast to traditional cultures, contemporary society lacks cultural supports to assist families in integrating the fact of death with ongoing life (Becker, 1973; Aries, 1974, 1982; Mitford, 1978). Geographical distances and emotional estrangement separate family members at times of death and dying. Medical advances have complicated the process by removing death from everyday reality, while at the same time confronting families with unprecedented decisions to prolong or end life.

Currently, we are seeing a heightened recognition of the importance of facing death and loss. The worldwide AIDS epidemic has forced greater attention to death and dying. Also, the approach of middle-age for the baby boom generation has prompted a shift in public consciousness from a preoccupation with youth to the realities of aging and mortality. Families are beginning to reclaim the dying process through such directives as living wills and more meaningful memorial rites. Amidst the social and economic upheaval of recent decades, families are dealing with multiple losses, transitions, and uncertainties. Through such dislocations as migration and job loss, the stability and security of increasing numbers of families have been disrupted. As families increasingly break apart through separation and divorce, they recombine, with both courage and confusion, in varying forms and new gender arrangements. This chapter focuses on loss through death, yet the family challenges and processes we will describe have broad application to other experiences involving loss, recovery, and resilience. In helping families to deal with their losses, we enable them to transform and strengthen their relationships as they forge new resiliencies to face future life challenges (Walsh, 1996, in press).

Loss in systemic perspective

By and large, the mental health field has failed to appreciate the impact of loss on the family as an interactional system. The extensive literature on bereavement has focused on individual mourning processes (Bowlby, 1961; Kübler-Ross, 1969; Parkes, 1972; Worden, 1982) and attended narrowly to grief reactions in the loss of a significant dyadic relationship. A systemic perspective is required to appreciate the chain of influences that reverberates throughout the family network of relationships with any significant loss. Insufficient attention has been given to the immediate and long-term effects of a death for partners, parents, children, siblings, and extended family. Legacies of loss find expression in continuing patterns of interaction and mutual influence among the survivors and across the generations. The pain of death touches all survivors' relationships with others, some of whom may never even have known the person who died.

Epidemiological studies have found that the death of a family member increases vulnerability to premature illness and death for surviving family members (Osterweis et al., 1984), especially for a widowed spouse and for parents who have recently lost a child (Huygen et al., 1989). Furthermore, family developmental crises have been linked to the appearance of symptoms in a family member (Hadley et al., 1974). In view of the profound connections among members of a family, it is not surprising that adjustment to loss by death is considered more difficult than any other life change (Holmes and Rahe, 1967).

Although family systems theory introduced a new paradigm for understanding family relationships, few in the field of family therapy approached the subject of loss, reflecting the cultural aversion to facing and talking about death. As Murray Bowen (1976, 1991), noted: 'Chief among all taboo subjects is death. A high percentage of people die alone, locked into their own thoughts, which they cannot communicate to others' (1991, p. 80). Bowen saw at least two processes in operation: 'One is the intrapsychic process in self, which always involves some denial of death. The other is the closed relationship system: People cannot communicate the thoughts they do have, lest they upset the family or others'.

Bowen advanced our understanding of the loss experience as profoundly influenced by and, in turn, influencing family processes. Bowen described the disruptive impact of death or threatened loss on a family's functional equilibrium. He viewed the intensity of the emotional reaction as governed by the level of emotional integration in the family at the time of the loss and by the functional significance of the lost member. The emotional shockwave may reverberate throughout an entire family system either immediately or long after a traumatic loss or threatened loss. It is not directly related to the usual grief or mourning reactions of people close to the one who died. Rather, it operates on an underground network of emotional interdependence of family members. As Bowen observed, 'The emotional dependence is denied, the serious events appear to be unrelated, the family attempts to camouflage any connectedness between the events, and there is a vigorous emotional denial reaction, when anyone attempts to relate the events to each other' (1991, p. 83).

Bowen maintained that knowledge of the shockwave provides valuable information for therapy, without which the sequence of events may be treated as unrelated. Therefore, it is essential to assess the total family configuration, the functioning position of the dying or deceased member, and the family's overall level of adaptation, in order to understand the meaning and context of presenting symptoms and to help the family in a healing process.

Another family therapy pioneer, Norman Paul, also commented on the reluctance of the therapist, as well as clients, to confront the topic of death. He noted the paradox that where there exists a constant shadow of death in everybody's life, all are entertaining notions of their own immortality. Paul found that however intense the aversion to facing death and grief, their force will find expression, nonetheless (Paul and Grosser, 1965; Paul and Paul, 1982). Grief at the loss of a parent, spouse, child, sibling, or other important family member, when unrecognized and unattended, may precipitate strong and harmful reactions in other relationships, from marital distancing and dissolution to precipitous replacement, extramarital affairs, and even incest. He cautioned that a clinician's own aversion to death and grief may hamper the ability to inquire about loss issues, notice patterns, and treat a systemic problem correctly as grief-related, resulting in unhelpful focus on secondary problems. Paul advocated an active therapeutic approach that confronts hidden losses, fosters awareness of their relational connections, and encourages mutual empathy in conjoint couple and family therapy.

In the early development of the field of family therapy, attention to observable here-and-now interactional patterns blinded many to the relevance of past or threatened losses that are out of view. More recent postmodern approaches may fail to grasp the significance of unmentioned loss events that are not 'storied' and remain disconnected, ambiguous, or distorted. Loss is a powerful nodal event that shakes the foundation of family life and leaves no member unaffected. More than a discrete event, from a systemic view it can be seen to involve processes over time, from the threat and approach of death, through its immediate aftermath, and on into long-term implications. Individual distress is not only due to grief, but is also a consequence of changes in the realignment of the family emotional field (Kuhn, 1981). Loss modifies family structure, often requiring major reorganisation of the family system. Perhaps most important, the meaning of a particular loss event and responses to it are shaped by the family belief system, which in turn, is modified by all loss experiences (Reiss and Oliveri, 1980).

A death in the family involves multiple losses: there is a loss of the person, a loss of roles and relationships, the loss of the intact family unit, and the loss of hopes and dreams for all that might have been. If we are to understand the significance of loss processes, we must attend to the past as well as the present and future; to both process and content; and to the factual circumstances of a death as well as the meanings it holds in a particular family in its social context.

Family adaptation to loss

The family life cycle model of Carter and McGoldrick (1989) offers a framework for taking into account the reciprocal influences of several generations as they move forward over time and as they approach and respond to loss (McGoldrick and Walsh, 1983). Death poses shared adaptational challenges, requiring both immediate and long-term family reorganisation and changes in a family's definitions of its identity and purpose. The ability to accept loss is at the heart of all skills in healthy family systems. In contrast, very dysfunctional families show the most maladaptive patterns in dealing with inevitable losses, clinging together in fantasy and denial to blur reality and to insist on timelessness and the perpetuation of never-broken bonds (Lewis *et al.*, 1976).

Adaptation does not mean resolution, in the sense of some complete 'once and for all' getting over it. Nor does resilience in the face of loss mean simply putting it behind you, cutting off from the emotional experience, and moving on. Mourning and adaptation have no fixed timetable or sequence, and significant or traumatic losses may never be fully resolved. Coming to terms with loss involves finding ways to make meaning of the loss experience, put it in perspective, and move ahead with life. The multiple meanings of any death are transformed throughout the life cycle, as they are integrated into individual and family identity and along with subsequent life experiences, including other losses.

Research on loss has found wide diversity in individual coping styles and in the timing and intensity of normal grief responses (Wortman and Silver, 1989). Children's reactions to death will depend on their stage of cognitive development, on the way adults deal with them around the death, and on the degree of caretaking they have lost. Our research and clinical experience suggest that there are crucial family adaptational challenges which, if not dealt with, leave family members vulnerable to dysfunction and heighten the risk of family dissolution. Two major family tasks tend to promote immediate and long-term adaptation for family members and to strengthen the family as a functional unit.

1. Shared acknowledgement of the reality of death and shared experience of the loss

All family members, in their own ways, must confront the reality of a death in the family. With the shock of a sudden death, this process may start abruptly. In the case of life-threatening illnesses (Rolland, 1991, 1994), it may begin tentatively, with the anticipation of *possible* loss, while retaining hope, then, to the *probability* and finally, the *certainty* of impending loss, as in the terminal phase of an illness. Bowen (1991) drew our attention to the importance of direct contact with the reality of death, and in particular to the inclusion of vulnerable family members. He urged visits to dying members whenever possible and ways to include children. Well-intentioned attempts to protect children or vulnerable members from the potential upset of exposure to death isolates them from the shared experience and risks impeding their grief process. They are harmed more by the anxiety of survivors than by exposure to death.

Acknowledgment of the loss is facilitated by clear information and open communication about the facts and circumstances of the death. Inability to accept the reality of death can lead a family member to avoid contact with the rest of the family or to become angry with others who are moving forward in the grief process. Longstanding sibling conflicts and cut offs can often be traced back to the bedside of a dying parent.

Funeral rituals (Imber-Black, 1991) and visits to the grave (Williamson, 1978) serve a vital function in providing direct confrontation with the reality of death and the opportunity to pay last respects, to share grief, and to receive comfort in the supportive network of the community of survivors. Sharing the experience of loss, in whatever ways a family can, is crucial to successful adaptation.

Family communication is vital over the course of the loss process. While keeping in mind that individuals, families, and cultures vary in the degree to which open expression of feelings is valued or functional, there is strong evidence from research on well-functioning families that clear, direct communication facilitates family adaptation and strengthens the family as a supportive network for its members (Walsh, 1993). A climate of trust, empathic response, and tolerance for diverse reactions is crucial. The mourning process also involves sharing attempts to put the loss into some meaningful perspective that fits coherently into the rest of a family's life experience and belief system. This requires dealing with the ongoing negative implications of the loss, including the loss of dreams for the future.

Families are likely to experience a range of feelings depending on the unique meaning of the relationship and its loss for each member and the implications of the death for the family unit. Strong emotions may surface at different moments, including complicated and mixed feelings of anger, disappointment, helplessness, relief, guilt, and abandonment, which are present to some extent in most family relationships. In American and British cultures the expression of intense emotions tends to generate discomfort and distancing in others. Moreover, the loss of control experienced in sharing such overwhelming feelings can frighten an individual and other family members, leading them to block all communication around the loss experience to protect one another.

When we take into account the multiple, fluctuating, and often conflicting responses of all members in a family system, we can appreciate the diversity and complexity of any family mourning process. Tolerance is needed for different responses within families and for the likelihood that members may have different individual coping styles, may be out of phase with one another, and may have unique experiences in the meaning of a lost relationship. Mourning may be blocked by roles and responsibilities, as in single parenthood, with children and well-intentioned relatives colluding to keep the sole parent strong and functioning (Fulmer, 1983). With parental grieving blocked, a child is more likely to become symptomatic.

When comunication is blocked, the unspeakable may go under-ground to surface in other contexts or in symptomatic behaviour. Unbearable or unacceptable feelings may be delegated and expressed in a fragmented fashion by various family members (Reilly, 1978). One may carry all the anger for the family while another is in touch only with sadness; one shows only relief, another is numb. If a family is unable to tolerate certain feelings, a member who directly expresses the unacceptable may be scapegoated or extruded. The shock and pain of a traumatic loss can shatter family cohesion, leaving members isolated and unsupported in their grief, as in the following case:

Mrs Campbell sought help for her 11-year-old daughter's school problems. Inquiry to understand 'why now?' explored recent events in the family. The therapist learned that the eldest son had been caught in the crossfire of a gang-related shooting. The shot that killed him had also shattered the family unit. The father withdrew, drinking heavily to ease his pain. The next eldest son carried the family rage into the streets, seeking revenge for the senseless killing. Two other middle sons showed no reaction, keeping out of the way. The mother, alone in her grief, turned her attention to her daughter's school problems.

Family therapy provided a context for family grief work, building resilience in the family by repairing the fragmentation and promoting a more cohesive network for mutual support and healing. It was especially important to involve the 'well' siblings, who had been holding in their own pain so as not to further burden their parents. On follow-up, the daughter's school problems and father's drinking had subsided. The experience of pulling together in dealing with their loss had strengthened their resilience, increasing their capacity to cope with other problems, as well.

2. Reorganisation of the family system and reinvestment in other relationships and life pursuits

The death of a family member disrupts the family equilibrium and established patterns of interaction. The process of recovery involves a realignment of relationships and redistribution of role functions needed to compensate for the loss, buffer transitional stresses, and carry on with family life. As in the following case, children can be harmed more by their family's inability to provide structure, stability, and protective caregiving than by a loss itself. The sibling bond can be a critical lifeline through such times.

Marie, a woman in her 50s, sought help for depression after the sudden death of her brother, who had been her mainstay in life. When she was seven years old, her mother had died of cancer. Marie vividly recalled that the night of the death, as relatives came and left, she put on her best dress and sat on the edge of her bed in her room, holding her brother's hand, waiting to be called to say their goodbyes. No-one came for them; nor were they taken to the funeral. In the upheaval of the aftermath, she and her brother were separated for a time, sent to stay with various relatives. When she returned home, her father, overwhelmed in his grief, turned to her sexually, coming into her bed late at night for comfort and contact. There was continued uncertainty about where she and her brother would live until her father's remarriage, a year later, brought stability and a caring stepmother, and ended her secret ordeal.

Promoting cohesion and flexible reorganisation in the family system is crucial to restabilisation and resilience. The upheaval experienced in the immediate aftermath of a loss leads some families to hold on rigidly to old patterns that are no longer functional to minimize the sense of loss and disruption in family life. Other families may make precipitous moves into new homes or marriages, taking flight or seeking immediate replacement for their losses. Further dislocations may make matters worse and replacement relationships are complicated by the unmourned losses. It is important to help families pace their reorganisation and reinvestment.

The process of mourning is quite variable, often lasting much longer than people themselves expect. Each new season, holiday, and anniversary is likely to re-evoke the loss. Over-idealisation of the deceased, a sense of disloyalty, or the catastrophic fear of another loss may block the formation of other attachments and commitments. Family members may refuse to accept a new member who is seen as replacing the deceased when the loss has not been integrated.

Family therapy with loss requires the same ingenuity and flexibility that families need to respond to various members and subsystems as their issues come to the fore. As changes occur in one part of a system, changes for others will be generated. Decisions to meet with an individual, couple, or family unit at various points are guided by a systemic view of the loss process.

Variables influencing family adaptation to loss

We can identify a number of variables in the loss situation and family processes surrounding it that influence the impact of a death (Bowen, 1976, 1991; Herz, 1989; Walsh and McGoldrick, 1991). It is important for clinicians to be aware of patterns that tend to complicate family adaptation and pose higher risk of dysfunction. In order to work preventively at the time of a loss, or to understand and repair long-term complications, these variables should always be carefully evaluated and addressed in any intervention plan.

The loss situation
Sudden or lingering death

Sudden deaths or deaths following protracted illness are especially stressful for families and require different coping processes. When a person dies unexpectedly, family members lack time to anticipate and prepare for the loss, to deal with unfinished business, or in many cases even to say their goodbyes. Clinicians need to explore and help family members with painful regrets and guilt over what they wish they had done differently, had they known that loss was imminent.

When the dying process has been prolonged, family caregiving and financial resources are likely to be depleted, with needs of other members put on hold (Rosen, 1990; Rolland, 1994). Relief at ending patient suffering and family strain is likely to be guilt-laden. Moreover, families are increasingly faced with the dilemma over whether, and how long, to maintain life support efforts, at enormous expense, to sustain a family member who may be in a vegetative state or in chronic pain, with virtually no hope of recovery. Controversy over medical ethics, religious beliefs, patient/family rights, and criminal prosecution extend to the most fundamental questions of when life ends and who should determine that end. Families can be torn apart by opposing positions of different members or coalitions. Clinicians can help family members to prepare and discuss living wills, to share feelings openly about such complicated situations, and to come to terms with any decision taken.

Ambiguous loss

Ambiguity surrounding a loss interferes with its mastery, often producing depression in family members (Boss, 1991). A loved one may be physically absent but psychologically present, as in those missing in wartime. The uncertainty about whether a missing family member is dead or alive can be agonising for a family. In the case of a missing child, for instance, a family may become consumed by efforts to maintain hope while fearing the worst, and by desperate searches and attempts to get information to confirm the fate of their child.

In other situations of ambiguous loss, a family member may be physically present but psychologically 'dead,' or unable to recognise loved ones, as in the mental deterioration of Alzheimer's disease (Boss, 1991). It is important to help family members to deal with the progressive loss of mental functioning and important aspects of their relationship without extruding the person as if already dead. At the same time, with prolonged strain over many years, it is important to validate the needs of a spouse or adult children to go on with their own life.

Violent death

The impact of a violent death can be devastating, especially for loved ones who witnessed it or narrowly escaped themselves, as in a bombing incident or a plane crash. Body mutilation or the inability to retrieve a body hinders family mourning processes. The senseless tragedy in the loss of innocent lives is especially hard to bear, particularly if it is the result of negligence, as in drunk-driving. The taking and loss of lives in war may haunt survivors and impact on their family relationships for years to come, as in post-traumatic stress disorders (Figley, 1989). A community may pull together in the wake of a major tragedy or a natural disaster. However, an entire community can be traumatised by persistent violence and the everpresent threat of recurrence, as experienced by poor families in blighted inner city neighbourhoods, much like living in a war zone (Garbarino, 1992). Lethal firearms have contributed to an alarming increase in homicides and accidental shootings, particularly of children by children. Murders are committed more often by relatives than strangers. Clinicians should be especially vigilant when marital conflict escalates into violence, and take threats of harm quite seriously, especially when women attempt to leave abusive relationships.

Suicide

Suicides are among the most anguishing deaths for families to come to terms with (Cain, 1972; Dunne *et al.*, 1988; Gutstein, 1991). The recent rise in adolescent death symbolism and suicide demands more attention to peer drug cultures and larger social forces, as well as family influences. Clinicians also need to be alert to family patterns, such as threatened abandonment or sexual abuse that may pose heightened risk of suicide. Current life-threatening family situations can trigger catastrophic fears of loss and self-destructive behaviour. A teenage girl was seen in the emergency room with a gunshot wound in her chest after a gun she had been carrying in her bra accidentally fired. In family crisis intervention, she revealed that, frightened by late night conflict between her parents, she removed the gun kept under their mattress and hid it on her to protect them from harm.

When a suicide has occurred, clinicians need to help family members with anger and guilt that can pervade their relationships, particularly when they are blamed or blame themselves for the death. The social stigma of suicide also contributes to family shame and cover-up of the circumstances. Such secrecy distorts family communication and can isolate a family from social support, generating its own destructive legacy. Clinicians should routinely note family histories of suicide or other traumatic loss that may predict future suicide risk, particularly at an anniversary, birthday, and holiday time. Although a therapist or loved ones cannot always prevent a suicide, the risk can be lowered by mobilising family support, making covert linkages to ongoing or past trauma overt, and helping them to integrate painful experiences and envision a meaningful future beyond their losses.

Family and social network

Consistent with leading research on family functioning (Walsh, 1993, in press), we observe that patterns of family organisation, communication, and belief systems are crucial mediating variables in adaptation to loss. The general level of family functioning and the state of family relationships prior to and following the loss should be carefully evaluated with attention to the extended family and social network. Particular note should be taken of the following variables.

Family cohesion and differentiation of members

Adaptation to loss is facilitated by family cohesiveness for mutual support, balanced with tolerance of and respect for different responses to loss by various family members. Extreme family patterns of enmeshment or disengagement pose complications. At one extreme, enmeshed families may demand a united front and regard as disloyal and threatening any individual differences, which then must be submerged or distorted. They may seek an undifferentiated replacement for the loss and have difficulty with subsequent separations, holding on to other family members at normal developmental transitions. At the other extreme, disengaged families are likely to avoid the pain of loss with distancing and emotional cut offs. In family fragmentation, members are left to fend for themselves, isolated in their grief.

Flexibility of the family system

Family structure, in particular family rules, roles, and boundaries, need to be flexible, yet clear, for reorganisation after loss. At the extreme, a chaotic, disorganised family will have difficulty maintaining enough leadership, stability, and continuity necessary to manage the transitional upheaval. An overly rigid family is likely to resist modifying set patterns to make the necessary accommodations to loss.

Open communication vs secrecy

When a family confronts a loss, open communication facilitates processes of recovery and reorganisation as described above. Situations in which certain feelings, thoughts, or memories are prohibited by family loyalties or social taboos can create secrecy, myths, and taboos which distort communication around the loss experience and contribute to symptomatic behaviour (Wright and Nagy, 1992). It is important for clinicians to promote a family climate of mutual trust, support, and tolerance for a range of responses to loss.

Availability of extended family, social, and economic resources

The family loss experience is buffered by the availability of kin and friendship networks as resources to draw upon (Anderson, 1982) and is especially crucial in widowhood (Parkes, 1972; Lopata, 1973; Parkes and Weiss, 1983). The lack of community or a spiritual connection for so many contemporary families makes loss more difficult to bear. The draining of family finances by costly, protracted medical care and the loss of economic resources with a death impair family recovery. When longstanding conflicts, cut offs, or social stigma have left families disengaged and isolated, clinicians working with loss can be helpful by mobilising a potentially supportive network and promoting a healing reconciliation (Gutstein, 1991).

Prior role and functioning in the family system

The more important a person was in family life and the more central his or her role in family functioning, the greater the loss. The death of a parent with small children is generally far more devastating than the loss of an elderly grandparent who has become more peripheral to family functioning. The loss of a leader or caregiver will be sorely felt, whereas the death of a quarrelsome troublemaker may bring a sigh of relief. The death of an only child, the only son or daughter, or the last of a generation, leaves a particular void. Families risk dysfunction if, at one extreme, they seek to avoid the pain of loss by denying the significance of an important family member or by seeking instant replacement. At the other extreme, they can become immobilised if they are unable to reallocate role functions or form new attachments.

Conflicted or estranged relationships at the time of death

Family relationships are bound to have occasional conflict, mixed feelings, or shifting alliances. When conflict has been intense and persistent, where ambivalence is strong, or when relationships have been cut off altogether, the mourning process is more likely to be complicated, with fallout for other relationships. In therapy, the coaching process (Carter, 1991) can be useful to address immediate or long-term complications of a loss. When death is anticipated, as in life-threatening illnesses, clinicians should make every effort to help patients and their families to reconnect and to repair strained relationships before the opportunity is lost. Often this requires overcoming hesitance to stir up painful emotions or to dredge up old conflicts for fear that negative confrontations would increase vulnerability and the risk of death. Family therapists need to be sensitive to these fears and actively interrupt destructive interactional spirals, helping family members to share feelings constructively with the aim of healing pained relationships, forging new connections, and building mutual support. A conjoint family life review (Walsh, 1989) can foster transformation by helping members to share different perspectives, to place hurts and disappointments in the context of the family's life cycle challenges, to recover caring aspects of relationships, and to update and renew relationships that have been frozen in past conflict.

Sociocultural context of death

Ethnic, religious, and philosophical beliefs

A family's belief system is a critical influence on adaptation to loss. Beliefs about death and the meanings surrounding a particular loss are rooted in multigenerational family legacies, in ethnic and religious beliefs, and in the dominant societal values and practices (McGoldrick *et al.*, 1996). Western notions of mastery and control hinder acceptance of what can not be controlled. Family members may despair that, despite their best efforts, optimism, or medical care, they cannot conquer death or bring back a loved one. Clinicians need to appreciate the power of belief systems for healing the pain of loss as well as the destructive impact of blame, shame, and guilt surrounding a death (Rolland, 1994). Such causal attributions are especially strong in situations of traumatic death where the cause is uncertain and questions of responsibility or negligence arise. Each member may hold a secret belief that he or she could have – or should have – done something to prevent a death. It is important to help families share such concerns, view them as normal, and come to terms with the extent and limits of their control in the situation.

Sociopolitical and historical context of loss

The impact for families of war-related deaths is heavily influenced by social attitudes about the war involvement. Loss can be assuaged by a common sense of patriotism and heroism for a noble cause and for victory. However, highly charged, conflicting positions about a war seriously complicate family adaptation. Bitter legacies of unresolved political, ethnic, and religious conflict are passed down from generation to generation.

Cancer and AIDS have become the epidemics of our times, each generating tremendous stigma and fear (Sontag, 1988). The AIDS epidemic has led many, including clinicians, to distance from persons with HIV, impairing family and social support, as well as the delivery of critical health care. Distinctions are too often made between 'innocent victims', such as children born with AIDS, in contrast to those who are condemned for having 'brought it on themselves' through homosexuality or drug use. Clinicians can help to reduce social stigma and unfounded fears of contagion so that death by AIDS is not made all the more painful and isolating for all.

More generally, societal attitudes toward homosexuality complicate all losses in gay and lesbian relationships (Laird, 1993). The death of a partner may be grieved in isolation when the relationship has been a secret or has been disapproved of by the family or the community. Lacking the legal standing of marriage, death benefits may be denied. The epidemic of AIDS is all the more devastating in the gay community – and increasingly, for men, women, and children in poor inner city neighbourhoods – because of the multiple losses and anticipated losses experienced in relationship networks (Klein and Fletcher, 1986). As one man lamented, 'Death and dying are all around us and any of us could be next'.

Gender role constraints

Although Western societies have been changing rapidly, normative expectations for men and women in families are still strongly influenced by gender-based socialisation and role constraints (McGoldrick et al., 1989). With a death in the family, mothers are particularly vulnerable to blame and guilt because of societal expectations that they bear primary caretaking responsibility for the well-being of their husbands, children, and aging parents. Women have been socialised to assume the major role in handling the social and emotional tasks of bereavement, from the expression of grief to caregiving for the terminally ill and surviving family members, including their husband's extended family. Now that most women are combining job and family responsibilities, they are increasingly overburdened in times of loss. Men, who have been socialised to manage instrumental tasks, tend to take charge of funeral, burial, financial, and property arrangements. They tend to remain more emotionally constrained and peripheral around times of loss. Cultural sanctions against revealing vulnerability or dependency needs block emotional expressiveness and ability to seek and give comfort. These constraints undoubtedly contribute to high rates of serious illness and suicide following the death of a spouse.

The different responses of men and women to loss can increase marital strain, even for couples with previously strong and stable relationships (Videcka-Sherman, 1982). For example, in a study of parents' reactions to sudden infant death syndrome (SIDS), fathers reported anger, fear, and a loss of control, wanting to keep their grieving private, whereas mothers responded more openly with sorrow and depression (DeFrain et al., 1982). Fathers are more likely to withdraw, to take refuge in their work or turn to alcohol or an affair. They tend to be uncomfortable with their wives' expressions of grief, not knowing how to respond and fearful of loss of control of their own feelings (culturally framed as 'breaking down' and 'falling apart'). Mothers may perceive their husbands' emotional unavailability as abandonment when they need comfort most, thereby experiencing a double loss. When husbands are expressive and involved in their child's illness and death and in the family bereavement process, the quality of the marriage improves markedly.

These findings have important implications for loss interventions. Individual approaches seem to have limited impact on recovery when marital relationship dynamics are not addressed as well (Videka-Sherman and Lieberman, 1985). Most commonly it is women who present themselves – or are sent by their husbands – for depression or other symptoms of distress concerning loss, while their husbands appear to be well-functioning and see no need for help for themselves. Interventions need to be aimed at decreasing the gender-based polarisation so that both men and women can more fully share in the full range of human experiences in bereavement. Moreover, encouraging mutual empathy and support in couple and family sessions builds resiliency in relationships to withstand and rebound from loss together (Walsh, 1996).

Timing of loss in the family life cycle

The meaning and consequences of loss vary depending on the particular phase of life cycle development the family is negotiating at the time of the loss (Shapiro, 1994). The particular timing of a loss in the multigenerational family life cycle may place a family at higher risk for dysfunction (Walsh and McGoldrick, 1988; McGoldrick and Walsh, 1991). Factors that influence the impact of a loss include (1) untimeliness of the loss; (2) concurrence with other loss, major stresses, or life cycle changes; and (3) history of traumatic loss and unresolved mourning. In each situation the nature of the death, the function of the person in the family, and the state of relationships will interact in crucial ways. Whatever our therapeutic approach with loss, a family life cycle perspective can enable us to facilitate adaptation in ways that strengthen the whole family in future life passage.

Untimely losses

Premature deaths that are 'off-time' in terms of chronological or social expectations (Neugarten, 1970), such as early widowhood, early parent loss, or death of a child, tend to be immensely more difficult for families to come to terms with. Such losses are experienced as unjust, ending a life before its prime and robbing hopes and dreams for a future that can never be. Prolonged mourning, often lasting many years, is a common occurrence. Long-term survival guilt for spouses, siblings and parents can block achievement of other life pursuits and satisfaction for years to come.

Children who lose a parent may suffer profound short- and long-term consequences (Furman, 1974; Osterweis *et al.*, 1984), including illness, depression, and other emotional disturbances in subsequent adult life. They may later experience difficulty in forming other intimate attachments and may carry catastrophic fears of separation and abandonment. A child's handling of parent loss does depend largely on the emotional state of the surviving parent (Rutter, 1966) and the supportive role of the extended family.

The death of a child, reversing the natural generational order, is perhaps the most painful loss of all for a family. It is often said that 'When your parent dies, you have lost your past. When your child dies, you have lost your future'. The untimeliness and injustice in the death of a child can lead family members to the most profound questioning of the meaning of life. Of all losses, it is hardest not to idealise a deceased child. Parental marriages are at heightened risk for discord and divorce (Kaplan *et al.*, 1976; Schiff, 1977). However, couples who are able to support each other through the ordeal may forge stronger relationships than ever before, underscoring the crucial role of couple and family therapy in child loss (Hare-Mustin, 1979). Many feel the impetus to have another child or turn to a sibling as a replacement (Cain and Cain, 1964). In the death of a child, it is crucial not to neglect the impact on siblings, who may experience prolonged grieving or anniversary reactions for years afterward (Cain *et al.*, 1964). A sibling's death is likely to be accompanied by an experienced loss of the parents who are preoccupied with care-taking or grieving. Normal sibling rivalry may contribute to intense survival guilt that can block developmental strivings well into adulthood.

A 13-year-old boy was hospitalised following an attempted suicide. The boy and his family were at a loss to explain the episode and made no mention of an older deceased brother. Family assessment revealed that the boy was born shortly before the death of an elder son at the age of thirteen. He grew up attempting to take the place of the brother he had never known in order to relieve his parents' sadness. The father, who could not recall the date or events surrounding the death, wished to remember his first son 'as if he were still alive'. The boy cultivated his appearance to resemble photos of his brother. Only when asked about his brother did he reply that he had attempted suicide to join his brother in heaven. The timing corresponded to his reaching and surviving the age of his brother's death and to his concern, with his growth spurt at puberty, that he was changing from the way he was 'supposed' to look. Family therapy focused on enabling the boy and his parents to relinquish his surrogate position and to move forward in his own development.

Untimely loss is complicated by the lack of social norms, models, or guidelines to assist in preparation and coping. Early widowhood (Parkes and Weiss, 1983; Butler and Lewis, 1983) or child loss (Rando, 1986) tends to be a shocking and isolating experience without emotional preparation or essential social supports. Other couples and peers at the same life stage commonly distance to avoid facing their own vulnerability. Well-intentioned relatives and friends may urge immediate replacement, which may lead to further complications (Glick *et al.*, 1975). One couple were seen in couples' therapy for conflict over their inability to name their baby, now almost a year old. The solution-focused therapy succeeded in two sessions in helping them to name the child; however, the mother then made a suicide attempt. It was learned that they had conceived this child only two months after she had lost a much desired pregnancy, for which she blamed herself. Urged to have another child 'to get over it', she found herself unable to attach to the new baby. It only made matters worse when, pressed to name their daughter, they gave her the name that had been chosen for the other child. Such cases underscore the need for a careful evaluation in every problem situation. Losses during pregnancy and perinatal deaths tend to be hidden and minimised (Lewis, 1976). The impact of such loss experiences will depend greatly on spousal support and on religious or cultural beliefs about the meaning of stillbirth, infertility, miscarriage, or abortion.

Concurrence with other loss or stressful life cycle changes

The temporal coincidence of loss with other major stress events, including multiple losses, and with other developmental milestones may overload a family and pose incompatible tasks and demands. In family assessment, a genogram and timeline are particularly useful in tracking sequences and concurrence of nodal events over time in the multigenerational family field (McGoldrick and Gerson, 1985). Sketching a timeline can alert clinicians to concurrence of losses and stressful transitions and their relation to the timing of symptoms. We pay particular attention to the concurrence of death with the birth of a child, since the processes of mourning and parenting an infant are inherently conflictual. Moreover, the child born at the time of a significant loss may assume a special replacement function that can be the impetus for high achievement or dysfunction. Similarly, a precipitous marriage in the wake of loss is likely to confound the two relationships, interfering with bereavement and with investment in the new relationship in its own right. When stressful events pile up, support by one's spouse and/or extended family are crucial buffers that facilitate adaptation.

Past traumatic loss and unresolved mourning

Some individuals and families are made hardier by past traumatic loss experiences, whereas others are left more vulnerable to subsequent losses that have not been dealt with by the family (Walsh, 1996). Past traumatic losses can intersect with current life cycle passage in many ways, such as the separation issues and self-destructive behaviour of substance abusers. It is crucial to explore possible connections to other traumatic losses in the family system (Coleman and Stanton, 1978; Coleman, 1991). Whenever issues of separation, attachment/commitment, or self-destructive behaviour are presented in therapy, an inquiry about past losses and their legacy is particularly relevant. In cases of marital breakdown, we are especially careful to inquire about losses that occurred at the start of the relationship and those coinciding with the onset of marital problems. We also note significant losses in the family that coincided with the birth of the symptom bearer. Studies by Walsh (1978) and Mueller and McGoldrick Orfanidis (1976) suggest that the death of a grandparent within two years of the birth of a child may contribute to later emotional disorder of the child, particularly around separation and launching attempts in young adulthood, which disrupt the family equilibrium.

We pay special attention to transgenerational anniversary patterns, when the occurrence of symptoms is found to coincide with death or loss in past generations at the same point in the life cycle. Individuals may become preoccupied with their own or their spouse's mortality when they reach the same age, or life transition such as retirement, at which a parent died. Some make abrupt career or relationship changes, or start new fitness regimens and feel they must 'get through the year', while others may behave self-destructively. Unresolved family patterns, or scenarios, may be replicated when a child reaches the same age or stage as a parent at the time of death or traumatic loss

(Walsh, 1983). It is crucial to assess a risk of destructive behaviour at such times. The more seriously dysfunctional a family, the more likely such linkages are covert and disconnected. In one chilling case, a 15-year-old boy stabbed a man in an apparently dissociated episode that the family ignored. Upon psychiatric referral after a third such stabbing, a family assessment revealed that the father, at the age of 15, had witnessed the brutal stabbing to death of his own father. In some cases, dissociation and denial may be functional and even essential for an individual to survive and master catastrophic trauma and loss, as occurred in the Nazi holocaust. However, the maintenance of such patterns over time may have dysfunctional consequences for other members of a family system, constricting relationships and risking serious fallout for the next generation.

An appreciation of the power of covert family scripts (Byng-Hall, 1991) and family legacies (Boszormenyi-Nagy and Spark, 1984) is important to an understanding of the transmission of such patterns in loss (McGoldrick, 1995). Anniversary reactions are most likely to occur when there has been a physical and emotional cut off from the past and when family rules, often covert, prohibit open communication about past traumatic events. In our clinical work, interventions are aimed at making covert patterns overt and helping family members to come to terms with the past and differentiate present relationships so that history need not repeat itself.

In order to help families with loss, family therapists must reappraise family history, replacing deterministic assumptions of causality with an evolutionary perspective. Like the social context, the temporal context provides a matrix of meanings in which all behaviour is embedded. Although a family cannot change its past, changes in the present and future occur in relation to that past. Systemic change involves a transformation of that relationship.

Conclusion

Mastery or dysfunction associated with loss is not simply a matter of individual bereavement, but is also a product of family mourning processes. Of all human experiences, death poses the most painful and far-reaching adaptational challenges for families. In this overview chapter, we have presented a systemic framework for clinical assessment and intervention with loss, examining the reverberations of a death for all family members, their relationships, and the family as a functional unit. An understanding of major adaptive challenges in loss and key interactional processes in recovery and resilience guides our intervention efforts in clinical practice. An awareness of crucial variables in the nature of the loss, in the family and social context, and in the timing of loss in the family life cycle alerts clinicians to issues that require careful attention in any systemic assessment and intervention approach.

Given the diversity of family forms, values, and life courses, we must be careful not to confuse common patterns with normative standards, nor assume that differences in family bereavement are pathological. Helping family members deal with a loss requires respect for their particular cultural heritage and encouragement to be proactive in determining how they will commemorate a death. While it is generally better to foster openness about death, it is also crucial to respect their pain and their timing in facing the emotional meaning of a loss. There are many pathways in family mourning and many ways for clinicians to approach loss systemically. Where family processes have become blocked or distorted, it can be a profoundly moving experience for clinicians as well as family members to collaborate in the creative transformations and deepening of relationships that can occur in the healing process.

References

Anderson, C. (1982) The community connection: the impact of social networks on family and individual functioning. In Walsh, F. (ed.) *Normal Family Processes.* New York: Guilford Press.

Aries, P. (1974) *Western Attitudes Toward Death: From the Middle Ages to the Present.* Baltimore: Johns Hopkins University Press.

Aries, P. (1982) *The Hour of Our Death.* New York: Vintage.

Becker, E. (1973) *The Denial of Death.* New York: The Free Press.

Boss, P. (1991) Ambiguous loss. In Walsh, F. and McGoldrick, M. (eds) *Living Beyond Loss: Death in the Family.* New York: W.W. Norton.

Boszormenyi-Nagy, I. and Spark, G. (1984) *Invisible Loyalties.* New York: Brunner/Mazel.

Bowen, M. (1976) Family reaction to death. In Guerin, P. (ed.) *Family Therapy.* New York: Gardner. Also in Walsh, F. and McGoldrick, M. (eds) (1991).

Bowlby, J. (1961) Process of mourning. *International Journal of Psychoanalysis* **42**:317–40.

Butler, R. and Lewis, M. (1983) *Aging and Mental Health.* St. Louis: C.V. Mosby.

Byng-Hall, J. (1991) Family scripts and loss. In Walsh, F. and McGoldrick, M. (eds) *Living Beyond Loss: Death in the Family.* New York: W.W. Norton.

Cain, A. (ed.) (1972) *Survivors of Suicide.* Springfield, IL: Thomas.

Cain, A. and Cain, B. (1964) On replacing a child. *Journal of the American Academy of Child Psychiatry* **3**:443–56.

Cain, A., Fast, I. and Erickson, M. (1964) Children's disturbed reactions to the death of a sibling. *American Journal of Orthopsychiatry* **34**:741–52.

Carter, B. (1991) Death in the therapist's own family. In Walsh, F. and McGoldrick, M. (eds) *Living Beyond Loss: Death in the Family.* New York: W.W. Norton.

Carter, B. and McGoldrick, M. (eds) (1989) *The Changing Family Life Cycle: Framework for Family Therapy*, 2nd edn. Boston: Allyn & Bacon.

Coleman, S.B. (1991) Intergenerational patterns of traumatic loss: death and despair in addict families. In Walsh, F. and McGoldrick, M. (eds) *Living Beyond Loss: Death in the Family.* New York: W.W. Norton.

Coleman, S.B. and Stanton, D.M. (1978) The role of death in the addict family. *Journal of Marriage and Family Counseling* **4**:79–91.

DeFrain, J., Taylor, J. and Ernst, L. (1982) *Coping with Sudden Infant Death.* Lexington, MA: D.C. Heath.

Dunne, E., McIntosh, J. and Dunne-Maxim, K. (1988) *Suicide and its Aftermath.* New York: W.W. Norton.

Figley, C. (1989) *Helping Traumatized Families.* San Francisco: Jossey-Bass.

Fulmer, R. (1983) A structural approach to unresolved mourning in single parent family systems. *Journal of Marital and Family Therapy* **9**:259–70.

Furman, E. (1974) *A Child's Parent Dies: Studies in Childhood Bereavement.* New Haven: Yale University Press.

Garbarino, J. (1992) *Children in Danger: Coping with the Consequences of Community Violence.* San Francisco: Jossey-Bass.

Glick, I.O., Parkes, C.M. and Weiss, R. (1975) *The First Year of Bereavement.* New York: Basic Books.

Gutstein, S. (1991) Adolescent suicide: the loss of reconciliation. In Walsh, F. and McGoldrick, M. (eds) *Living Beyond Loss: Death in the Family.* New York: W.W. Norton.

Hadley, T., Jacob, T., Miliones, J. *et al.* (1974) The relationship between family developmental crises and the appearance of symptoms in a family member. *Family Process* **13**:207–14.

Hare-Mustin, R. (1979) Family therapy following the death of a child. *Journal of Marital and Family Therapy* **5**:51–60.

Herz, F. (1989) The impact of death and serious illness on the family life cycle. In Carter, B. and McGoldrick, M. (eds) *The Changing Family Life Cycle: A Framework for Family Therapy*, 2nd edn. Boston: Allyn & Bacon.

Holmes, T. and Rahe, R.H. (1967) The social adjustment rating scale. *Journal of Psychosomatic Research* **11**:213–18.

Huygen, F.J.A., van den Hoogen, H.J.M., van Eijk, J.T.M. and Smits, A.J.A. (1989) Death and dying: a longitudinal study of their medical impact on the family. *Family Systems Medicine* **7**:374–84.

Imber-Black, E. (1991) Rituals and the healing process. In Walsh, F. and McGoldrick, M. (eds) *Living Beyond Loss: Death in the Family.* New York: W.W. Norton.

Kaplan, D., Grobstein, R. and Smith, A. (1976) Predicting the impact of severe illness in families. *Health and Social Work* **1**:71–82.

Klein, S. and Fletcher, W. (1986) Gay grief: an examination of the uniqueness brought to light by the AIDS crisis. *Journal of Psychosocial Oncology* 4:15–25.

Kubler-Ross, E. (1969) *On Death and Dying.* New York: Macmillan.

Kuhn, J. (1981) Realignment of emotional forces following loss. *The Family* 5:19–24.

Laird, J. (1993) Lesbian and gay families. In Walsh, F. (ed.) *Normal Family Processes,* 2nd. edn. New York: Guilford Press.

Lewis, J., Beavers, W.R., Gossett, J. and Phillips, V. (1976) *No Single Thread: Psychological Health in Family Systems.* New York: Brunner/Mazel.

Lewis, E. (1976) The management of stillbirth – coping with an unreality. *Lancet* 2:619–20.

Lopata, H. (1973) *Widowhood in an American City.* Cambridge, MA: Schenckman Books.

McGoldrick, M. (1995) *You Can Go Home Again.* New York: W.W. Norton.

McGoldrick, M. and Gerson, R. (1985) *Genograms in Family Assessment.* New York: W.W. Norton.

McGoldrick, M. and Walsh, F. (1983) A systemic view of family history and loss. In Aronson, M. and Wolberg, D. (eds) *Group and Family Therapy.* New York: Brunner/Mazel.

McGoldrick, M. and Walsh, F. (1991) A time to mourn: death and the family life cycle. In Walsh, F. and McGoldrick, M. (eds) *Living Beyond Loss: Death in the Family.* New York: W.W. Norton.

McGoldrick, M, Anderson, C. and Walsh, F. (eds) (1989) *Women in Families.* New York: W.W. Norton.

McGoldrick, M., Giordano, J. and Pearce, J. (eds) (1996) *Ethnicity in Families and Family Therapy,* 2nd edn. New York: Guilford Press.

McGoldrick, M., Almeida, R., Hines, P. *et al.* (1991) Mourning in different cultures. In Walsh, F. and McGoldrick, M. (eds) *Living Beyond Loss: Death in the Family.* New York: W.W. Norton.

Mitford, J. (1978) *The American Way of Death.* New York: Touchstone Books.

Mueller, P.S. and McGoldrick Orfanidis, M. (1976) A method of co-therapy for schizophrenic families. *Family Process* 15:179–92.

Neugarten, B. (1970) Dynamics of transition of middle age to old age: adaptation and the life cycle. *Journal of Geriatric Psychiatry* 4:71–87.

Osterweis, M., Solomon, F. and Green, M. (eds) (1984) *Bereavement: Reactions, Consequences, and Care.* Washington DC: National Academy Press.

Parkes, C.M. (1972) *Bereavement: Studies of Grief in Adult Life.* New York: International Universities Press.

Parkes, C.M. and Weiss, R.S. (1983) *Recovery from Bereavement.* New York: Basic Books.

Paul, N. and Grosser, G. (1965) Operational mourning and its role in conjoint family therapy. *Community Mental Health Journal* 1:339–45. Also in Walsh, F. and McGoldrick, M. (eds) (1991).

Paul, N. and Paul, B.B. (1982) Death and changes in sexual behavior. In Walsh, F. (ed.) *Normal Family Processes.* New York: Guilford Press.

Rando, T. (1986) *Parental Loss of a Child.* Champaign, IL: Research Press.

Reilly, D. (1978) Death propensity, dying and bereavement: a family system's perspective. *Family Therapy* 5:35–55.

Reiss, D. and Oliveri, M. (1980) Family paradigm and family coping: a proposal for linking the family's intrinsic adaptive capacities to its responses to stress. *Family Relations* **29**:431–44.

Rolland, J. (1991) Helping families with anticipatory loss. In Walsh, F. and McGoldrick, M. (eds) *Living Beyond Loss: Death in the Family*. New York: W.W. Norton.

Rolland, J. (1994) *Families, Illness, and Disability: An Integrative Treatment Model*. New York: Basic Books.

Rosen, E. (1990) *Families Facing Death: Family Dynamics of Terminal Illness*. Lexington, MA: Lexington Books.

Rutter, M. (1966) *Children of Sick Parents*. London: Oxford University Press.

Schiff, H.S. (1977) *The Bereaved Parent*. New York: Penguin Books.

Shapiro, Esther (1994) *Grief as a Family Process*. New York: Guilford Press.

Sontag, S. (1988) *AIDS and its Metaphors*. New York: Farrar, Straus, & Giroux.

Videka-Sherman, L. (1982) Coping with the death of a child: a study over time. *American Journal of Orthopsychiatry* **52**:688–98.

Videka-Sherman, L. and Lieberman, M. (1985) Effects of self-help groups and psychotherapy after a child dies: the limits of recovery. *American Journal of Orthopsychiatry* **55**:70–82.

Walsh, F. (1978) Concurrent grandparent death and birth of schizophrenic offspring: an intriguing finding. *Family Process* **17**:457–63.

Walsh, F. (1983) The timing of symptoms and critical events in the family life cycle. In Liddle, H. (ed.) *Clinical Implications of the Family Life Cycle*. Rockville, MD: Aspen.

Walsh, F. (1989) The family in later life. In Carter, B. and McGoldrick, M. (eds) *The Changing Family Life Cycle: A Framework for Family Therapy*, 2nd edn. Boston: Allyn & Bacon.

Walsh, F. (1993) Conceptualization of normal family processes. In Walsh, F. (ed.) *Normal Family Processes*, 2nd edn. New York: Guilford Press.

Walsh, F. (1996) The concept of family resilience: crisis and challenge. *Family Process* **35**:216–31.

Walsh, F. (in press) *Strengthening Family Resilience*. New York: Guilford.

Walsh, F. and McGoldrick, M. (1988) Loss and the family life cycle. In Falicov, C. (ed.) *Family Transitions: Continuity and Change*. New York: Guilford Press.

Walsh, F. and McGoldrick, M. (eds) (1991) *Living Beyond Loss: Death in the Family*. New York: W.W. Norton.

Williamson, D.S. (1978) New life at the graveyard: a method of therapy for individuation from a dead former parent. *Journal of Marriage and Family Counseling* **4**:93–101.

Worden, W. (1982) *Grief Counseling and Grief Therapy*. New York: Springer.

Wortman, C. and Silver, R. (1989) The myths of coping with loss. *Journal of Consulting and Clinical Psychology* **57**:349–57.

Wright, L. and Nagy, J. (1992) Death: The most troubling family secret of all. In Imber-Black, E. (ed.) *Secrets in Families and Family Therapy*. New York: W.W. Norton.

CHAPTER 2

The Relevance of Tears: Reconstructing the Mourning Process from a Systemic Perspective

Pauline Sutcliffe with Guinevere Tufnell

Much of what is know about the process of recovery after a bereavement focuses on the individual's experience and the emotional processes involved in mourning. Therapeutic intervention has traditionally been based upon the view that the therapist's role is to assist the bereaved individual to express feelings, thus aiding the resolution of mourning. With the resolution of mourning, grief passes and the tears of the bereaved no longer flow. Conversely, where tears continue to flow, it is often assumed that they are a symptom of chronic grief, indicating that mourning is unresolved. But are tears always a sign that mourning is unresolved? This chapter challenges that assumption, exposing hazards that await the therapist who accepts uncritically the 'easy fit' between traditional therapeutic approaches and the values embedded in our social context. The relevance of a systemic approach to bereavement is explored in relation to the experience of two families who have experienced loss. Within this framework, traditional ideas about the tears of the bereaved are reinterpreted and reworked, pointing to new ways of assessing the effects of loss and of defining the therapeutic tasks. The focus of therapy now encompasses not only the bereaved individual but the family group and also the interfacing wider systems.

Developing a systemic approach to bereaved families: raising the issues

In a recent supervision session with a colleague whom I shall call Anne, she told me 'now I think I've understood what the homeostasis is in this family'. When I asked her to describe what she meant, she said that the family contained 'many generations of unresolved losses'. This had struck her in the last session with them, when Mary, the mother, broke down into inconsolable tears about the loss of her husband. She had concluded that what this mother needed was to be in individual therapy. I asked Anne to remind me of the presenting problem. She told me that Mary had requested help because her 13-year-old daughter Tracy had recently begun to miss school and steal. The school and the police had become involved, but to little effect. It later emerged that Tracy's father, Bill, had died several years before. I was puzzled about the nature of the link that Anne had made between the loss of Bill and Tracy's school non-attendance and stealing. Anne explained that the mother's tears seemed to indicate unresolved grief, and that the child's 'problem behaviour' was a further indication of this. Anne then assumed that Mary needed individual therapy to help her to come to terms with her loss. But how, I wondered, would this address Mary's wish to get Tracy back into school and stop her stealing? At this point, Anne smiled and said 'Oh, I see, I've fallen into that old trap, haven't I? I've stopped thinking systemically and I'm thinking in a very linear way about loss'. I replied that I was not surprised, because the main theoretical framework we have for thinking about the effects of loss is a linear one. It is easy to fall back on this when there is no clear systemic alternative to put in its place. I have supervised many family therapists over the years, and it is almost inevitable that whenever a person becomes tearful in a session when recalling a loss, the therapist will make an assumption that the loss is 'not resolved', and that the tears indicate some 'pathological' process. In my view, this usually means that the therapist is in retreat from their systemic framework, and is reverting to more linear models of understanding loss.

There is, in fact, a strongly held belief even among some systemic practitioners that 'not to treat a systemic problem correctly as grief-related results in an unhelpful focus on secondary problems' (Paul and Paul, 1982). There are a number of important ideas here which I, working with a structural model, would question. The first is the suggestion that grief should always be seen as the primary problem, and that other problems should be seen as secondary. The second suggestion is that the therapist's role is to address the feelings of grief, by helping the bereaved individuals to express them, and ultimately to work through the mourning process. This is consistent with the idea that if feelings of grief are not expressed, there is a risk of the mourning process being delayed and giving rise to secondary problems. It is implied that if feelings of grief are expressed, for example as tears, there will be a reduction of the need to 'act out' in a way that causes symptomatic behaviour (in Anne's case, Mary's helplessness and her daughter's behaviour problems).

Anne's story and her assumption that the mother's tears were an expression of unresolved mourning reminded me of my own experience of family bereavement and its aftermath, and of the way in which tears continued to be shed for many years after the event – the sudden death of my older brother Stuart Sutcliffe. It was my mother's tears that I found particularly moving. For years afterwards, she would weep when reminiscing about Stuart, often whilst being interviewed about him by journalists in search of memorable anecdotes about his life as a member of the Beatles pop group, or as an undiscovered artist. 'Beatlemania' and the continuing public interest in the group has ensured that, over the years, the media appetite for interviews of this kind has persisted, erupting from time to time in response to particular events. I had always assumed that my mother's tears on these occasions were an expression of continuing grief. However, as time went on and I gained experience as a therapist, I began to question this, because in many other ways my mother did not show the signs of chronic grief. Working with bereaved families, I found myself beginning to ask a series of questions about the basis of our understanding about the way in which people adjust after a loss, and what the meaning of such late tears might be. These questions were the beginning of a long journey in the development of my thinking about the effects of bereavement on the family and on the wider systems to which the family is linked; the nature of the adjustments which follow bereavement, including the mourning process; and the process of change that occurs in the emotions of bereaved individuals during this process of adjustment. In this chapter, I will attempt to describe this journey in the development of my thinking, and to show how it has influenced my approach to therapeutic work with families who have experienced loss. I will show how this thinking was used by Anne in her therapy with Mary and Tracy, enabling her to address the systemic issues which lay behind Mary's tears. By way of introduction, however, I will say a little more about the circumstances linked to my brother Stuart's death, since these played an important part of the context in which my initial thinking was formed.

Stuart died suddenly and unexpectedly at the age of 21. Several years later, two of his closest friends – Brian Epstein and John Lennon – also died tragically young. Stuart died in 1962, just after the Beatles had made their first hit record. He had been a founder member of the group and had helped create the name, style and image. For my family, Stuart's death came as a devastating blow. Not only was his death shockingly premature, it also came completely unheralded. Stuart appeared to be a healthy young man on the verge of a brilliant career as an artist. Within the family, he had always been a great help and support to my mother. With my father away at sea in the Navy all the years of my childhood, and my mother working full time as a teacher, Stuart had grown up to feel very responsible for looking after my mother, my sister and me. Looking back, family relationships were extremely close and interdependent.

Stuart became involved with the Beatles group through his friendship with John Lennon, who was also a student at the Liverpool Art School. John had been raised as an only child by his mother Julia, her sister, Mimi and Mimi's husband, George. John's natural father Freddy had vanished when John was very young, leaving Julia alone and in difficult circumstances with her baby son. It was natural for Mimi and George, who had no children of their own, to want to help out. Julia continued to live nearby, and often visited John at her sister's home. They remained in close and frequent contact, even though Julia later had several more children. In 1955, John's family was devastated by the sudden and premature death of George, John's surrogate father, and, three short years later, by the death of his mother Julia, who was run over by a police car outside Mimi's home. With George's death, Mimi became in effect, a single parent. John was only eighteen when Julia died. At this stage of his life, he was an angry, rebellious young man, who often cut classes and mocked authority figures. His sculpture teacher, Philip Hartas, described him as 'like a car without brakes', crashing his way through life, and through everyone's sensitivities. Mimi, unsure of her own authority as a parent, and struggling to come to terms with the death of her husband and sister, must have found it hard to cope. Nevertheless, she and John remained very close, and when John was gunned down in 1980, outside his apartment building in New York, it was as if Mimi had lost her only son.

John and Stuart soon became close friends. They were drawn together by their love of music and a mutual admiration for each other's talents. Stuart was also one of the friends who was allowed to glimpse the vulnerability that lay behind John's 'hard man' façade. Stuart taught John to draw out of class and was part of a close group of fellow students who helped John with his exam submissions. It was about this time that John met up with schoolboys Paul McCartney and George Harrison. They were all taking part in a church garden fête which featured a number of performing skiffle groups. Drawn together by their love of music and admiration for each other's musical talents John, George and Paul began to spend a lot of time making music together. Soon Stuart, who was fanatically interested in rock 'n roll, became a member of the group and as convinced as John, Paul and George that they would soon become pop stars.

They were helped on their way to success by Brian Epstein, who became the group's manager. Brian had also been born and raised in Liverpool. He was the elder of two brothers and part of a close-knit family unit. Brian was a few years older than John and Stuart, whom he met when he went to see them play at the Cavern Club in 1961. At that time Brian was working in his family's music store and had become intrigued by the many requests he received for the group's one and only recording. Brian was the second of this group of young men to die. His sudden death, only six weeks after the death of his own father, left his family devastated and his mother Queenie doubly bereft. Brian died five years after Stuart and thirteen years before John.

The deaths of these three young men devastated their families. Not only had they all died unexpectedly young, but all of them were 'special' in a number of different ways. All had been eldest sons, close to their mothers, and had filled a very special role within their families. In addition, each one had achieved considerable success. Brian had become perhaps the best known manager of his time. John had become a superstar, and his achievements continue to attract media attention. For Stuart, fame came more slowly. His death attracted a lot of media attention at the time because of his member-ship of and continuing association with the group. At the time of his death Stuart had left the group at the end of yet another of their gruelling stints, playing for long hours in dingy Hamburg clubs, to return to his painting. Regarded as a one of the brightest young talents of his generation at art school, Stuart had recently been awarded a prestigious postgraduate scholarship to study in Hamburg with Eduardo Paolozzi. With his death, it seemed inevitable that none of his early promise would be fulfilled. It also seemed at the time as though his talent and his achievements as a painter would be forever overshadowed by his membership of the Beatles. However, by 1996, 34 years after his death, Stuart has gained an international reputation as an artist and performer. By a strange twist of irony, in 1995–6, Stuart was back performing with the Beatles on their number one world-wide hit record, *Anthology 1*, and participating in a TV documentary of the same name made possible from old tape recordings and images made before his death. So Stuart, since his death, has gained a reputation both as a significant young painter and as a performer with the most famous pop group of all time.

The popularity and success achieved by the group as a whole, and by each of its members was accompanied by enormous media attention and public interest. Media attention became a part of every-day life for the group. It also became an important challenge for the families. The invasion of journalists, hungry for news and for interviews, is a major factor for family members to contend with. When such an onslaught happens only hours after the death of one of the family's members, the effect can be overwhelming. Relatives struggling to comprehend what has happened, feeling that their world has been shattered, may be glad of the opportunity to express this, or may feel further traumatised. The potential of media intrusion for causing further harm to survivors has been increasingly recognised in recent years in the wake of coverage of mass disasters such as the bombing of the Pan American flight over Lockerbie, the Zebrugge ferry disaster, and the shooting of primary school children in Dunblane, Scotland in 1996. Following the tragedy at Dunblane, a news blackout was considered by the media and restraint was requested by the families. However, for the journalists at the scene, there must have been intense conflict between the wish to shield survivors from further trauma and the need to inform the nation of what had taken place. A similar conflict between the need to report and the need to protect can also occur in the case of the death of public figures. Here too, the emotional vulnerability of the survivors is often exposed by such encounters in a way that creates a naked intimacy between the casual viewer and the bereaved. For me, for example, the television image of the grief-stricken face of Yoko Ono following her husband's murder is etched in detail on my memory – a testimony to the ability of the camera to penetrate even the most painfully intimate moments, and of the way in which the survivor can become a victim of a different kind. In the case of the famous Beatles, media interest following the death of each young man was considerable. What is less widely known is the degree to which it affected not only close relatives of the deceased but also the families of all the members of the group. Thus it was that, many years after Stuart's death, my mother found herself being asked to talk about her reactions to the deaths of Stuart's friends, Brian and John, and she was in tears once more as she spoke to the reporters.

After Stuart's death, family life was radically changed. After the funeral my father went back to sea, and my mother and sister and I were left alone at home. There was little open expression of grief, and looking back now, I think that my mother and I did our best to resume our lives and tried to hide our grief from one another. My mother seemed to lose her zest for life and the house seemed sad and empty. At the time, I remember the visits that Mimi and Queenie made to my mother, and being very touched by the concern and affection which they showed. They had met in the very early days of the group and had become firm friends. After Stuart's death they would often come for tea and their visits would always involve tears. At these times I would be grateful that they provided solace and companionship for my mother, but at the same time I would be concerned that the wounds would not heal if their tears continued to flow.

After Stuart's death I abandoned my plans to go to art school and instead decided to train in social work. By the time of John Lennon's death in 1980 I was an experienced social worker and trained family therapist. My professional training inevitably added new dimensions to my personal perspective on the deaths and their aftermath. Looking back over the years, it seems to me that society's present ways of responding to death are very different from those which prevailed in the 1960s. I also realise, looking back, that my own way of thinking about these losses and their aftermath has undergone a number of significant revolutions over the years. By the mid-1970s, for example, my thinking was heavily influenced both by my training and experience as a social worker and family therapist, and by the psychodynamic theory of mourning that was prevalent at that time. This was rooted in the individual's experience of loss and the normal stages through which the experience of loss was thought to be resolved. According to mourning theory, as I understood it, a healthy resolution would entail the cessation of grief and the resolution of mourning. Where grief persisted long after the loss, I had learned, as a therapist, to expect some sort of emotional disturbance or pathology. Therefore, when it came to observing the tears of my mother, Mimi and Queenie, I perceived them as not having adjusted to their losses. Yet knowing them all personally, it was clear to me that they had moved on in their lives, appeared to be functioning well in many ways, and did not seem to be suffering from chronic grief. Over time, I found it increasingly difficult to make sense of the fact that their tears continued to flow, even though they were coping well. This simply did not seem to fit with the theory which informed my professional work. Eventually I began to wonder if the apparent contradiction might, in fact, be explained by some conceptual flaw or limitation in the theory itself. However, it was only later, with the development of systemic ideas, that I began to be able to resolve this apparent conflict. In the next section I will describe how this came about.

The evolution of a systemic approach

After Stuart died my mother flew to Germany with George and Brian to identify the body and bring it home for burial. John met them at the airport. My mother told me that he had showed no emotion about Stuart's death and shed no tears. He also showed no concern for her, and did not visit my parents to 'pay his respects' for more than a year. Then, still outwardly unmoved, he asked my mother if she would give him Stuart's big black scarf and one of his paintings. To my mother, John's wish to wear Stuart's scarf close to his body – which he did for a long time – was the closest he could get to being able to show her how painfully he had been affected by Stuart's death. John became more open about his vulnerability only in the late 1960s, when he undertook Primal Therapy with Arthur Janov and recorded songs such as *Julia*, with its heart-rending cries, and *Woman*, a passionate love song. In the late 1950s, however, it would have been considered unmanly to grieve openly. It was only much later that such expressions of feeling were to become socially acceptable. At that time grief was to be suffered bravely and in silence. The experience was conventionally regarded as one that should not be talked about by others, for fear of increasing the pain of the bereaved individual. There was no place for talking about the experience, and certainly no place for therapy with its emphasis on the expression of feeling. After the funeral there was a respectful silence on the subject and an assumption that the process of mourning had to be endured, and that grief would gradually cease over time if left alone. At that time my family's community leaned heavily on the Church for emotional support, and the response to a death in the family was one which was at once both extremely ritualised and organisationally hierarchical. All the procedures, including the order of the funeral procession, the way in which the service was conducted, the reception, the letters of condolence and so on, served to underline this. In the case of Stuart's death these procedures also underlined a hierarchy in which parents were seen as the individuals who had sustained the most important loss. Within the parental couple it was, of course, generally accepted that it was the mother who would express feelings of grief, whilst the father preserved a rock-like strength and silence. In those days of ritual and formality there was little of the understanding that we have today about the importance of the family being able to share feelings openly, and the tendency of adults was to attempt to protect themselves and other family members by excluding them from events and by keeping their feelings very much to themselves. In this climate of ritual and emotional restraint, the emotional expressiveness and human warmth of Mimi and Queenie must have meant more to my mother than even I realised at the time.

Although, by the 1960s, the work of Freud (1915) and Lindemann (1944) had done much to develop awareness of the psychological process of mourning among mental health professionals, the world of therapy was still very much seen as the preserve of the 'mentally ill' and was tainted with the stigma of mental illness and 'pathology'. The 'talking cure' would certainly not have been regarded as something which might be helpful for a family experiencing loss and who were suffering the normal process of recovery following bereavement. Indeed, this would have gone against the prevailing beliefs of the time. Not even the most enlightened family doctor of those days would have dreamed of considering that therapy might be helpful or even relevant in these circumstances. Of course, this view was to change radically over the next 20 years. It is now much more widely accepted that in some situations, therapeutic intervention may be useful or even necessary. For example, on his recent review of the literature, Frude (1990) draws attention to the fact that nowadays grief is commonly regarded *either* as a form of depression following the loss of an important attachment *or* as a response to the impact of a major life stress or trauma. These different explanations are associated with different ways of looking at the nature of the processes involved. To quote Frude:

According to the depression model, grief is a form of depression triggered by loss. The emotional reaction of grief is seen as having much in common with clinical depression and the origins, nature and functions of grief are therefore explained by reference to general theories of depression... [In] the stress model, bereavement is regarded principally as a stressful life event that taxes the survivor's resources.... It is well established that major stressors bring about emotional and physiological reactions, and grief is regarded as the stress response to bereavement. (p. 343)

In either case, therapy is now seen as having a part to play in helping individuals to cope with bereavement. This is particularly true of those individuals who are exhibiting 'abnormal reactions' to loss or who are 'at risk' of doing so. Since the 1970s, an extensive body of research has accumulated which identifies particular risk factors for poor adjustment following bereavement (for a review, see Frude 1990). According to the results of research with bereaved spouses described by Parkes and Weiss (1983), poor adjustment is associated with the presence of at least one of the three commonly recognised patterns of 'abnormal grief reaction'. The first of these is the 'conflicted grief syndrome', and commonly occurs in situations where the marital relationship was conflicted or ambivalent. The second type of abnormal grief reaction is the 'chronic grief syndrome', which can arise when the marital relationship was highly dependent. The third type is the 'unexpected loss syndrome', in which the death occurs in circumstances which do not allow any preparation by the surviving members of the family. The sudden unexpected death of a young person, for example, is likely to be much more difficult to come to terms with than the death of an older person after a long illness. Sudden bereavement as a result of suicide or murder can also present particular problems (see for example, Schneidman, 1980). Abnormal grief reactions are said to be associated with poor outcome for the survivors and with increased likelihood of psychiatric disorder.

In summary, the notion that there are mourning processes which follow a universal series of stages has now become widely accepted. It is often assumed that, no matter who dies, the processes are the same, and that deviation from this process produces pathology. The role of therapy is seen as helping those whose mourning process did not seem to be conforming to the normal pattern, and as helping to avoid chronic mental health problems or depression. The identification of risk factors for mental health problems of this kind led to the idea that therapy might also have a preventative role for those at risk. The most prevalent type of therapy concentrated on individuals, particularly bereaved spouses. Time spent in the process of mourning was seen not only as normal, but as necessary. In the epilogue of her seminal book *Death and the Family* (1974), Lily Pincus writes:

> There is no growth without pain and conflict; there is no loss which cannot lead to gain. Although this interconnection is what life is all about, it is difficult for the newly bereaved to accept. Only slowly may he, who has been in touch with death through the loss of a significant person, regain touch with life. A life which may bring new growth through the acceptance of death and pain and loss, and thus become truly a new life, a rebirth. (p. 278)

She points to the fact that this has always been known, and is engrained in Christian culture:

> Writers, artists, thinkers have always known about it, and on some level so have we all. It is explicit in the Christian conception that Satan, on bringing sin into the world, introduced with it sex, death, and painful birth, where before the Fall there had been love, joy and eternal life. (p. 276)

Psychotherapeutic practice was thus very much in line with the Christian belief that the acceptance of death, through suffering, is followed by recovery and rebirth. If, therefore, therapeutic intervention is justified, it is to promote the process of mourning. The therapist is able to facilitate this by encouraging the expression of emotion. This was, in fact, very much my own experiences when, as a therapist in training, I undertook psychoanalysis. My analyst took the by then conventional view that my own inability to shed tears about Stuart's death was an indication that I had not resolved the mourning process, and progress could not be expected until I had.

Questions unanswered by mourning theory

By the time I had trained as a systemic therapist, in the late 1970s, I was beginning to find that the prevailing mourning theory left me with a number of unanswered questions about the response of the family system as a whole. It also left me puzzled as to how to account for the tears of my mother, Mimi and Queenie. If not a symptom of unresolved mourning, what was the significance of these tears? Were they a sign that therapeutic help was needed? I often wondered how they would have responded to such a suggestion. If not a sign of pathological mourning, what other meaning might these tears have, I wondered? Perhaps the normal processes of mourning could vary, depending on the particular circumstances of the loss. It might, for example, be harder to get over the loss of a child than the loss of a spouse. For a parent, the death of a partner of the same generation as oneself might be easier to live with. For the family system as a whole, it is clear that the impact of a child's death would be very different from that of a spouse. The impact of the loss would be far reaching in terms of the structure of the family, the normal order of events across generations and the developmental transitions within the family. Perhaps a combination of factors could entail prolonged duration of the recovery process, including grief.

By the end of the 1970s, research was beginning to address some of these questions, and it became apparent that there were at least three things that the systemic therapist needed to take account of when exploring the effect of a loss on the family system. First, the *role* of the person who died, second, the *circumstances* of the death and third, the *support* available to the family. Research began to show the importance of contextual factors not only for the way in which the family was affected by loss, but also for the way in which it was able to cope. These are briefly reviewed below (for a more extended review, see Frude, 1990). This work has taken our understanding of the processes following a loss beyond the private experience of the individual into a broader context. For the systemic therapist this research has helped to extend perspectives on the systemic effects of loss, to identify the risk factors likely to impede recovery and has also suggested new possibilities for therapeutic intervention.

Some effects of loss on the family

Most of the research I had read described the effects of loss of a partner on a bereaved spouse. What, I wondered, of the effects of losses of a different kind? Would the process of mourning follow the same stages; and what other processes of adjustment might be needed? What of the effects of the death of a child on the mother, and on younger brothers and sisters? From a systemic point of view, the roles and relationships would be altered in very different ways. It therefore seemed likely that the effect of the death of a child on the parent would be different in many respects from the effects of the death of a spouse. It also seemed likely that the effects on a child of the death of a sibling would be very different from those resulting from the death of a parent.

Given my own experience of my brother's death, I was particularly interested in the way in which siblings were affected, but found that there was a dearth of literature on this topic. However, the ways in which death affects a young child have recently become better understood (Bentovim, 1986; Black and Urbanowicz, 1987). Once again, the research highlights the importance of the role of the deceased, the circumstances of the loss and the amount of support available to the child. Children do not necessarily manifest the effects of loss in the same way as adults (Black, 1993a). Their responses depend on their age, stage of psychological development, the degree of trauma involved (Black, 1993b) and the impact of the loss on how their needs are met. In a study of young children who have suffered the loss of a parent, Raphael (1982) describes a range of emotional and behavioural responses. She notes that the nature of the young child's response will vary enormously depending on the way in which adults respond. Very young children may appear to lack any grief reaction but commonly manifest a variety of behavioural problems. The degree to which these may give rise to longer-term difficulties seems to depend largely upon how sensitively adult carers respond to the child's needs (Bifulco *et al.*, 1992).

There is increasing evidence that both depression and anxiety in adult life are linked to the experience of loss in childhood, and that these effects are mediated by the effects of the lower quality of care they receive after the loss (Brown and Harris, 1993). It has been suggested that the psychological unavailability of parents, insecure attachment relationships between parent and child and the child's development of depression or precursors of depression may be seen as interrelated processes (Cummings and Cichetti, 1990). Where parental loss occurs as a result of suicide there are particular risk factors for the surviving children. Cain and Fast (1972), in their paper on the suicide of a parent, shed further light on the importance of the circumstances in which a death occurs. They suggest that, for the children of the deceased, the fact that death was chosen rather than inevitable, implies rejection and accusation of survivors, and raises unresolvable questions about the role of emotional and interpersonal factors in the events leading up to the death. Children also suffer from the effects of stigma following a suicide, especially where the wider family and community offer blame rather than support. The role of the extended family in providing support can obviously be very important, but is not always reliable (for example, Tufnell, Sutcliffe and Cornish, this volume). Raphael (1977) found that extended families were not always helpful, and that parents-in-law sometimes became embroiled in bitter conflict with the surviving parent. The effects of this could be considerable. For example, in a much later study of the effects of bereavement on children, West *et al.* (1991) found evidence to suggest that these effects were mediated indirectly through four variables which affect the family. The first variable was the degree of demoralisation and depression in the surviving parent, who may become withdrawn and have difficulty in responding to the child's needs. The second factor was the change in 'family warmth' following the loss. 'Negative family events' such as loss of home and familiar surroundings, loss of contact with friends and relatives, financial difficulties and change of schooling, was the third variable identified as having a powerful potential to compound the difficulties following the death of a parent. The fourth variable was that of 'family stability', with very positive effects on the children noted when there was good social support, communication and ability to share feelings. Lieberman and Black (1987) suggest that the response of the individual may be dampened or enhanced by the response of the family system, and that where the system enhances individual pathology, such as an abnormal grief reaction, the behaviour of the family will mirror those of the individual.

The importance of systems beyond the family

The importance of the role of the extended family in providing support to the family is self evident. But beyond this, what of wider systems which impinge upon the family? The effect of a death may, after all, be felt well beyond the confines of the nuclear family, and the response of wider systems can be expected to inform or even to pattern the social context within which the family's process of adjustment will take place. For example, in the case described by Anne, the family had (because of Tracy's stealing and school non-attendance) become embroiled with at least two such systems – the school and the police. In a similar way, the families of disaster victims may become embroiled with the media in a way that impacts massively on their ability to cope. In the case of my own family, and those of John Lennon and Brian Epstein, the public fascination with the Beatles meant that a enormous network of fans were affected by their deaths, and that the families were inevitably caught up in the wave of concern and interest that followed. Of course, the attention of the media that this entailed was considerable. What effect, I wondered, did this involvement of such wider system have on the process of mourning, and the ability of individuals to resolve their grief, and to move on? I have already mentioned that, during media interviews, the mothers would often cry when talking about their sons. Why was this, I wondered. Was it the way in which the interview prompted memories of the lost child, and reflections on what might have been and all the promise that was lost? Did such interviews open up old wounds? If that were the case, why did they not simply refuse to give further interviews? Or was it that this media interest served a useful purpose for them? Did it help them to hold onto cherished memories of their lost sons? Did it somehow help them to believe that they did not need to be forgotten? Alternatively, was it possible that interviews provided some sort of opportunity for 'debriefing' after a trauma that would otherwise have been overwhelming. Whatever the answers to these questions, it was clear that the impact of a death on the surviving family could be affected not only by the circumstances within the family itself, but by systems outside the family. If the person who dies is famous, for example, and is therefore part of a wider system, the impact on the family and the process of adjustment are bound to be affected. Perhaps the burden of loss is greater for the family if the deceased is well known. On the other hand, perhaps the family is helped by knowing that millions of people care about the death, and derive support from sharing their memories in public. But if it causes grief, could this be harmful? I have found it easier to think about these questions within the framework of a systemic approach. In the following sections I will describe how this came about.

The advent of systemic thinking

Systemic thinking, with its focus on the family system as a whole, brought a number of new perspectives to the world of psychotherapy. Whilst it did not deny the proposition that the mourning process is an important one for individuals who have experienced loss, systemic ideas challenged the primacy of this conceptualisation as a way of understanding the impact of death both on individuals and on the family as a whole. It also offered an approach that moved the focus away from the internal world of the individual and its attendant pathologies, towards one that attempted to address the issues for the family system as a whole. Therapeutic interventions of this kind were directed towards changing very much more than the feelings and beliefs of a single individual. However, Walsh and McGoldrick (1991) comment on the paucity of literature which looks at the impact of death on the entire family and the narrowness of existing models of adjustment following loss. There has also been a dearth of information both about how to organise therapeutic work with a bereaved family and how to intervene effectively using a systemic approach. Their volume represents a major attempt to develop a broad systemic perspective. McGoldrick (1991), highlights the importance of mourning as a family process, and the influence of life cycle and developmental issues:

> It is important to track patterns of adaptation to loss as a routine part of family assessment, even when it is not initially presented as relevant to chief complaints. It is most useful to construct a three-generational genogram and a family chronology or timeline of major stress events as part of each family evaluation. These tools allow you to organise information gathered in an interview quickly and easily, without taking an elaborate family history... . It is then easier to scan for patterns relevant to presenting problems, as well as for coping strategies and resources that will influence the family members' adaptation to their presenting problem. (p. 52)

For Walsh and McGoldrick, it is important that, from a systemic point of view, there can be no 'normal' process equivalent to the mourning process for the individual:

> The meaning and consequences of loss vary depending on the particular phase of life cycle development the family is negotiating at the time of the loss. We are mindful of the variability in family life cycle patterns, given the diversity of family forms and ethnic norms. (McGoldrick and Walsh, 1991, p. 30)

For them,

> The uniqueness of each life course in its context needs to be appreciated in every assessment of the multigenerational family life cycle and in our understanding of the meaning of loss. (*ibid.*, p. 47)

This claim, that the response of each family system will be unique, determined by its own specific circumstances, constituted a new challenge to the idea that the process of accommodation to a death follows a predictable course – at least in individuals. If true, it confronts the systemic therapist with a number of questions about the function of therapy and the role of the therapist. If, from a systemic point of view, there is no normal process of mourning, what are the criteria for recognising an 'abnormal' response to loss? What role, if any, does therapy have? How and when is it appropriate to intervene? The traditional view of mourning has been that it is not only a private and personal experience but a universal one. In therapeutic terms, are universal experiences of this kind a legitimate cause for therapeutic intervention? Perhaps referrals should not be made before problems arise – a child who steals or refuses to go to school, as in Anne's case, for example. In the latter case, should such problems be the primary focus of work, with the mourning issues becoming of secondary importance? If so, perhaps there might be a case for preventative intervention in 'high risk' situations.

The answers to these questions from within the field of systemic therapy have been varied, reflecting the range of ideologies within the umbrella of the systemic approach, and accounts to some extent for the lack of anything like a coherent systemic approach to working with bereaved families. The question as to how a systemic therapist might intervene appropriately, therefore remains very much open, reflecting the lack of consensus about how to conceptualise family organisation (that is, democratic or hierarchical) or theory of change (based on expression of feeling, alteration of beliefs, or organisational restructuring). Space in this chapter precludes a detailed review of these different approaches, and the interested reader is referred to Walsh and McGoldrick (1991). However, despite the diversity of views and the lack of consensus at a theoretical level, it is clear that everyone agrees that a death in a family has a major impact on all aspects of the family system's functioning.

A structural approach to family bereavement

Following Stuart's death I trained as a social worker, then as a therapist. Later, whilst I was working at the Tavistock Clinic in London, I became interested in the work of Salvador Minuchin, who was there as a visiting trainer. Minuchin had developed a particular application of systemic ideas for use in therapeutic work with families. This became the basis of a model of systemic intervention that conceptualised the family as an open communication system, whose function was determined by the elements it contained, and by the nature of the rules governing the interactions between them. In this model, the therapist working with the family was seen as part of the system, whilst interventions by the therapist were aimed at changing the interactional patterns between elements of the system. This became known as the structural model of systemic therapy. Minuchin's approach appealed to me both because of the way it took account of the importance of the social context of the individual, and because of the clarity of its principles for intervention. In the following section I will briefly summarise the main points and show how these can be applied to working with families who have experienced loss. Readers in search of a more detailed account are referred to Minuchin (1974) and Minuchin and Fishman (1981).

For the purpose of therapeutic work using the structural model, the individual is conceptualised as an integral part of his social context, but as interacting *with*, rather than acting *on* his environment. Where the environment in question is the family, this is seen as a hierarchically organised system, within which there is a circular, continuous process of mutual influence and reinforcement which tends to maintain a fixed pattern of relationships (homeostasis). In Minuchin's (1974) view

> therapy designed from this point of view rests on three axioms. Each has an emphasis quite different from the related axiom of individual theory. First, an individual's psychic life is *not entirely an internal process*. The individual influences his context and is influenced by in constantly recurring sequences of interaction.... . His actions are governed by the characteristics of the system, and these characteristics include the effects of his own past actions. The individual responds to stresses in other parts of the system, to which he adapts; and he may contribute significantly to stressing other members of the system. The individual can be approached as a subsystem, or as part of the system, but the whole must be taken into account. The second axiom underlying this kind of therapy is that changes in the *family structure* contribute to changes in the behaviour and the *inner psychic processes* of the members of that system. The third axiom is that when a therapist works with a patient or a patient family, his behaviour becomes part of the context. Therapist and family join to form a new, *therapeutic system*, and that system then governs the behaviour of its members. (p. 9, emphases added)

All these, as Minuchin points out, have been taken for granted as part of the *background* to therapy for many years. However, for the therapist who uses a structural approach they provide the *foreground* to intervention.

What are the implications of these three axioms for the therapist dealing with loss and the family? The first is that loss will have a major effect not only upon specific individuals but upon the family system as a whole. The effects of the loss will affect both the structure of the family and the way in which the system functions. How these effects are manifested will depend upon the position in the hierarchy of the individual who has died, and their specific roles and responsibilities. In Anne's case, for example, the mother had lost her husband, and the daughter a father, so that in structural terms both the spouse subsystem and the parental subsystem had been depleted. The therapist maps the effects of such losses by asking members of the family to describe them. This is in marked contrast with the approach of therapies which focus more on the feelings of the bereaved individual.

The effects of the loss on the family system will also depend on the way in which it has functioned prior to the loss. This depends on the degree of 'enmeshment' or 'disengagement' that is present between family members (Minuchin, 1974, p. 55). Where the family's transactional style has been enmeshed, there is often a lack of 'autonomous exploration and mastery of cognitive problems', and this is (in psychodynamic terms) associated with particular difficulties in dealing with issues of separation and individuation. Conversely, where the family's transactional style is disengaged, 'members may function autonomously, but have a skewed sense of independence and lack feelings of loyalty and belonging and the capacity for interdependence and for requesting support when needed' (*ibid.*, p. 55). Both types of relating can cause problems when the family is faced with the need to adapt to change. It is often at this point that families come to therapy.

However, as Minuchin points out:

> To focus on the family as a social system in transformation, however, highlights the transitional nature of certain family processes. It demands an exploration of the changing situation of the family and its members and of their stresses of accommodation. (*ibid.*, p. 60)

The family who has experienced a death of one of its members is also a family in a state of transition. The therapist will need to learn about the family's transactional style and also to explore the nature of the changes required, and the stresses associated with these.

A family will tend to respond to stress in a way that maintains family continuity while making restructuring possible. If a family responds to stress with rigidity, dysfunctional patterns occur. These may eventually bring the family into therapy. (*ibid.*, p. 66)

The therapist will observe how members of the family respond to each other during the interview, noting behaviour which indicates support, cooperation, conflict, and so on. She will ask about the way in which the specific situations were dealt with, and use this to understand the family's patterns of interaction and the degree of flexibility available. The structural therapist will also intervene in these processes directly, by inviting the family to show (enact) what happens, and then intervening to change the process.

Symptomatic behaviour is seen as resulting from dysfunctional patterns of family interaction, rather than a matter of individual psychopathology. Symptoms are particularly associated with the family failing to accommodate to a developmental transition. The therapist's role is to make active efforts to change these patterns of behaviour in such a way as to help the family to be able to cope more effectively. This contrasts with the intervention of the psychodynamic therapist working individually, who would be more concerned to focus on helping the bereaved individual to express and ultimately transform their feelings. The way in which the structural therapist deals with feelings derives from the theory of change which is central to this model:

When the structure of the family group is transformed, the positions of members in the group are altered accordingly. *As a result, each individual's experience changes.* (*ibid.*, p. 2, emphasis added)

This is not to say that the structural therapist does not address directly the emotions that are inevitably expressed in the process of therapy. However, these do not become the primary focus for the therapeutic work, because the expression of feeling alone is not – within this model – assumed to promote change and resolution. Rather, the therapist will explore the feelings expressed by individuals in the light of awareness that these may have important significance for the way in which the family as a whole is coping with loss. For example, if one member is grieving, then all family members will be affected. Respect for the feelings and needs of all the individuals within the family also requires the structural therapist to hold in mind the fact that the feelings and needs of one family member may be very different from those of another. Within the context of the family group, the therapist will respond to the expression of emotion by exploring not only what emotion is being expressed by someone, but also how this affects and is affected by processes in the wider system, especially relationships with others.

From the foregoing discussion it can be seen that the structural approach offers a radical departure from the methods of psycho-therapies which focus on the subjective experience or 'truth' of a single individual (as described in verbal narrative), on the importance of past events (history-taking) and on feelings, rather than on patterns of interactional behaviour. The concept of pathological reaction, too, is conceptualised in a very different way.

> The identified patient's symptoms occupy a special position in the family's system's lines of transaction. They represent a concentrated nodule of family stress. Frequently, they are one of the family's ways of handling this stress. In any case, the identified patient's symptoms are supported by a number of significant family transactional patterns. (*ibid.*, p. 152)

Symptomatic behaviour, therefore, may arise *from* a family's reaction to stress, and can also represent the family's way of dealing *with* stress. This double valence, and the way in which family transactions become organised to maintain the *status quo*, mean that the family will find it difficult to change. In psychodynamic terms this would be described as 'resistance' to change. For the systemic therapist resistance to change occurs because of the tendency of all systems to maintain stability. This is known as homeostasis. Stability and change within any system are mediated by the way in which incoming information (or an event) is transmitted within it. All systems need to be able both to maintain stability (homeostasis) and to bring about structural changes (morphogenesis), and also to facili-tate interactions with other systems. These processes are controlled by the use of feedback loops, which regulate change within the system in much the same way as does a thermostat in a central heating system. When the system's stability is maintained, a negative feedback loop is said to be operating, and this reduces the system's response and preserves the *status quo*. Where the system behaves in a 'goal seeking' or change-orientated way, positive feedback loops are operating, and structural changes (morphogenesis) may ensue. The family that is either enmeshed or disengaged will be particularly vulnerable to homeostatic influences and these may prevent the family from being able to make the changes and transitions that are needed following a death. The stresses involved in maintaining stability and lack of change following a death may be very considerable. The therapist will need to anticipate this normal response, and help to identify the factors maintaining it in order to be able to help the family to move on. Given that there is likely to be not one, but a series of changes which will follow a death, the therapist will need to be alert for homeostasis at each locus of change.

In the case reported by Anne, which was described earlier, the structural therapist would see the loss of Bill, Mary's husband, as initially creating a situation in which the family has to adapt to being a one-parent family. If the family structure is not flexible enough to make the transition, dysfunctional patterns of behaviour may arise. In this case the dysfunctional pattern includes Tracy's school non-attendance and stealing and Mary's inability to deal with these. Mary might, for example, be reluctant to take on the responsibility for disciplining and controlling Tracy, because this is a role more traditionally associated with fathers. If so, her attempts to exercise discipline might therefore appear ambiguous, and Tracy's challenging behaviour might be understood as a response to the way her mother behaves. In circumstances of this kind, the therapist will need to address transactions of this kind by setting up enactments (Minuchin and Fishman, 1981) which will illustrate the ways in which Mary feels that Tracy obeys or disobeys her. Enactment will allow the therapist to track the process that has taken place over a recent event and to make interventions which will strengthen the mother. This might take the form of a task which will involve both Mary and her daughter behaving in a new way. For example, using a task concerned with school attendance the therapist would put mother in charge, help her to define her expectations clearly and coach her in being able to set more effective rules and limits. She would also aim to put mother and daughter into a relationship with a clearer hierarchy, with a higher level of control and attention, thus enabling Tracy to feel more cared for and Mary to feel more effective as a parent. This would change Mary's view of herself, enabling her to feel competent rather than a failure.

Beyond the family – the power of wider belief systems

I had just completed my training with Salvador Minuchin and Marianne Walters in Philadelphia when the news of John Lennon's murder broke in 1980. I can still remember the shock and disbelief I experienced on hearing the news. I felt as if I had been rooted to the floor, and then, after what seemed like a period in which time stood still, rushing to turn on the television and checking from one channel to another, hoping against hope that there had been a mistake. When the truth finally hit home my thoughts went automatically to my mother. How would she react? Would this be the last straw for her? Would she be able to cope? Her tears had often made her seem so vulnerable, and once again I found myself worrying that this new disaster would finally precipitate a crisis in her 'unresolved mourning'. Looking back on my responses now, I am struck by the ease with which, even whilst I was in the heartland of structural family therapy, I reverted to such a linear and pathologising view of my mother's emotional state. At the time, the conventional wisdom – even among some systemic therapists – was that, over time, the tears would stop. In fact, by 1980 my mother was, like Mimi and Queenie, a widow living alone, apparently coping well. Within a few hours of John's death my mother, Mimi and Queenie were all besieged with requests for media interviews. As they had done many times before over the years, they rose magnificently to the occasion. Their tears flowed once more, along with their personal reminiscences and amusing anecdotes. But the breakdown that I feared for my mother did not materialise. What, I asked myself, did this say about the meaning of their tears?

Discussing my puzzlement later with a colleague, I was surprised to be asked why I continued to associate tearfulness long after a tragic event with unresolved mourning. These mothers were fine examples of the cultural tradition in which each had been raised and exposed to all their lives, she said. They were conforming to the expectations of society. Viewers and readers expected them to be sad when plumbing the depths of their memories as mothers. Surely, she suggested, it must be possible to account for such behaviour within the framework of the structural approach, at the heart of which lies the concept of the individual as part of a wider interacting system. My colleague's observations reminded me that it is important not to lose sight of the fact that, just as the individual can be influenced by the wider system of the family, so too the family itself can be affected by systems which operate in society at large. The media, with its claim to represent the interests of the public, is clearly a system with the power to influence the social status of individuals, the families of the famous and prominent individuals, and beliefs and reactions to significant events. Up to now I had not taken account of the possibility that wider systems of this kind might influence the way in which a family deals with loss; nor had I considered how this might impact on therapists working with bereaved people. Could media expectations about the effects of loss, the inevitability of sadness and the appropriateness of tears, be influencing the behaviour of the mothers in the context of the interviews they gave? Could this be perceived as supporting them in the role of 'grieving mothers', or, years later, as reviving this role within the context of the interview? Could there, in fact, be a homeostatic influence here?

The wider system, homeostasis and therapy

Whilst society and psychotherapists are committed to the belief that tears are always an indication of mourning, then tears long after the event may well be understood as mourning that is unresolved. For these therapists, stopping the flow of tears might be a therapeutic goal in itself. However, systemic therapists, whether working with families, couples or individuals, will want to be more cautious about making assumptions about the meaning of such tears, and want to consider the implications of such an expression of emotion for the system or systems involved. Almost every therapeutic encounter involves us in some way with loss, for example the loss of a relationship, the death of a spouse, parent or child, redundancies from work, road traffic accidents. It is all too easy to assume, as Anne did, that tears are an indication that loss is emotionally 'unresolved', and further to assume that this is the primary problem. However, the therapist who is working systemically will also need to consider carefully what is the impact of the loss on this particular family at this particular stage of their development.

The case described by Anne at the beginning of this chapter provides an example. Here the therapist had fallen into what I considered to be a familiar trap by recommending individual psychotherapy for the tearful mother. But this would have left the presenting difficulties (the child's school non-attendance and stealing) untouched. When the meaning of Mary's tears was explored in terms of the effects that they produced both within the family and with the wider system, a very different set of possibilities became visible. It became clear that the mother's tears occurred only when she was describing how unable she felt to deal with Tracy's behaviour. The therapist's sympathetic assumption that Mary needed support in her grief mirrored the effect on the wider system. It now transpired that the authorities (police and school), had also expressed sympathy for Mary's tearful state. Her distress had the effect of causing the authorities to withdraw, and they had therefore not helped Mary to correct Tracy's behaviour. The tears in this case could be seen as having a homeostatic function, preserving the status quo in the relationship between Mary and her daughter.

As my discussion with Anne progressed, a new hypothesis began to emerge about the nature of the structural problem for the family at this stage, and the interventions that might be needed to help the work to progress. Tracy's school non-attendance enabled her to stay at home with her mother and to maintain the close relationship that they had developed after Bill had died. There had initially been no problems with her behaviour. Mary had often talked about how much she valued this closeness with Tracy and how they had become more like best friends than mother and daughter. She had always hated arguments and tended to give in to Tracy, whom she preferred to treat like an adult, and whom she (unrealistically) expected to act like a responsible adult. Anne commented on the enmeshed quality of the relationship between Mary and her daughter, adding that she felt that Mary was finding it very painful to lose her sense of closeness as Tracy became more adolescent. As a single parent, this was particularly hard for her and she often felt lonely and bereft. As our discussion came to an end Anne decided that the question now facing her was 'What can be done to help Mary to become a more effective parent for Tracy?' rather than 'What would help Mary resolve her grief?'

For the structural therapist the primary problem following loss is usually conceptualised as a systemic one. The therapist helps to identify the structural difficulty and to assist the family to make the necessary adaptations. In Anne's case it now appeared that although Mary had adapted to being a single parent of a young child after Bill's death, she now needed to make a further transition to being effective as the single parent of an adolescent. This was, in fact, very much linked to the problem that Mary had presented as her primary concern and her reason for seeking help, namely her daughter's school non-attendance and stealing, and her own inability to deal with these effectively. Following our discussion Anne decided to see Mary on her own, in order to explore what kind of help Mary might find most useful, and who might need to be involved. Her aim was to support Mary as a parent and to help her to develop ways of dealing with Tracy more effectively. In order to do this the importance of the wider system needed to be acknowledged and its homeostatic influence needed to be overcome. Mary decided that it was important for Tracy to return to school as soon as possible, but felt that she would not be able to achieve this alone. She would need practical help from the school. This led to a meeting being set up at school, and a plan being made to provide help and support for Tracy to attend school regularly. Meanwhile, Anne continued to work with Mary and Tracy, helping them to create a mother–daughter relationship in which rules and limits were more clearly defined and where conflicts could be negotiated more successfully. Mary decided to return to work part time and to take steps to expand her social life. A year later Tracy had been able to return to school successfully and had done well in her end of year exams. Mary had returned to work full time and was feeling much more positive and cheerful.

In Anne's case the issue of loss turned out to be a complex one, needing more than the resolution of grief for the presenting difficulties to be resolved. However, when grief is presented as the primary concern brought by the family/couple/individual seeking help, many systemic therapists feel ill-equipped to conceptualise and to construct systemic interventions. The reasons for this are eloquently explored by Walsh and McGoldrick (1991 and this volume). In Anne's case the mother's tears turned out to serve a homeostatic function at the interface between the family and the wider system, forestalling effective joint intervention of parent and authority. By assuming that the mother's tears were a symptom of 'unresolved grief', as she initially did, the therapist lost sight of the wider context and might have lost sight of the focus of therapy. It is of course possible that in another such case the mother's view might be that the 'real problem' was her overwhelming sadness about the death of Bill, which made her unable to deal with her daughter. In my view, the therapist using a structural approach would be mistaken if she were to assume – as many therapists would indeed do – that tears could only be a sign of unresolved grief, and furthermore only amenable to individual psychotherapy. Not that the importance of the 'loss' of a father and spouse should be ignored; but the main focus of structural therapy would be on the way in which family life had been affected, rather than on the feelings of the individuals concerned. The mother would be asked 'So what did your husband do when Tracy did not do as you asked... what would he be doing now about her not going to school?' and so on. The issue of grief would be worked as a subtext to the focus on the mother's primary concerns. Thus, using the structural approach, both the feelings of grief and the problems of transition following bereavement can be dealt with simultaneously. This is indeed a radical departure from approaches which would conceptualise the 'primary' issues as concerned with feelings of grief (and thus part of the mourning process) and the behaviour problems as 'secondary' to this. If Ann had, in fact, recommended individual grief work for Mary, there could have been a number of difficulties. Not only would this approach have excluded the other important systemic influences from the therapy system, it might also have entailed delay in getting Tracy back to school. The therapist might have had some difficulty in convincing Mary that her definition of 'the problem' was incorrect (located not in Tracy but in Mary), and in doing so would have risked further undermining Mary's self-esteem and competence as a parent. Such an approach might also have resulted in an abrupt disengagement from therapy.

Anne's case provides an example of the way in which wider social systems (school, police and therapy) can'impinge on the process of adaptation in the family, powerfully inhibiting or potentiating change. Before Anne's intervention the initial response of the school and the police had inadvertently added weight to the homeostatic forces preventing change. What had caused them to respond in this way? Perhaps their response of withholding normal sanctions in response to Mary's tearfulness was, like Anne's, simply ordinary human sympathy for a bereaved woman who appeared to be grieving for her loss. However, in our society such a response is also rooted both in what has now become the social norm in terms of the meaning of bereavement, but beyond that, in beliefs that continue to define women primarily in terms of their role as spouses, and their social status in terms of the occupation of their husbands. Their initial response effectively undermined Mary's sense of herself as a competent adult and effective parent. In my view, until these issues were addressed in the therapy it was not possible for change to occur, hence Anne's feeling that therapy was making no progress. However, when Anne was able to address these issues in therapy, she was able to empower Mary and to help her to regain her effectiveness with appropriate support from the school.

In the case of my mother, Queenie and Mimi, the impact of social context in the form of media attention might also be seen as homeostatic in its effect. From the perspective of the journalists who were sent to interview them, these women's views were of interest primarily because they were the mothers of the pop stars who had been so idolised by the public. From the point of view of the interviewer or the viewer, the tears that they shed when reminiscing about their sons and remembering their deaths lent credibility both to their involvement and to the reality of the events being described. For the media, then, they were defined by their role as mothers of the stars, and in this sense the effect of media involvement put them back into a role which they had long since left behind. In the sense that it involved the denial of change, this influence might be seen as manifestation of homeostasis. But was it? To what extent was this true homeostasis, and how much simply a temporary regression, or even simply behaviour which was appropriate for the context of the interview? In fact, however sad the mothers became when reminiscing about their sons they always appeared to remain emotionally in control. Their answers were relevant to the journalist's current concern, they always retained a coherent story line and showed no sign of being preoccupied with their own grief. Their tears were not an indication of breakdown, and had the effect of adding emotional depth to the interview, rather than causing it to be abandoned. Later, they would resume the ordinary pattern of their lives. They were not left weeping, preoccupied by grief and unable to cope.

The ability of the individual or family to influence wider systems, and to change public perceptions and beliefs also deserves mention here. It should not be forgotten that the family's response is not only shaped and altered by these wider systems, but is also able, through this interaction, to alter public beliefs and attitudes. The ability of individuals to retain a passionate commitment following a loss has been an important motivating factor in the creative work of many pioneering survivors of disaster. For example, the grief of the parents of the children killed at Dunblane has led many of them to become involved in a political campaign against handguns. The horrific rape and murder of a daughter inspired her mother to set up the Lamplugh Trust which offers help and support for bereft parents. For my mother, my sister and me, it has involved work to establish public recognition for Stuart's work and a memorial to him in the form of a scholarship for young artists.

Minuchin's pioneering work in drawing attention to the importance of social context in therapeutic work created a radical shift in the way in which therapists think about their role in relation to the family system and the ways in which they intervene. Using the structural approach that he and his colleagues developed, it becomes possible to see that the occurrence of tears is not necessarily an indication that the person who sheds the tears is suffering from chronic grief. However, within the social context of today there are a number of embedded beliefs which will tend to promote this assumption. I have tried to show how, for the systemic therapist, herself embedded in this social context and subscribing to many of its values and beliefs, it can be very easy to slide unwittingly into making such an assumption. When confronted by the emotional impact of working with a bereaved family, and the complexity of the subsequent processes of transition and adaptation, the therapist can at times feel overwhelmed. At such times it is easy to revert to traditional, normative or conventional ways of responding and to lose sight of a systemic perspective. Tears have a particularly powerful appeal as a signal of personal distress and the need for comfort. The therapist's feelings of concern and pity may draw them towards a response which is rooted not only in human fellow-feeling but also in a more linear way of thinking. The social acceptance of mourning theory, with its focus on the importance of the expression of grief as a means to resolution, can represent a trap for the systemic therapist. This may lead the therapist unintentionally to contribute to homeostasis rather than change. How can this be avoided? Before deciding how to respond to a particular behaviour, such as the shedding of tears, the therapist will need to consider the possible function of the behaviour in systemic terms. Does the expression of emotion signal a problem or an attempted solution? It is important to look at the function of the behaviour, the effect that it has on the process (of decision-making, problem-solving or change, for example), and the possibility that it fulfils a homeostatic function. Does it stop dialogue or problem-solving, does it deflect focus away from the problem under discussion towards the feelings of the individual? Minuchin's structural model – unlike some other systemic approaches – provides a clear framework for addressing these questions. However, in some ways this model does not go far enough for therapists working in the 1990s. For although Minuchin acknowledged the importance of the social context of the individual and the family, his writings do not explore in depth the degree to which the beliefs, values and norms which are embedded in our social context can permeate our work.

Conclusion

For the therapist using a structural model, the impact of loss on the family group will be conceptualised primarily in terms of the structure of the family system, the role that the deceased played within that structure, the family's developmental stage and the structural adaptations required to adjust to the loss.

The possible influence of wider systems also needs to be considered, in terms of the effect these may have on the ability of individual and family to adapt, and for therapeutic work to proceed. Socially accepted beliefs about what constitutes a 'normal' process of adaptation following loss permeate the family's social context, influences expectations about what constitutes socially acceptable conduct and may shape behaviour – even provoke tears on occasion. Such belief systems can exert powerfully homeostatic effects upon the family as a whole as well as within its subsystems. Such homeostatic influences may be particularly powerful at the interface between the family and the outside world.

Therapists need to be mindful of how powerfully homeostatic such belief systems can be, not only in determining conventional attitudes to death, but also the process of recovery. For the therapist, such influences are important in terms of the way in which they may impede constructive change. Such belief systems will often require the therapist both to challenge existing beliefs where these are homeostatic, and also to help the family to develop counter propositions with which to replace them. The construction of a more therapeutic reality with the family is likely to entail not only reframing of expectations and beliefs, but also a process whereby unhelpful social norms and values can be deconstructed to their component themes and issues (see also Levner, this volume).

All the people who have close affectional bonds to someone who has died will need to find a way of coming to terms with the loss. Grief is central to the experience of the bereft survivor and to the mourning process. It is undoubtedly important for the therapist to address directly the issues that are primarily grief-related. However, it is also important not to assume that family problems of adaptation after a loss as *necessarily* primarily grief-related. Tears are a potent expression of distress but do not always indicate unresolved mourning. The possibility that they are an expression of emotions other than grief needs to be considered, as does the possibility that they may have a homeostatic function in systemic terms.

References

Black, D. (1993a) Children and bereavement. *Highlight No. 120*. London: National Children's Bureau.

Black, D. (1993b) Traumatic bereavement in children. *Highlight No. 121*. London: National Children's Bureau.

Black, D. and Urbanowicz, M.A. (1987) Family intervention with bereaved children. *Journal of Child Psychology and Psychiatry* **28**(3):467–76.

Bentovim, A. (1986) Bereaved children. *British Medical Journal* **292**:1482.

Bifulco, A., Harris, T. and Brown, G. (1992) Mourning or early inadequate care? Re-examining the relationship of maternal loss in childhood with adult depression and anxiety. *Development and Psychopathology* **4**:433–49.

Brown, G.W. and Harris, T.O. (1993) Aetiology of anxiety and depressive disorders in an inner city population. 1. Early adversity. *Psychological Medicine* **23**:143–54.

Cain, A. and Fast, I. (1972) *Survivors of Suicide*. Springfield, IL: Thomas.

Cummings, E.M. and Cichetti, D. (1990) Towards a transactional model of relations between attachment and depression. In Greenberg, M., Cichetti, D. and Cummings, E. Mark (eds) *Attachment in the Pre-school Years*. London: University of Chicago Press, p. 346.

Freud, S. (1915) Mourning and melancholia. In Strachey, J. (ed.) *Standard Edition of the Complete Works of Sigmund Freud*, vol. 19. London: Hogarth Press.

Frude, N. (1990) *Understanding family problems*. Chapter 10 Bereavement. Chichester: J. Wiley & Sons.

Lieberman, S. and Black, D. (1987) Loss, mourning and grief. In Bentovim, A., Gorell Barnes, G. and Cooklin, A. (eds) *Family Therapy. Complementary Frameworks of Theory and Practice*. London: Academic Press.

Lindemann, E. (1944) Symptomatology and management of acute grief. *American Journal of Psychiatry* **101**:141–8.

McGoldrick, M. (1991) Echoes from the past: Helping families mourn their losses. In Walsh, F. and McGoldrick, M. (eds) *Living Beyond Loss: Death in the family*. New York: W. W. Norton.

McGoldrick, M. and Walsh, F. (1991) A time to mourn: death and the family life cycle. In Walsh, F. and McGoldrick, M. (eds) *Living Beyond Loss: Death in the Family*. New York: W.W. Norton.

Minuchin, S. (1974) *Families and Family Therapy*. London: Tavistock.

Minuchin, S. and Fishman H.C. (1981) *Family Therapy Techniques*. London: Harvard University Press.

Parkes, C.M. and Weiss, R. (1983) *Recovery from Bereavement*. New York: Basic Books.

Paul, N. and Paul, B.B. (1982) Death and changes in sexual behaviour. In Walsh, F. (ed.) *Normal Family Processes*. New York: Guilford Press.

Pincus, L. (1974) *Death and the Family: The Importance of Mourning*. London: Faber.

Raphael, B. (1977) Preventive intervention with the recently bereaved. *Archives of General Psychiatry* **34**:1450–4.

Raphael, B. (1982) The young child and the death of a parent. In Parkes, C.M. and Stevenson-Hinde, J. (eds) *The Place of Attachment in Human Behaviour*. London: Tavistock.

Schneidman, E.S. (1980) *Voices of Death*. New York: Harper & Row.

Walsh, F. and McGoldrick, M. (1991) Loss and the family: a systemic perspective. In Walsh, F. and McGoldrick, M. (eds) *Living Beyond Loss: Death in the Family*. New York: W.W. Norton.

West, S.G., Sandler, I., Pilow, D.R. *et al.* (1991) The use of structural equation modelling in generative research: toward the design of preventative intervention for bereaved children. *American Journal of Community Psychology* **19**(4):459–80.

CHAPTER 3

Death of a Parent in a Family with Young Children: Working with the Aftermath

Guinevere Tufnell, Ursula Cornish and Pauline Sutcliffe

Death of a parent in a family with young children is a tragic event which can have traumatic consequences for all members of the family. Therapeutic work with such families has received little attention in the research or clinical literature. However, there are indications from the work with bereaved individuals that therapy may have an important role to play in providing support and reducing dysfunction, both in the short and longer term. This chapter describes therapeutic work done with a family following the sudden, accidental death of the mother of two young children. The chapter shows how a systems approach was used in work with an individual member of the family. A structural model was used for the purpose of organising, directing and executing the work.

Recovery from the death of a loved one and the role of therapy

It is generally agreed that people recovering from bereavement are in a state of transition (Walsh and McGoldrick, this volume). Parkes and Weiss (1983) see the process of recovery as involving three tasks. The first of these is accepting the loss (rather than engaging in denial or displacement activity). Second, the bereaved person will have to construct a new 'model of the world' which matches their new

situation. Third, they will need to get used to new kinds of relationships with other people, and a new social status such as that of a
single or widowed person. Therapeutic help may be required where
these transitions are not taking place and where the process of
change has in some way been stopped. What might therapy aim to
achieve? This will depend not only on the kind of explanation the
therapist uses to understand the processes that take place after a loss,
but also on what model of therapy (and theory of change) is
employed. These in turn will determine both the therapist's goals
and the means by which those goals are achieved. It is well
documented that bereaved individuals can be helped effectively, and
how this may be achieved. Less is known about how to do effective
therapeutic work with the family. However, given the evidence
pointing to the impact of loss on the family as a whole, it seems
obvious that help will often be needed by the family group,
especially in cases where there are a high number of risk factors.

What will determine the effectiveness of therapeutic intervention
with the family group? The therapist will first need to be able to
understand how the family as a whole has been affected by what has
happened. Are there any clear models to help the therapist develop
this understanding? The models of mourning as an *individual*
psychic process are not designed to address the impact of loss on the
family system. Black and Urbanowicz (1987), describing their work
with bereaved families, do not discuss the theoretical framework
underlying their particular treatment approach and do not indicate
the type of interventions made. Elsewhere, in the context of work
with families where traumatic loss has occurred, Black and her
colleagues discuss the importance of considering the wider
consequences of the traumatic event on the family, and describe
'debriefing' traumatically bereaved children in order to prevent
post-traumatic stress disorder (Harris Hendricks *et al.*, 1993).
Other studies describing family intervention following bereavement
provide vivid accounts of the clinical work but appear to be based
on a very eclectic theoretical approach (for example, Sills *et al.*,
1988). These accounts, notwithstanding the apparent benefits to
the family, often leave the reader somewhat bemused. The broad
eclecticism employed, and the difficulty of identifying any unifying
theoretical framework often makes it difficult for the reader to
deduce why particular interventions were chosen by the therapist
and how the overall therapeutic intervention was planned. This
means that it can be difficult to know how appropriate it is to

generalise from the examples given and apply the described techniques in other circumstances. In one study that attempts to address these conceptual difficulties, the author describes how he made use of the concepts of attachment theory within a systemic framework (Fulmer, 1983). He provides a useful summary of the developmental and environmental influences which form the context for the individual's mourning process, explains how this can be seen in terms of attachment theory and shows how this was used in structural family therapy with a bereaved single-parent family. However, these elements, while informing and enriching the therapy, do not in the end seem to unify into a fully integrated framework at the level of the family system.

Issues for the family therapy team

The referral of a family to our team for therapy following the sudden death of the mother of three young children, provided an opportunity for us to consider the potential scope of our model for providing appropriate therapeutic help within a clear framework. Minuchin (1974) states that 'the scope of the therapist and the techniques he uses to pursue his goals are determined by his theoretical framework'. This is, of course, a particularly crucial consideration for therapists who aim to work as a team. Our own theoretical framework is based on a view of the family as a system, an approach which derives from the application of systems theory to therapeutic work with family groups. However, given the emphasis of much of the available literature on the conceptualisation of bereavement in terms of individual experience and of effective grief work in terms of *individual* processes that are essentially intrapsychic, we had some doubts initially as to how appropriate our way of working might be for the needs of the bereaved individuals within this particular family. What adaptations might be needed ? How should we begin to structure and organise the work so as to address the numerous issues that were likely to be important? Would we able to find an effective balance between working with the issues affecting the bereaved adults and children and those affecting the family as a whole?

In the next section we will summarise what we mean by the 'the systems approach' and we will then go on to look at the way in which structural family therapy is related to this.

The systems approach

The systems approach allows the therapist to view the individual in the social context of the 'system' of the family group. It offers not only a way of looking at the family but has come to be associated with a number of different applications to therapeutic work with families. Frude (1990) provides a useful introduction to thinking about the family as a special kind of system, which he defines as

> a set of elements, the relationships between them, and the relationships between the attributes or characteristics of the elements. A system is more than simply a collection, because there are comparatively stable relationships between the elements (i.e. there is structure) and because the different parts of the system are causally linked. (p. 38)

In the next section we will briefly outline the way in which the systems approach has been applied within structural family therapy.

Structural family therapy

Structural family therapy represents an application of systems theory to therapeutic work with family groups. According to Minuchin (1974), it consists of

> a body of theory and techniques that approaches the individual in his social context. Therapy based on this framework is directed towards changing the *organisation* of the family. When the *structure* of the family group is transformed, the positions of members in the group are altered accordingly. As a result, each individual's experience changes. (p. 2, emphases added)

The structural family therapy approach conceptualises the family group as a communication system, consisting of a hierarchical structure with elements organised into identifiable subsystems. The elements of the structure are the individual members of the family; the subsystems usually include marital, parental and sibling groups. The boundaries which separate these subsystems are defined by rules which determine the participants in the decision-making activities within each subsystem. In order to function well, family systems need to find a balance between the autonomy of individual members or subsystems, and the cohesiveness of the family as a whole. Stability within the family system is maintained by homeostatic processes, involving negative feedback processes, which operate to preserve the *status quo*. This stability however, will be challenged both by discrete events and by normal developmental processes in family life which necessitate change over time.

Different types of family structure have been described (Minuchin and Fishman, 1981), each with its own characteristic way of functioning. The structure of the family system may be more or less clearly defined, depending on the elements involved and the degree to which boundaries can be identified. A family system may, for example, contain a marital subsystem, a parental subsystem, a sibling subsystem, and a grandparental subsystem. The system is said to be 'enmeshed' when boundaries are poorly defined, and 'disengaged' where boundaries are overdeveloped. The way in which the family functions will depend not only on the way it is structured but also on its stage of development. For example, the patterns of behaviour seen in a family with pre-school children will be very different from those in which the children are adolescent or leaving home.

The process of structural therapy

Therapeutic intervention, observes Minuchin (1974), is based on three assumptions: that the individual's social context affects his or her inner processes, that changes in context produce changes within the individual, and that the therapist's behaviour is significant in facilitating change. Within the structural framework, 'pathology may be inside the patient, in his social context, or in the feedback between them' (p. 9). Structural family therapy intervenes at the level of the process of feedback between the individual and his/her family and social context.

> The therapist joins the family with the goal of changing family organisation in such a way that the family members' experience changes. (p. 13)

Structural family therapy provides the therapist with a very clear set of techniques for achieving this (for example, Minuchin and Fishman, 1981, to whom the reader in search of further details is referred). Basically, in order to work with the family the therapist will need to 'join' the system or particular subsystem with which he intends to work. Joining techniques allow the therapist to form working alliances with individuals and sub-groups within the family. Joining includes the process of making an assessment and also providing support, education and guidance. Once the therapist has joined the system he or she will then need to create a focus for the work and to begin to challenge the existing patterns of interaction. Minuchin describes a range of 'restructuring' techniques which enable the therapist to overcome homeostasis and facilitate change. Restructuring involves challenging the existing structure and transactional patterns of behaviour between family members. This is done by means of 'unbalancing' (altering the established hierarchy), 'boundary making' (changing the participation of members within a subsystem) and 'reframing' (creating the possibility of different meanings for a familiar sequence of events).

Minuchin compares the therapist orientated towards working with the individual to a technician using a magnifying glass. He contrasts this with a structural family therapist who is compared to a technician using a zoom lens, who is thus able to observe with a broader focus as well as zoom in for an intrapsychic focus if he wishes (Minuchin, 1974, p. 3). Thus the therapist expects to work not only with the system as a whole but from time to time with particular subsystems or individuals. This enables detailed work to be done on restructuring different aspects of the family system. In recent years there has been increasing interest in how possible it is to do effective systemic work *primarily* with dyads (such as couples) or individuals (for example Jenkins and Asen, 1992).

Working with a bereaved family

From the point of view of the structural family therapist, the effect of loss of a family member on the family will depend upon a number of factors. First, the effect will depend upon the roles and functions previously carried out by the member who has died. Loss of a parent, for example, would be expected to have a very different effect to the loss of a child. Second, the loss will disrupt family structure, changing previously stable hierarchies and familiar patterns of behaviour. For example, the loss of a parent in a family with young children may result in the parenting subsystem becoming dysfunctional, and if stability is to be maintained changes in routine will be required. The type of family organisation will also be a factor which affects the way in which death will impact upon the family. A third factor likely to have a significant impact on the effects of loss is the family's developmental stage at the time the loss occurs. Where the loss is that of the mother of pre-school children there is likely to be significant negative impact on a number of different levels of the systems simultaneously, including grandparents, spouse and children. In order to make the transition to life in the absence of the dead member the family will need to reassign the functions of the deceased in an appropriate way. The therapist will have to consider what are the problems caused by the death and what will need to change for these to be overcome. Where problems are not being resolved the therapist will have to look at what alliances are currently maintaining the problem and whether the problem is serving some stabilizing function for the family. The family's developmental stage and level of previous functioning has to be taken into account, as will the family's religious, cultural and economic status.

Work with a family after the death of a young mother

We will now describe work done with a family that was referred to us following an apparent suicide. We will describe the work somewhat schematically in order to demonstrate the way in which the systems framework was used and the structural model applied. Areas of exploration will be described in extremely condensed form, with strings of questions or comments used to indicate the direction in which a line of exploration was developed over a more extended time. The work took place in a series of more or less well-defined stages over a period of two years. During most of this time, the father was seen on his own. The first stage consisted of six sessions in the two months immediately following the death. These focused on crisis intervention work aimed at helping the family cope with the aftermath of the death. It also allowed an assessment to be made of the family's structure, its mode of functioning, the existing risk factors, and the opportunities for work to be done. The second stage of therapy took place over a period of about four months and focused mainly on work with the parental subsystem. The third stage of work extended over a period of about four to five months and work focused on the marital subsystem. The fourth stage dealt mainly with issues involving the wider system and took place over a period of approximately six months. Meetings took place approximately weekly, with longer gaps over holiday periods. There was a total of 19 meetings. The final stage of work took place over a period of one year, with 12 sessions at monthly intervals and was concerned with helping to consolidate the gains made at the earlier stages of the work.

Stage 1 – Crisis intervention and assessment

Mr B (aged 30) and his two children, Jim, aged two, and Annie, aged five, were referred for help shortly after the sudden death of Mrs B, following an overdose. At the time of Mrs B's death the family had been in the process of adopting Alf, a two-year-old Romanian orphan fostered by them for the last nine months. They were referred by the adoption social worker immediately after Mrs B's death and had been seen by an experienced bereavement counsellor and family therapist who referred them to us for more extensive work. Six meetings were held over the next eight weeks. During this time the family sought help in dealing with a series of transitional events including Mr B's return to work, moving house, the inquest, and the funeral of Mrs B.

Before meeting the family the team's initial hypotheses were based largely on general knowledge of how families are likely to be affected by sudden loss. We considered the effects that Mrs B's death was likely to have had on the system: Mr B and the three children, the extended family and the adoption agency. We decided that the therapist's first task would be ask the family why they had come and what type of help was wanted. It would then be important to get to know more about the family in terms of it structure (composition) ways of functioning (alliances, interactional patterns, type of attachment, degree of enmeshment and so on) and how death had affected these. Mr B arrived at our first meeting with his two natural children and his dead wife's sister, who said she had come to look after the children while Mr B talked to us. Alf was being looked after by friends. Mr B said that the adoption social worker felt that the children needed help. He told us that he was worried about how to deal with the funeral arrangements because Mrs B's parents felt that the children should not attend, but the adoption social worker's advice had appeared to contradict this. Mr B felt very unsure what to do for the best and was afraid of harming the children if he made the wrong decision. He also wanted someone to explain to the children what had happened to their mother. As we explored what particular questions were being raised by the children, and how these might be approached, it became clear that Mr B himself was struggling to make sense of what had happened. Had Mrs B committed suicide or had there been a tragic accident? In fact, there was still some doubt about the cause of death and the funeral had been delayed so that an inquest could be held to establish the cause of it. The therapist asked Mr B to describe the circumstances surrounding his wife's death. It gradually emerged that there had been a great deal of tension and difficulty in the marriage over the last year or so. Mr B was being treated for depression by his GP, who had advised him to take a holiday alone. He had eventually decided to go away for a while, despite his wife's objections. On the day his wife died he had been away about two weeks. He had arranged with Mrs B that he would collect the children from nursery and bring them home. On arrival he had found her body on the bathroom floor and had immediately called an ambulance. Earlier that day Mrs B had taken out a year's subscription to a gym and had appeared cheerful when her sister had spoken to her on the telephone. She seemed to have taken an overdose of antidepressants but there was no note or other indication that she intended to kill herself.

The effects of loss on the family system

The main theme emerging from the initial session was the degree of Mr B's concerns about his difficulties as a parent, particularly his fear of harming the children by making 'wrong' decisions. Mr B clearly expected us to talk to the children about their mother's death in 'the right way', saying that he did not know how to do this. During the interview he appeared calm, still in a state of emotional numbness about his wife's death, but was warm and responsive to the children, who appeared both over-active and clingy within the session. His behaviour contrasted sharply with his portrayal of himself as an 'incompetent' parent. The team wondered if this could be a manifestation of homeostasis, arising from the fact that until now it would have been primarily Mrs B's role to talk about such issues to the children. The therapist decided to challenge the homeostasis and to restructure the situation by using her 'expert' position to support Mr B's sense of competence as a parent. She commented on how impressed she was that he could think so clearly about the needs of the children at a time which was obviously so difficult for him, and complimented him on his sensitive and affectionate approach to the children. She invited him and his sister-in-law to describe how things were going with the children at home, and what particular help the children seemed to need in understanding what had happened. The therapist asked how he felt the children were reacting to the loss of their mother, and whether he was worried about any aspect of their behaviour. In response to Mr B's questions about how to help the children understand and cope with the loss of their mother, the therapist encouraged Mr B to discuss what Mrs B's absence might mean for them in terms of disruption of daily routine. Mr B was encouraged to describe the practical ways in which he was caring for the children, how he was responding to their questions, how they could be helped to feel secure and understood, and how he might prepare them for the funeral. In fact, he appeared to be coping well, with help from family members. This provided the therapist with opportunities to comment positively on areas where Mr B was coping well with parenting (challenging his 'one down' position), and to offer information or practical alternatives where appropriate. However, Mr B persistently portrayed himself as helpless and incompetent, expecting the therapist to tell him the 'right' thing to do. The therapist's attempts to reassure and encourage only seemed to increase Mr B's discomfort and she wondered whether Mr B's 'one down' position had some homeostatic function in the family before his wife's death. The therapist therefore attempted to unbalance this position by emphasising the enormity of the tragedy, validating and normalising Mr B's concern and uncertainty ('given what has happened... how could you feel otherwise'), and to reframe ('your wish to "get it right" for the children shows how sensitive you are to their needs'). She also commented that Mr B's task was made more difficult because he appeared to be caught in a 'no win' situation between two conflicting sets of advice. If he followed the advice of the family he would not be following professional advice as to what was 'best' for the children. On the other hand, if he followed professional advice he risked provoking disapproval and conflict within the family. Mr B agreed that this was indeed a major problem for him.

The sharp differences of opinion within the family were clearly threatening to disrupt crucial support to the family. It was therefore suggested that perhaps all members of the family who were involved in helping with the children could be invited to come to the next meeting. However, Mr B arrived bringing only the two children. He was also accompanied by his own sister, who knew the children well and had been helping to look after them. He told us it had not been possible for him to arrange for his wife's side of the family to come along to the meeting. He added that he felt that their reason for not joining him was that they blamed him for his wife's death.

The therapist noted that the children appeared more settled in the session, and asked Mr B how he saw their behaviour at home and whether there were any particular issues that he wanted to discuss. Mr B felt that he was coping reasonably well with the ordinary childcare. However, he still felt very uncertain about whether the children should attend the funeral. He was also finding it difficult to know how to talk to them about the meaning of their mother's death. The therapist asked when the funeral was to take place. Mr B said that it would have to be delayed until an inquest had been held. The therapist then asked if this meant that although it was known that Mrs B had taken an overdose, questions remained about the reasons for this. Mr B confirmed that the cause of death remained to be established. This enabled the therapist to comment that in this case no-one yet had an explanation of Mrs B's death, and not only Mr B but the whole family was in a state of uncertainty. No wonder, then, that Mr B was finding it hard to know what to say to the children. The therapist then asked Mr B whether it would be more helpful to talk more about arrangements for the funeral or whether he would prefer to spend some time, perhaps without the children, thinking about why his wife had died. Mr B chose to discuss the broader issues and asked his sister to take the children out for the remainder of the session.

The background to the tragedy

Mr B then went on to talk about the background to his wife's death. He described his relationship to his wife as an idyllic love affair that resulted in marriage when both were in their early twenties. Mrs B was a vivacious, fun-loving person, with lots of friends. For Mr B she became a soul-mate, someone whom he could feel blissfully and effortlessly close to without the need for talking about feelings. He himself was rather quiet and shy, like his father, a rather withdrawn, unresponsive man who left the more extrovert mother to organise everything. He had attended a boarding school before becoming an officer in the Navy. He met Mrs B after leaving the Navy. Following their wedding Mrs B wanted to have children immediately but her first pregnancy had been ectopic. Failing to conceive again she became depressed and took two overdoses. When the children were eventually born she became a happy and devoted mother with an active social life. For a while things went well. Mr B's business was growing and was demanding a lot of his time. He was working long hours, which included a three-hour commute. As time went on the couple spent less and less time together and lost their previous sense of closeness. Mrs B now wanted another child and made plans to

adopt Alf. Feeling increasingly 'depressed' and excluded, Mr B tried
to discuss the difficulties but this only made Mrs B angry. Despite his
wife's objections ('How will I manage to look after the children
without you?') Mr B decided to follow his GP's advice and go on
holiday. After her death he was plagued with conflicting feelings. On
the one hand he worried that his departure had caused Mrs B's death,
as his parents-in-law seemed to feel. On the other hand he wondered
why a woman who cared so much for her children would abandon
them so carelessly? Would someone who, on the day of her death,
seemed to be coping well, had just renewed annual membership of
the health club and arranged to see her husband really have intended
to take her own life? It was the first time that Mr B had been able to
speak openly about these concerns and he expressed relief at being
able to talk without the children being present.

A month later Mr B attended the inquest with his own family and
his in-laws. Shortly afterwards the funeral took place, with neither of
the children present. At the inquest the coroner had initially returned
a verdict of suicide. However, Mr B had found himself impelled to
challenge this in court. As a result he had been asked to give evidence.
He had argued that Mrs B's death could have been accidental. There
was no clear indication that she had intended to die despite the
overdose of antidepressants found at autopsy. In fact there were a
number of indications to the contrary. Mr B had actually made a plan
to meet Mrs B on the day she died. She seemed to have taken the
tablets only a short time before he was due to arrive with the children.
Perhaps she expected him to find her as he had when she had taken
overdoses in the past. As a result of Mr B's evidence the coroner
returned an open verdict. Mr B felt that this was more accurate, as
well as less stigmatising for the family, especially the children. On the
other hand, it did nothing to resolve the uncertainties about his own
role in his wife's death. He continued to ruminate about why his wife
had acted as she did and tended to blame himself for causing her
death. By assuming he was guilty in this way, the therapist
commented, he seemed to be choosing a position that had the
advantage of avoiding continuing conflict in his own mind, and also
of helping him to avoid discord with his wife's family, whom he
continued to perceive as blaming him. On the other hand, there
seemed to be heavy price to pay, because it left Mr B feeling as if he
alone had to carry all the responsibility. In the longer term, if only for
the sake of the children, it might be better to avoid jumping to
conclusions too quickly. Mr B then said that he could still not make

sense of what had happened but that it had been very helpful to be able to talk to someone who was not taking sides. This had given him the courage to stand up in court and put forward his point of view, despite his own uncertainties and the hostility of his wife's relatives. But he remained full of doubts as to whether he could be a good parent for the children, even though they now seemed well settled. The therapist asked Mr B whom he could confide in and share his worries with. Mr B said that he had felt very isolated since the recent house move. In fact, there was no-one with whom he felt he could share his worries. He felt that if he were going to be able to continue to cope he would like to have further meetings with the therapist.

Reviewing the first stage of work

At the end of the assessment phase the team reviewed its initial hypotheses and considered how to proceed. Briefly, the family system seemed to have been fragmented as a result of the death of Mrs B, but there seemed to be no possibility of working directly with this because other members of the family did not wish to attend. Mr B had been left carrying all the responsibility for the family but his position of authority was weak, being both poorly supported and subject to criticism. He was now expressing depressive ideas (guilt, self-blame, lack of confidence, poor self-esteem) and was describing numbness in relation to the bereavement. Considerable marital conflict had been present and there were indications that the system had been very enmeshed. The children were at a stage where they would need considerable time and careful attention, and as well as losing their mother had been bereft of all familiar daily routines, contacts and surroundings.

How was the therapist to 'join' with such a system, and how should the work be taken forward? In the case of the B family the initial sessions helped to clarify that there were a number of possible choices for the therapist to consider. For example, would it be more appropriate to join with Mr B as a bereaved spouse or as a bereft parent (spouse or parent subsystem)? Second, given Mr B's incipient conflict with his in-laws, how feasible would it be to join with the extended family system and to work with the issues of blame and stigma? Third, what was the task involved in joining with the child subsystem and how appropriate would it be at this stage to undertake direct work with the children in the absence of support from the wider family? Might this further undermine Mr B or deepen the split that was already evident between him and his in-laws? To some extent the agenda for the therapist had already been set by the referring professionals and involved, at least in Mr B's view, an implication that he was incompetent as a parent. Beyond this, however, there was an unspoken implication that he had, by his absence, also been incompetent as a spouse. Painfully, it emerged that in Mr B's view others saw him as directly to blame for his wife's death.

Joining

The joining process at this stage involved finding ways of acknowledging Mr B's difficulties whilst not colluding with his negative views of himself. It also involved creating an opportunity for him to consider the possibility that he might have a therapeutic agenda of his own. This was achieved by the therapist showing Mr B that she did not view him as an unfit parent but rather as a poorly supported one, facing many real practical difficulties in providing care for the children. By encouraging Mr B to describe these problems and the steps he was taking to solve them, it became possible for the therapist to reframe Mr B's worries about his parental competence as a sign of his caring and thoughtfulness, and as quite normal given the traumatic family circumstances. The therapist's support enabled Mr B to 'own' for the first time that he himself wanted help in continuing to cope. It also enabled him to participate in sessions without having to accept blame for being an unfit parent or spouse. In structural terms, the therapist initially 'joined' the parental subsystem in order to create an initial focus for the work.

Stage 2 – Transition to a single-parent family

At the end of the initial assessment our working hypothesis was that the primary loss currently being experienced by the family was that of the loss of a mother for the children. Mr B was presenting primarily an unconfident and unsupported parent of two small children. At the end of the assessment phase an important shift had taken place. Mr B was now no longer attending sessions simply because he had been sent, but for reasons of his own. It was therefore possible to agree a new focus for the work with him around the parenting issues. In structural terms the family system could now be thought about in terms of the need for an important developmental shift. The primary task at this stage was that of making a successful transition from a two-parent family to an effective one-parent structure. The main homeostatic issue here was Mr B's position as 'incompetent parent', which enabled him to maintain a clear focus on doing the best for the children and to seek and receive support on their behalf. It also served as a temporarily shield from his overwhelming feelings of guilt and confusion about his wife's death. The task for the therapist at this stage was to create a clear focus of work around reconstructing an effective parenting subsystem and to find a way of 'joining' this subsystem in order to facilitate this change.

What would be involved in achieving a successful transition to a single-parent system? The therapy team's hypothesis involved a series of complex and interrelated issues which would need to form the main focus for the work. First, there would be the need to establish new patterns of daily living and new routines. Mr B would, at least initially, have to take on many of the roles and responsibilities of his dead wife and find ways of meeting the needs of the children in a new way. This would involve thinking about how parenting had been managed in the past. He would have to cope with the ordinary tasks of parenting and probably also cope with a lot of upset and difficult behaviour from the children without the support of his wife. He would be likely to feel very lonely and there would be a risk of depression compounding his difficulties in coping. The children's care would then be likely to deteriorate. There might be a risk of the older child being drawn into a pseudo-partner or pseudo-parent role, with disruption of the sibling subsystem. Beyond this, it seemed likely that the search for an explanation of Mrs B's death would continue.

Mr B was seen alone eight times between January and May. At first he was kept extremely busy with practical tasks and caring for the children. After some months, and as soon as Mr B was able to sell his previous home, the family moved to a permanent new home 'that Mrs B would have liked'. At times he became quite elated about how well he was managing on his own. He had always enjoyed looking after the children and had been very involved with them in the past. Now he was very moved by how attached they were to him and how pleased they were to see him on his return from work. The children gradually became more settled in their new daily routine. A nanny was found for Jim, and Annie settled well in her new school. The behaviour problems that had appeared after Mrs B's death (bed-wetting, nightmares, clinginess and tantrums) gradually subsided. He also found it easier to respond to Annie's questions (for example, 'Can we buy another mummy at the supermarket, Daddy?') and remarks (for example, 'Did you know, my Mummy's dead?' when introduced to strangers) about her mother's death. In the early phase of this stage of therapy the role of the therapist was primarily aimed at supporting Mr B's sense of competence and self-esteem as a parent. As before, this involved resisting Mr B's invitations to blame and condemn him for incompetence, repeatedly reframing his uncertainty and indecisiveness as the normal response to difficult circumstances, and helping him to formulate solutions as well as to describe problems.

The work around parenting inevitably involved explorations of how things had been when Mrs B was alive and how they were different now. What were their different roles and responsibilities as parents and how did they work together as a team? Mr B portrayed his wife as competent, decisive and always able to be clear about what she wanted. By contrast, he saw himself as incompetent, inarticulate, indecisive and often unclear about what he wanted – in fact the complete opposite of his wife. He was used to leaving family decisions to her. He increasingly began to talk about how things had been when his wife was alive and how she had liked to do things. He found himself talking to her when confronted with the need to make the 'right' decision about things such as a nanny for the children, a school for Annie, the choice of a new house. Often he found himself thinking 'what she would have done', imagining what she would have said and the choices she would have made. The therapist noted his continuing lack of sadness and wondered whether to acknowledge his continuing denial of Mrs B's death at this point. However, she decided it would be more helpful to use this as an opportunity to challenge the homeostasis around 'incompetence' once more. Given how well Mr B was now coping, making decisions and discussing things in therapy, she now said that she was puzzled by his claims of incompetence. Furthermore, his reports of his business affairs seemed to indicate that he was extremely competent in some areas of his life. She also encouraged Mr B to say more about how he and his wife had come to decide to divide the labour on decision-making in the way that they had, thus reframing 'incompetence' as a conscious decision about roles and responsibilities.

Mr B's descriptions about how family life had been in the past were initially very idealised but gradually, through discussions of how he and his wife had coordinated their parenting activity, began to reveal some real areas of conflict. When talking in more detail it became clear that Mrs B had not always been vivacious and confident. In fact, after their idyllic courtship she had often been quite depressed. Her depression had lifted following the birth of her first child but she had retained a tendency for depressive mood swings, and also a tendency to blame her husband when things were not going well. Because of his wife's previous overdoses he feared her disappointments and tended to accede to her demands in order to avoid this. With the arrival of the children Mrs B's need for support from her husband increased. He therefore became very involved in the day-to-day care of the children, which he enjoyed very much. However, he began to feel he needed some time for himself. This tended to create problems. The therapist commented on how common such problems were for families with young children. Had they managed to sort things out? Mr B described how he would try to get home as soon as possible so that his wife could have a break and get out of the house. He would play with the children and put them to bed. He tried not to be late but sometimes he would get stuck in a traffic jam and would arrive home late. This tended to make Mrs B angry and she would accuse him of not understanding how she needed a break and that he had made her late for her appointment. Whatever he did, he had begun to feel she did not value his contributions and did not recognise that he too needed time for himself. On the other hand, he seemed to feel that perhaps he should have done more.

By this stage Mr B was beginning to be much more confident in his parental role but was still tending to denigrate and blame himself, in contrast to idealising his lost soul-mate. The therapist now decided to challenge this homeostatic position more directly. In order to do this she expressed astonishment that, following a long day at work and an exhausting journey home, such a sensible and competent person would respond to her husband in this way. Surely Mrs B would have at least offered him a cup of tea and a few moments breathing space before expecting him to take over looking after the children. Mr B seemed surprised. Mrs B never responded in this way, he said. The therapist commented that if Mrs B was always so inconsiderate, she was not surprised he had been feeling so fed-up and depressed. But given the couple's 'closeness', how could Mrs B have been so unaware of her husband's needs? Mr B explained that in most things he and his wife were so close that they did not really need to talk. Did this mean, the therapist asked, that they had not had much practice at discussing things where they might not automatically agree? Mr B said that this had only started to happen recently. There had not been much talking because Mrs B would get so upset and then the tension would get worse. Did this mean, the therapist asked, that Mr. B's need to protect his wife had prevented him being able make his wife more aware of his needs? How far did Mr B's fear of upsetting his wife lead him to conceal his feelings from her? Had he ever explained to her that he too needed time for himself? Mr B felt that he had begun to try but that his decision to take some time for himself had resulted in his wife taking her final overdose.

Stage 3 – Working with the marital subsystem

At the end of the first stage of therapy, Mr B was coping confidently and effectively as a parent but was increasingly feeling that a life of work and parenting no longer seemed enough. He began to long for adult companionship and time for himself. These feelings echoed themes that had begun to emerge in the marriage prior to Mrs B's death. Now Mr B began to confide in a male friend who was having marital difficulties, and was surprised and relieved to discover that they had many of problems in common. It now seemed clear that in order to move forward and build a new life for himself and the children, Mr B would have to face the issue of his own needs and wishes more directly. How would he be able to make friends? What activities might be able to fill the emptiness? Would he ever be able to have a close relationship with a woman? What did he really want? Mr B seemed to find it very difficult to know. Instead, he talked more and more about how much he missed the companionship of his wife and the blissful relationship that they had had before the birth of the children.

The therapy team noted that a new stage had been reached. Mr B was now feeling the effects of bereavement much more in terms of the marital relationship. The issues about what had gone so tragically wrong now required exploration in terms of the rules of intimacy and the ways in which the needs of the individual can be met within a close relationship. The main focus of the work now shifted to the marital subsystem. What exactly were the difficulties here? It seemed clear that the couple's relationship had been very enmeshed. What Mr B described as 'closeness with no need to talk' was accompanied by a lack of ability to identify the needs of the partners as individuals. This avoidance of possible areas of conflict, however, prevented the couple from learning how to communicate and negotiate solutions to problems. Mr B's great difficulties in expressing his thoughts and feelings in the therapy sessions were now understood in a new way as part of this generalised pattern of behaviour and one that had blighted the development of his relationship with his wife. The anger and frustration that could find no expression were turned inwards, giving rise to 'depression'. The therapy team, which had been focused on supporting Mr B's sense of competence as a parent, decided to challenge directly his feelings of responsibility for the marital problems. The team believed that Mr B would now feel well enough supported by the therapist to be able to look more closely at the serious issue of his 'incompetence' in the marriage. The team's focus now shifted to helping Mr B to be clearer about his own present needs, and from this to consider why these had been so poorly met within his marriage. This might throw a different light on the question of responsibility for things going wrong, and perhaps add to our understanding of why Mrs B had died. Mr B needed a lot of encouragement and reassurance from the therapist to be able to feel that he had any right to look for opportunities and choices in the present. His idealisation of his wife and his longing for her and sadness at having lost her gradually began to emerge, reinforcing the homeostatic forces of self-denigration and self-blame.

In this phase of the work the therapist helped Mr B to describe the relationship in more detail and to begin to explore how the apparently idyllic relationship had gone so badly wrong. How, for example, given the tremendous sense of closeness, had it been possible for the couple to become so out of touch with each other's needs? Mr B began to speak in more depth about his sense of guilt and failure in the marriage. He felt he had let his wife down by not giving her more support and by wanting space for himself. It became clear, that as they became more involved in looking after the children there had been less and less time for themselves or each other. Although Mrs B had developed a number of activities outside the home she had found it difficult to understand that Mr B might also need to have some time for himself. The couple had, in fact, not been able to negotiate at all about the ways in which family life would have to change following the birth of the children. There was little time for talking and listening, and too much unspoken expectation and resentment. Just before the separation they had begun to have arguments which tended to involve a lot of angry demands and blaming, but little in the way of discussion of practical problems and how these might be solved. The therapist now tried to help Mr B to identify and describe the marital difficulties that had formed such an important context for the suicide. It was a task that he found particu-

larly difficult, having never attempted to do so before. The therapist
challenged Mr B's portrayal of himself as selfish and irresponsible by
asserting that it was quite normal for individuals within a marriage to
have personal needs. She acknowledged that some couples had more
trouble than others in working out solutions where conflicts of
interest were involved. More experienced couples would take for
granted that time is needed for talking and listening, she said. Of
course, most people found that practice was needed in working out
sensible compromises about things like having time for oneself. How
much practice did Mr B think they had had?

The roots of enmeshment and conflict avoidance

What slowly began to emerge, on exploring this area, was that the
couple had discussed such things very little. Beneath her bright façade
Mrs B was an insecure and needy young woman who relied heavily
on Mr B's support. But what about her family and friends nearby, the
therapist asked. Would they not have been able to help her, and
provide babysitting for the children when he was away? Mr B said
that, according to Mrs B's sister, when he decided to take a break, her
parents apparently simply told her to forget him. They said that the
marriage was clearly over, he must have gone off with another woman
and that it seemed unlikely that he would be coming back. They had
then, themselves, gone on holiday. The therapist expressed astonishment that Mrs B's parents should have gone away, given their
daughter's situation. Was this an unusual way for them to behave? Mr
B then revealed that although Mrs B was 'very close' to her parents
she never liked to bother them with her problems, but always tried to
appear cheerful and coping. Why was this? Mrs B's mother tended to
rely on Mrs B for support. Since childhood Mrs B had felt very
responsible for the difficulties in her parents' marriage. In fact, after
Mrs B and her sister had left home the parents had gone though a
period of not speaking for five years and eventually they were
divorced. Later, however, they were reunited and had been living
together for the two years prior to Mrs B's death.

    The therapist wondered if there might be some important clues
here about how Mrs B's background might have affected her expectations during the period just prior to her death. She decided to explore
this further and commented that it sounded as if Mrs B might never
have had much nurture and support from her parents, given all these
problems. She asked Mr B how he, in the light of his experience

looking after two young children, thought a young child would have
been affected by such a situation. The therapist encouraged Mr B to
reflect with her on a number of questions. How likely was it that such
troubled parents would have been able to provide a secure and
nurturing family for a child? How responsive would they have been
to a child's needs, given how preoccupied they might have been with
their own difficulties? How likely was it that such a child would grow
up feeling secure and confident? Might this have any relevance to Mrs
B's experience? Had they always been unable to offer reassurance?
Could Mrs B's cheerfulness and self-confidence been more apparent
than real, perhaps developed to help her cope with the lack of nurture
from her parents? Did it perhaps mask a more depressed, needy and
dependent side to her personality?

Mr B began to see that there might, in fact, be a needy child side to
his wife's personality. At times this would have made it very difficult
for her to respond to him as a caring spouse, to notice his needs, to
show concern about his depression, and so on. Perhaps these might
even have made her feel as though he was withdrawing support.
Furthermore, Mr B's inability to express his own needs to his wife was
now understandable as, in part, due to Mrs B's need for him to protect
and care for this needy child aspect of her. Mr B's role had been to
provide support that was more parental than marital in nature.

The team realised that a false hierarchy had been established in the
relationship, with Mrs B in a pseudo-dominant position identified
with the children's needs, and with Mr B being increasingly marginalised. By helping Mr B to acknowledge that his perfect wife was at
times like a needy child, it was possible for him to think about his
responsibility in connection with her death in a different way. Having
previously established that he was able to be a sensitive and competent
parent with his own children, it was possible to link his feelings of
responsibility for his wife's death to his sensitivity to the needy child
part of her. It also began to be possible to challenge more openly his
sense of total responsibility for her decision to take an overdose.

As this stage of the work progressed, the therapist helped Mr B to
begin to identify his own position more clearly, to express his thoughts
and feelings and to understand his part in the marital difficulties in a
new way. This in turn led to a reframing of his role in the spouse
subsystem and also of the nature of his responsibility for things going
so tragically wrong. The problem was not so much that he had been
selfish about his needs, and failed to protect his wife as if she really
were a needy child. Instead, he was now able to grasp the idea that he

had been part of a couple where both partners had failed to communicate and to solve problems. This realisation brought with it new
feelings of sadness and also of regret that they had not sought help
sooner. However, Mr B began to feel freer to begin to develop a social
life and to go out occasionally in the evenings with a male friend.

Stage 4 – Working with the wider system

At the end of the previous stage of work Mr B was feeling less guilty
and confused. However, he was increasingly complaining about
isolation. He found it impossible to initiate contact with his wife's
family or any of their old friends. When he had attended a family
wedding he had felt people were avoiding him. There had been no
mention of Mrs B's death, although opportunities had arisen when
the children were invited to visit their grandparents. The aim of the
therapy during this stage was to help Mr B to rebuild the social
support system and also to understand the contribution of the wider
family to Mrs B's death. This involved a shift in emphasis away from
the issues of the spouse subsystem to the wider systemic issues. Mr B's
attempts to develop new interests and new friends remained limited
by acute feelings of unfaithfulness or disloyalty to his wife, or fear of
disapproval by his in-laws. Now the main homeostatic position was
that of 'grieving widower', a position relating to the wider system that
enabled Mr B to ensure a balance between his need to maintain his
relationship with his wife's family, and his need to gradually build a
new life.

Mr B was reluctant to make contact with old friends because he
feared they would blame him. Vague fears also arose in relation to
making contact with new neighbours. The therapist encouraged Mr
B to formulate ways in which these fears might be overcome. As luck
would have it, many of Mr B's new neighbours were families with
young children. He was able to explain simply to them that his wife
had recently died, and to share more with them about this as he got
to know them better. He greatly appreciated the companionship,
sympathy and support he was offered, and was more able to accept
these as he allowed himself to relinquish some of his feelings of being
to blame. Shared childcare and babysitting with neighbours meant
that it was possible to go out and he began to talk with the therapist
about the possibility of a range of activities and relationships,
including relationships with women. The therapist encouraged Mr B
to imagine getting involved in a broader range of activities, as well as

his occasional tentative experiments. Why not go out in a foursome if he felt like it? Why not include women among his new friends? Of course it would feel strange at first, but perhaps it might also be fun. Perhaps in time he might even meet someone he could grow fond of... .

Mr B's explorations in these new areas were often interrupted by memories of the past and his longing for his wife. He described himself more and more in love with her and as feeling as being unfaithful even to imagine a life without her. These feelings made him increasingly unhappy about the lack of contact and communication with her family. He also found himself worrying that they might telephone and find him out, and that they would take this as confirmation that he had been unfaithful to their daughter. He spoke of how much he missed the frequent contact and close communication with Mrs B's parents since moving house. Lack of contact also tended to perpetuate Mr B's feeling that they blamed him for their daughter's death. The therapist encouraged Mr B to explore in more depth how and why Mrs B's family could have come to blame Mr B for their daughter's death. Mr B reported that he had been estranged from Mrs B's family since the funeral, when her father had more or less directly said that if Mr B hadn't left, she would still be alive. Mr B had been unable to challenge this, and in fact there had never been any discussion with the family of why Mrs B had taken the overdose. Furthermore, Mrs B's parents had never been made aware of how insecure and depressed their daughter had often felt, and Mr B had been unable to tell them of her previous overdoses.

Why had Mr B been unable to talk more openly with his parents-in-law? Or to his own family? Was this purely attributable to his own tendency to communicate indirectly, so as to avoid conflict and to protect others? The therapist encouraged Mr B to reflect upon what communication patterns were like in the two families. This exploration revealed that enmeshment was a powerful force on both sides of the family and that this extended back into the previous generation. It was now easier to understand that these powerful patterns of behaviour contributed to Mr B's difficulties in talking to his relatives. If he had explained to them about his wife's fragility, the marital problems and the reason for his absence, how might they have responded? How would they have felt about having told their daughter that her marriage was over? How would they have felt about departing on holiday rather than providing reassurance and practical support? Could they have done more to help the two young people to find ways of resolving their problems? Indeed, was it possible that they themselves bore some responsibility for the tragic turn of events?

Contact between the children and their maternal grandparents had become very infrequent since the family had moved to their new house. Annie's birthday provided an occasion for Mr B to take the initiative and invite them over. He also began to think about how important it might be for the children to have more regular contact. On the one hand, Mr B felt that the children might benefit from contact, on the other, it had still not been possible for him to talk to his in-laws about Mrs B's death and he still felt that they blamed him. The therapist encouraged Mr B to think beyond his fears about how his in-laws might view him, and to focus on what he would like to happen in terms of contact. Would it be in the children's interests to maintain the contact? If so, what would need to change in order for this to happen? It seemed clear that communication needed to be improved, but it was also clear that neither Mr B nor his parents-in-law had been able to initiate discussion. The difficulty involved in achieving any shift in this situation indicated that powerful homeostatic forces were at work. Did Mr B's role, as a grieving widower carrying all responsibility for his wife's death, in some way protect her relatives from becoming more aware of Mrs B's depression and her need for support? Given that Mrs B had always protected her parents from this knowledge, how easy would it be for them to learn the truth about their daughter?

Mr B remained doubtful about his ability to talk with his parents-in-law, but he was clear that he wanted the children not to lose touch with their mother's side of the family. A year after the death, and with much support and encouragement from the therapist, he was able to create an important opportunity for closer contact and more open communication. He had decided to choose a headstone and inscription for his wife's grave, and invited his mother-in-law to help with this. For Mr B this was an opportunity to share some of his feelings of loss for his wife and also create a focus for visits of remembrance by the family. However, having invited his mother-in-law to join him, he soon found himself having difficulties in coping with her attempts to take the project over. His natural response was to become silent and withdrawn, allowing her to take over and thus avoiding any potential upset or difference of opinion. The therapist helped Mr B to see that this might be only one of a number of possible ways of responding to his mother-in-law's enthusiasm. Mr B was encouraged to be specific about what the best outcome could be for him and the children. He was quite clear that he wished to retain control of the design of the headstone rather than allow his in-laws to take control. However, he was completely at a loss as to how this might be achieved. To assist with this the therapist invited Mr B to consider a number of possible approaches whereby he would be able to declare to the in-laws his intention of remaining in charge of the headstone project, whilst at the same time showing outwardly that he valued their suggestions and support. It was suggested that, given his sensitivity to the feelings of his in-laws and his own wish to create an appropriate memorial for his wife, he might wish to imagine exactly how he would like to handle the meeting with his mother-in-law, and to rehearse how he would put his views across to her. Mr B's ability to negotiate this crisis successfully represented a turning point in the therapy. He became more hopeful about being able to build a 'more open' relationship with his in-laws and began to have more frequent contact, especially with his mother-in-law.

Review of the first year of therapy

The end of the first year of therapy coincided with the anniversary of Mrs B's death and was followed a few weeks later by the first Christmas in the new house. This seemed a natural time for reflection and review. What had been achieved? Mr B felt that he had survived a catastrophe but now felt overwhelmed with sadness, regret, and longing for his wife. His confusion and feelings of self-blame reappeared strongly. The decision to place a headstone on her grave was one way of giving expression to all this. It had also provided the first real opportunity for Mr B to begin to share his loss in a more open way with other members of the family. However, the increase in contact and warmth with his wife's family was not accompanied by the greater openness in communication that he had hoped for. Christmas was a particularly difficult time, leaving Mr B feeling that his life was empty, that he was 'back to square one' and that therapy was going nowhere. The therapeutic team considered whether this might be a good moment to encourage Mr B to explore these feelings once again. Perhaps he needed time to grieve. Perhaps the therapist ought to encourage him to ventilate his feelings of anger, with himself, with the therapist, with his wife, and so on. Perhaps this would help him to work through these feelings, and to shake off some of the guilt that still weighed on him so heavily. The team decided, however, that this would involve too confusing a change of therapeutic approach. A more structural intervention should be considered, and one aimed more at the homeostatic influences that appeared to be at work. The therapist now attempted to restructure the situation by responding in a strongly positive way to Mr B's feelings of frustration and stuckness. At last he was feeling he wanted more from life! This was a very positive sign. She encouraged Mr B to give himself credit for having come through the past year's difficulties so well and wondered if he might now be at a point where he could begin to think beyond simply surviving for the sake of the children. His feelings of emptiness were positively reframed as helpful indications that he was now beginning to be ready to build a more positive future for himself and the children. He was encouraged to think about what would need to change in order for him to begin to fill the emptiness in his life.

Stage 5 – The second year of therapy: deconstructing enmeshment and improving relatedness

The main work of the second year of therapy was centred around helping Mr B to build a life in which his needs could not only be acknowledged but satisfied. Socially this meant being able to communicate more directly and effectively with others and to act assertively. Being able to achieve this in intimate relationships was a particular challenge. Much of the ground covered in the first year of therapy now needed to be reworked. The position of 'grieving widower' was gradually relinquished as Mr B began to gain confidence, and to accept that his wife's decision to take the overdose did not necessarily mean that he would be condemned to a life of solitude. For the sake of both himself and the children other options now needed to be considered. During the second year of therapy the frequency of meetings was reduced to monthly at Mr B's request. Progress was reviewed after six months, just before the summer holidays.

At the beginning of the year Mr B continued to need considerable encouragement to see and be able to talk about his own position in relationships. He remained tremendously solicitous of the wishes of others, although he very rarely enquired as to whether his assumptions were, in fact, correct! Furthermore, his habitual response was either to comply with what he perceived others to wish of him, or to take steps to avoid the situation. In other words, he showed the pattern of conflict avoidance that is classically associated with enmeshment. Both Mr B and the therapist by now agreed that in the past this pattern of behaviour had not only made it very difficult for his needs to be met, but had actually played an important part in the breakdown of his marriage. If things were to be different in the future this would need to change. Many of the themes of the first year of therapy were reworked in this new context. Mr B was now more able to identify the situations he found difficult to deal with, rather than relying on the therapist to point these out. For example, the 'sensitivity' which had been much discussed as a reason for Mr B avoiding conflict in the past was now seen as a potential obstacle to him achieving the 'openness' and 'honesty' which he now often talked of seeking in his relationships with those closest to him. He began to see that in order to achieve his aims he must first give himself time to work out what they might be! Second, he would need to change his habit of responding automatically to the demands of others, and also find ways of informing them of his own position. Third, he needed to be able to develop strategies for negotiating how his aims might be achieved. Finally he needed better skills in solving problems and conflicts. With help, he was able to deal increasingly competently with conflictual situations at work, with his in-laws and at home. For example, was eventually able to acknowledge his increasing dissatisfaction with the children's nanny, to discuss what might be done about this and then to rehearse a plan for telling her that he wished to terminate the contract.

So much for defining rules and boundaries more clearly. But what of Mr B's great longing for closeness and intimacy, including sexual intimacy? Mr B began to talk more and more about these aspects of his relationship with his wife and his conflicting feelings about whether he would ever again be able to replace her. On the one hand the children would often ask him when they were going to have another mummy, and on the other he could not imagine being unfaithful to his wife. He had a brief passionate encounter with a young woman who had been a friend of his wife's. However, he found himself alarmed by her constant telephone calls and apparent neediness. After a few weeks he decided to stop seeing her. The encounter stirred up many conflicting feelings. It had been wonderful to feel excitement and intimacy. But how could he have been unfaithful to his wife? The young woman's neediness made him feel that he should look after her. Perhaps even marry her. He experienced feelings of revulsion, wanting to be rid of her, yet at the same time, deeply ashamed. The therapist responded by saying how normal it was for all of us to have sexual feelings. Feeling attraction and excitement with women was a natural thing for him to begin to feel. She thought that this was an encouraging sign that he was beginning to feel more confident, confident enough to experiment a little more with intimacy and closeness. But choosing not to jump into a close relationship with a very needy woman was probably very wise. Perhaps this was an indication of how much his ideas had matured over the last year, and how much more realistic he had become about being able to solve other people's problems. All this brought back to Mr B the feeling of being tremendously in love with his wife and the impossibility of having a new relationship, which would feel like a betrayal of his wife. The therapist acknowledged that it was likely that Mr B would always remember and love his wife, in spite of the way in which she had left him and the children. However, she observed that one can love people in different ways, and we have all experienced loving different people in different ways at the same time. Furthermore, people who have experienced great love tend to be people who form more than one loving relationship in their lives. She asked whether Mrs B would have wanted him and the children to live out the rest of their lives alone following her death. Although she had sometimes been very needy when she was alive, the therapist asked, would the more caring and mature part of her have been able to understand the tremendous need they all had for closeness and intimacy? Mr B said that he felt his wife would have wanted him to have a new partner and someone to help him look after the children. The therapist noted that Mr B was caught in a dilemma in which the desire to move on was held back by his loyalty to the past. She then asked if Mr B had ever found himself talking to his wife about the dilemma he was in. This question was based on the discovery that Mr B did, in fact, have frequent imaginary conversations with his wife. The therapist suggested that Mr B might wish to consider planning a visit to his wife's grave and speak to her directly about how he and the children now needed to move on, and his intention to do this. It would be important to emphasise his wish to do his best for them and how much they all still loved her, even though she was no longer with them. Mr B was encouraged to rehearse what he would say out loud, so that he could be sure of saying the right thing at the graveside. Soon afterwards he began to talk more about having formed a special relationship with a woman friend.

Mr B's gradual increase in confidence and widening social circle now included contact with a few old family friends, including the family who had by now adopted Alf. He found himself able to talk more about the past and was very moved by the affection and support he was offered. Sadly, however, his relationship with his in-laws did not develop the openness and honesty that he had so much hoped for. He began to question the value of maintaining the relationship with his in-laws under these circumstances. He also began to be less anxious about needing to please and placate his parents-in-law, and to feel freer to begin to think about his own needs in a way that he had not been able to do since before his wife's death. Meanwhile, his 'special' relationship ran into problems and Mr B came to realise that he might need to give himself time to get used to being close without repeating harmful patterns from the past. Perhaps he would need time to make mistakes and to work towards the 'openness and honesty' he wanted.

Deciding to end the therapy

Progress was reviewed just before the summer holidays. Mr B expressed a sense of growing frustration and lack of progress, particularly about the lack of improvement in his relationship with Mrs B's parents. On the other hand he continued to report a stream of problems that he felt unable to cope with. There seemed to be a number of possible ways of resolving this. The first would have been to engage the wider family in therapy, thus supporting Mr B more directly with realigning his relationships with the extended family. The second option that was considered was whether Mr B might benefit from a different therapeutic approach. The third option was to work towards ending therapy. Mr B and the therapist agreed to consider these separately over the summer period and to meet two months later to make a plan.

The team felt that a considerable attachment had developed between Mr B and the therapist. As a part of the system the therapist, too, was involved in its enmeshment. Given the quality of dependency that had been worked with, and the evident anxiety about separation, it was felt that there might be difficulties in completing the work without a plan which allowed these issues to be addressed more directly. The team favoured an approach which would entail working towards the end of therapy at a time when things were going well, whilst acknowledging that problems would continue to crop up from time to time.

When Mr B returned from holiday he chose to work towards ending the therapy before the end of the year. He would find it helpful, he said, to have some time in which to work towards an ending. Three more meetings were arranged, at monthly intervals. This allowed time for a review of the achievements he had made since the beginning of therapy. Mr B said that he felt that things were going very well for him. Of course, he still thought about his wife and missed her sometimes. He had decided that he would probably need some time before making any new permanent commitments. He spoke of feeling sad that he did not have a better relationship with his in-laws but accepted that this might not be possible. He spoke very positively about his plans for the future, including his plans for re-training and possibly moving abroad. The therapist asked how the children were progressing? Mr B reported that the children were doing very well and that they seemed happy, secure and confident. Both were playful, doing well in school, and had lots of friends. Annie enjoyed looking at photos and videos of her mother, and liked to draw pictures of her. Alf, too, seemed well settled in his new family. The therapist took this opportunity to think about difficulties that might arise in the future. Was Mr B worried about the children's future well-being? Might there be a need for couple or family work if Mr B decided to get married again? It was agreed that these were possibilities that might need to be considered. Different sorts of therapeutic resources were described for Mr B's future reference. Mr B became noticeably more assertive about the content of the sessions leading up to termination. On one occasion he arrived with a list of prepared topics and also ventured to disagree with the therapist on occasion. Two months following the final session Mr B wrote to the therapy team expressing 'heartfelt thanks' for the help he had received, not only in relation to the death of his wife but also in relation to helping him deal more effectively with all his relation-ships, particularly those with people whom he cared for. He reported that he had formed a happy partnership with another woman and his feelings for the future now looked 'rosy'.

Discussion

Issues raised by the work

It is never easy to know quite how to intervene when one starts to work directly with a bereaved family. So much depends on the specific circumstances of the family system, the way in which its structures and patterns of interaction have been disrupted, the stage at which problems are presented and what the family's wishes are.

What might therapy aim to achieve? Some families will have extensive needs requiring a complex series of interventions, whilst others will have more limited needs that call for a brief, focused approach. The effects of bereavement on the family will depend upon a variety of factors, including the family's current circumstances, pre-bereavement functioning and the degree of trauma associated with the loss (Black, 1993). The therapist will first need to assess the overall situation (Raphael, 1982) in order to identify the needs and wishes of the family so that an appropriate plan or set of treatment options can be formulated (Street et al., 1991). A number of different approaches may need to be considered and the therapist will need to consider whether or not his or her preferred approach will offer the most appropriate way forward.

For the therapy team offering therapy as described above, a number of practice issues arose in the course of therapy, some of which we would like to discuss. The first of these was concerned mainly with the need to achieve clarity at a theoretical level to enable the team to function effectively. Given the apparent absence of a clear paradigm for working with bereavement within the structural model and the range of the issues which appeared to require therapeutic attention, would our approach be able to accommodate the therapeutic agenda adequately? Second, how would our work within this model be able to relate to models of bereavement rooted in other frameworks. In particular, would it be feasible to adapt our structural model and its techniques to work with an individual, and what types of adaptation would be required ? Finally, in terms of the outcome of the therapy, to what extent could we be said to have achieved our aims? These issues will be discussed further below.

The use of a systems approach to bereavement work

We found that the systems approach can provide a helpful framework for a broad assessment of the effects of loss on the family, and in developing hypotheses to guide the process of therapeutic work. It permits the effects of loss on the individual to be thought about in a broad context, including risk factors at a variety of levels. By facilitating work with the extended family system, subsystems and individuals, the possibilities for intervention are multiplied. In order for the therapeutic work to be effective, the systems approach needs to be informed by the more historical and individually based models of bereavement that describe the process of mourning and coping with stress. These models, however, are based on a linear view of causality (Walrond Skinner, 1986). We found that in order to be able to exploit them within the therapy process it was necessary to find some means of conceptualising the issues in terms of a view of causality consistent with the circularity of a systems approach. This led us to think about the different theories of change that underlie the application of these ideas to the process of carrying out therapeutic work.

The theory of change associated with the systems approach prescribes an approach to family work which is focused *primarily* on interactional processes between family members. This contrasts with the psychodynamic or cognitive approaches, where the main focus of work is primarily on the feelings of the individual. These approaches utilise a linear theory of causality and the aim of therapy is to achieve 'insight', in other words to transform the way in which the client feels about events. By contrast, the theory of change within the structural approach is not insight-orientated. Rather, the aim is to create a process of change within the system by means of repatterning interactions between the people present in the room. This does not necessarily negate the possibility of discussing individual feelings as an issue of content within the therapy, but simply that affective change is usually not the primary focus of the therapeutic process. The aim of our work with Mr B at an emotional level was to support him through the mourning process *primarily* by providing support focused on helping him to function effectively in daily life. This included assisting him to express his feelings of bereavement and to see these as normal, and helping him to identify confidants from whom he could derive emotional support. It was not the aim of the therapy to provide the principle space for him to talk about his feelings, but rather to help Mr B to avoid the development of a pathological mourning process which would put both himself and the children at risk.

The use of a structural model

The structural model represents a particular application of systemic ideas and provides both a particular method of conceptualising the family system and a range of techniques for intervening in such a way that process can be changed. The therapist aims to achieve change during the therapeutic session and uses techniques which are specifically designed to promote novel interactional possibilities between the family members who are present. How far was this applicable in terms of the work with the B family? The team found it helpful to conceptualise the B family in terms of a system composed of a series of identifiable subsystems, both in order to be able to form working hypotheses at different levels and in order to be able to construct a manageable process for what turned out to be quite a complex piece of work. Using a structural model to look at pre-bereavement relationships, the team's hypothesis was that this had been an enmeshed family showing signs of breaking down in the face of negotiating the issues of separation and conflict which arose following the birth of the children. Enmeshed families, as described by Minuchin and Fishman (1981) are characterised by over-involvement, conflict avoidance and lack of conflict resolution. At the individual level, attachments are likely to appear rather dependent, insecure or ambivalent, and to be associated with problems of separation and individuation. There are likely to be particular difficulties in dealing with traumatic loss. Given the degree of enmeshment that had been present in the relationships prior to Mrs B's death, it seemed highly likely that Mr B would develop a pathological grief reaction, that he would blame himself for his wife's death and become very depressed. Therapy using a structural model attempted to take account of the attachment issues by addressing these in terms of the enmeshment in family relationships. With the B family, the aims of therapy were to provide support and thus reduce feelings of insecurity, to clarify individual roles and responsibilities so as to reduce over-involvement, to identify individual needs and thus enhance autonomy, and to assist conflict resolution within the system by promoting better communication between family members. Our strategy for achieving these changes was aimed primarily at changing interactional patterns, and interventions attempted to target these patterns wherever they were manifested – in the therapeutic relationship, in the patterns of daily life, and in terms of descriptions of the relationship patterns of the past. Wherever possible, the emphasis was on promoting different transactions rather than on reflecting or interpreting material, as it would have been if we had been using an insight model of therapy.

Some ways of working systemically with the individual

How possible is it to do effective therapeutic work if the family is not actually present? In a recent paper, Jenkins and Asen (1992) suggest that work with the family system is more a question of the theoretical framework and techniques used by the therapist, than one of how many people are seen. They suggest that the therapist must focus on creating new connections between different patterns of relationships for the client as the first stage in developing a climate for change. Does the structural model provide any tools with which to create different patterns of this kind? And second, how does this differ from the change achieved within the psychodynamic approach? Are there any particular difficulties or dilemmas in the path of the systemic therapist who is using the structural model?

The structural therapist's primary aim is to construct 'therapeutic opportunities' with which to create a *process* of change, rather than to help the client work through feelings or create insight, as the psychodynamic therapist does. This is achieved by taking the different points of view of individuals in the family and generating new patterns of transaction between them. When working with the individual, therefore, the first challenge to be overcome is the absence of significant others in the room. This entails the lack both of observable transactional patterns and also of the different points of view, or 'propositions' about the 'reality' or meaning of the situation, that provide much of the therapist's raw material when working with a family. Instead, there is only the client's proposition about 'the way life is', and it is not possible to create transactions between individual points of view in the same way. There are a number of ways in which this may be overcome using techniques already available in the structural model. First, the therapist will need to take special care to invoke the appropriate dyadic or subsystem context for the work and second, by using him or herself to create transactions. These are discussed in more detail below.

Working with dyads and subsystems

When working systemically with the individual, the therapist will need to work with subsystems and the dyads within these just as he or she would when working the family group. The client's point of view, or propositions about his situation (for example, 'X is the way it was') can be translated into dyadic terms by asking questions which translate these into statements about transactions which invoke the presence of absent family members (for example, 'How was your wife involved in this event?… What was it about your wife's behaviour in that situation that made you feel X?'). It then becomes possible to enquire about the interactional processes with the person in the outside world (for example, 'How did you respond to her behaviour?... How typical was this of the way the two of you used to deal with situations of this kind?'). The therapist can also use the questions to create 'as if' transactions in the room ('If your wife were here now, what would she say about this?'). By means of circular questioning techniques it is possible to construct a complex picture of the transactional patterns involving the extended family system.

Work with different subsystems can also take place, by using similar techniques. Here the challenge for the therapist is to be able to hold in mind which subsystem is being worked with, to resist the temptation to stray to other levels and to preserve a consistency of approach. This can be particularly difficult to judge when working with enmeshed systems, in which boundaries are necessarily poorly defined. When working with Mr B on the issues within the marital relationship, for example, it was important for the therapist to hold in mind that although there was only one member of the dyad actually in the room, the focus of work was on the patterns within the spouse subsystem. Mr B's descriptions of 'the way it was' in linear terms would need to be reconstructed in terms of the appropriate system level, in this instance the spouse subsystem. A simple example of this would be to ask something like 'How did you see your contribution to this... and what was your wife's contribution?' This might then be expanded along the lines of how they would have liked things to have happened differently, how they could have been improved and what factors might have influenced their negotiations over the issue, and so on. The use of such techniques enabled roles and boundaries to be defined more clearly, permitting more detailed mapping of the infrastructure of the system at each level. In order to achieve this the therapist will need to make choices about the way that material offered by the client is taken up, and will find it helpful to select early in the session which themes will be most relevant to develop.

Therapist's use of self, and the role of the team

Within the structural model, the therapist has a powerful role as instigator of the process of interactional change, and this role becomes particularly important when working with an individual member of the family. The risks of the therapist becoming inducted is particularly high, especially when working with enmeshed systems. These difficulties are compounded when the client not only avoids conflict but also provides low levels of feedback, as can occur when the client is depressed or withdrawn. In our experience, the effects of induction were often observable as a lack of clarity and crispness in the transactions between therapist and client. When working with Mr B the therapist found herself working harder and harder to express, make links and explain in response to Mr B's apparent difficulty in formulating and expressing his ideas. Sometimes Mr B would, for example, launch into recounting a lengthy chain of events which appeared to the therapist completely at a tangent to the theme under discussion. The therapist would then struggle to make sense of these, and to link them back to the theme as follows 'You seem to be saying that X, Y and Z are the case, and this means so and so, is that right?' This, of course, only created a tendency for Mr B to produce more and more material and to rely on the therapist's 'superior' powers of understanding and expression, just as he used to rely on his wife.

Mr B's evident vulnerability and his difficulty expressing himself also created a particularly powerful tendency for patterns of enmeshment to be repeated. Linked to this, there was a tendency for a hierarchical relationship to be established in which the therapist was placed in an 'expert' or parental role, while Mr B took up a position of incompetence and dependency. In the early stage of therapy it was possible for the therapist to make use of this situation to provide authoritative support for Mr B. However, in the second year of therapy this hierarchy needed to be gradually replaced with a relationship which was more likely to foster Mr B's sense of independence and autonomy. The supervising team had an important role in identifying these issues, and in suggesting strategies that would enable the therapist to regulate her position. On occasions, for example, the therapist would take the 'expert' position for strategic reasons rather than because of processes of induction. This allowed repeated patterns to be reflected upon with Mr B, and challenged in such a way as to create new perspectives. It was also a useful stance to take when helping Mr B to try out new or unfamiliar strategies for problem-solving, when the therapist would sometimes engage in modelling or giving instructions. However, when the therapist was attempting to enable Mr B to develop a less dependent relationship, different strategies were required. For example, in order not to reinforce Mr B's difficulties in identifying and expressing his feelings, it became important for the therapist to learn to resist the need to 'explain', and to encourage Mr B to express himself more fully. In order to achieve this more explicit feedback was given to Mr B about the therapist's level of understanding and her need for information. For example, she might say 'I am not sure whether your story about X, Y and Z means you are agreeing with me or not!' or 'I don't fully understand how this follows, please could you explain?' or 'You seem to feel that this is an excellent example of what we were talking about. Which bit strikes you in particular?'

Working in a one-to-one situation creates a need to think about the nature of the therapist–client subsystem that is thereby created. In structural terms this dyad becomes an arena in which the therapist can expect to take on, as it were by proxy, a series of transactional positions, as well as developing his or her own relationship with the client. The therapist needs to be particularly aware of the tendency for interactional patterns to be reconstructed and repeated within the therapist–client relationship. When the family is actually in the room such tendencies are less likely to become a major focus for the work. However, where the relationship with the therapist becomes the main arena for direct intervention in transactional patterns, it inevitably becomes a more central issue. In this case, for example, the therapist was aware that the patterns of enmeshment within the family were being repeated in her relationship with Mr B, and that these were likely to be accompanied with intense feelings of attachment and difficulty with separation. Such feelings might lead to patterns of behaviour likely to perpetuate the therapy, thus avoiding the issue of ending. Thus homeostatic forces were as likely to present themselves within the therapist–client relationship as much as within any other part of the system and needed to be taken account of when forming hypotheses, strategies and interventions. Because of vicissitudes of this kind, the screen team remains a valuable resource for the therapist working systemically with the individual client. The team can assist the therapist to maintain the systemic focus of the work, preserve boundaries and prevent induction.

The outcome of therapy

To what extent were the aims of therapy achieved? Our assessment of this is necessarily somewhat limited and subjective because our impressions are based on our own clinical impressions, and on information from Mr B. Questions remain both about the way in which the wider system is functioning and in terms of the longer-term stability of the changes that appeared to have taken place. Within these constraints, however, outcome can be assessed in relation to the agreed aims of therapy. To what degree were these achieved? At the end of therapy Mr B's confidence and competence as a parent were much improved. His descriptions of how the children were functioning suggested that the disturbed behaviour observable during the assessment had disappeared, and that the children's development was progressing well. The aims of the initial stage of therapy (transition to a single-parent family) has apparently been successfully achieved. In the short term, therefore, despite the multiplicity of factors indicating that the family would make a poor adjustment to Mrs B's death, Mr B and the children are functioning well. Hopefully this will reduce the risk of family dysfunction and psychiatric disorder in later life for both Mr B and the children.

Looking at the wider system, however, the gains of therapy are less clear, and clear risk factors remain. On the one hand Mr B has been able to function effectively at work and to establish contact and communication with friends and family. Sadly, however, his relationship with his in-laws remains problematic. Though it was possible using this approach to go some way to improving Mr B's relationship with his in-laws, only limited improvement was possible without more direct access to the wider system. In other areas Mr B himself has made considerable progress. He has come to terms with the loss of his wife and has been able to understand his contribution to the situation that caused her death. He has also been able to see himself as needing to work on being aware of his own needs and to be more assertive about getting them met. Nevertheless, there are indications that Mr B is still at some risk both of getting depressed and of recreating an enmeshed partnership. There may be a need for additional therapeutic work in the future, perhaps with him as an individual, perhaps with the new partner and family unit. Also it seemed possible that the children too may need to be involved in work at a later stage. However, though not necessarily claiming credit for all these achievements, we would regard the overall risks that were present at assessment as having been significantly reduced.

Conclusion

The accidental death of a healthy young mother was a catastrophe for the whole family, and precipitated a multiplicity of risk factors for the individuals involved. Bereavement work with the family attempted to reduce these risks, with some degree of success. It was possible to work in an effective though limited way with the family system, through an individual member. The enmeshment present in the family created particular challenges for the therapist in being able to 'keep the system open' (Jenkins and Asen, 1992). The changes reported to have taken place within the family suggest that the greatest benefit has been derived from therapy by the children and their father.

The structural approach to therapy was useful in helping to organise an approach to a complex post-bereavement situation. It was also able to accommodate theories and models which adopt a more linear approach within the overall structural framework. It was also possible, within this paradigm, to provide effective therapeutic work with an individual member of the family system.

References

Black, D. (1993) Traumatic bereavement in children. *Highlight No. 121*, London: National Children's Bureau.

Black, D. and Urbanowicz, M.A. (1987) Family intervention with bereaved children. *Journal of Child Psychology and Psychiatry* 28(3):467–76.

Frude, N. (1990) *Understanding Family Problems*. Chapter 10 Bereavement. Chichester: J. Wiley & Sons.

Fulmer, R. (1983) A structural approach to unresolved mourning in single parent family systems. *Journal of Marital and Family Therapy* 9(3):259–69.

Harris Hendricks, J., Black, D. and Kaplan, T. (1993) *When Father Kills Mother. Guiding Children Through Trauma and Grief*. London: Routledge.

Jenkins, H. and Asen, K. (1992) Family therapy without the family. *Journal of Family Therapy* 14(1):1–14.

Minuchin, S. (1974) *Families and Family Therapy*. London: Tavistock.

Minuchin, S. and Fishman, H.C. (1981) *Family Therapy Techniques*. London: Harvard University Press.

Parkes, C.M. and Weiss, R. (1983) *Recovery from Bereavement*. New York: Basic Books.

Raphael, B. (1982) The young child and the death of a parent. In Murray Parkes, C. and Stevenson-Hinde, J. (eds) *The Place of Attachment in Human Behaviour*. London: Tavistock.

Sills, C., Clarkson, P. and Evans, R. (1988) Systemic Integrative Psychotherapy with a young bereaved girl. *Transactional Analysis Journal* 18(2):102–9.

Street, E., Downey, J. and Brazier, A. (1991) The development of therapeutic consultations in child-focused family work. *Journal of Family Therapy* 13(3):311–34.

Walrond Skinner, S. (1986) *Dictionary of Psychotherapy*. London: Routledge & Kegan Paul.

CHAPTER 4

Death of a Pupil in School

Ursula Cornish

This chapter provides a theoretical framework for working to mitigate the effects of a pupil's death on other pupils and teachers, and describes how such help can be given in practice. Two cases are discussed, one involving the murder of a schoolboy, the other the accidental death of a teenage girl in school. They illustrate the usefulness of combining bereavement work with systemic thinking in developing treatment for members of schools. Issues of assessment and intervention are described using a systemic framework, which allows boundaries to be established while analysing and working with subsystems.

Introduction

When the strangled body of Steven, a 9-year-old schoolboy, was found naked on the local golf course during the summer holidays, teachers, parents and pupils felt traumatised and the school was enveloped by a crisis that was both unforeseen and overwhelming. When Shareen, a 12-year-old girl, took a fatal overdose during an art lesson in school, the response was similar. The question in both cases was what kind of help would be most effective. This chapter describes the way in which an educational psychologist helped pupils and teachers to cope with the crisis by adapting methods developed by systemic family therapy.

Naturally a school will be shocked and saddened by the sudden death of one of its members. Is the reaction to such a death likely to be similar to or qualitatively different from the reaction to the loss of a close relative? What happens after the initial shock? What can be done to prevent long-term harmful effects? What kind of support, if any, is required? As with death in a family, the death of a pupil will remind some of their own mortality. Traumatic events may also evoke unpleasant memories associated with previous painful life experiences and loss. The death of a pupil is unlikely to result in long-term grief in the majority of the teachers and pupils but it will, nevertheless, have a considerable impact on the school community, which will take time to adjust to the loss and its implications. The school may require assistance in making the adjustments required. It will certainly need to find ways of coping with the crisis.

Any therapeutic intervention with a school will need to be negotiated with the head teacher who, with the school authorities, carries responsibility for the school. Often help is requested at short notice, as most unexpected deaths throw schools into a state of crisis that requires an immediate response. Normally there is no time for lengthy negotiations, especially in situations where the public and press are involved. The school may feel exposed and under scrutiny. The running of the school may be subjected to critical examination and the head teacher may feel particularly vulnerable at a time when sound and speedy decision-making is crucial. These pressures on the system as a whole may seem so overwhelming that the head teacher may try to contain the crisis by restricting therapeutic intervention to particular subgroups within the school. This in turn may restrict the freedom of choice of the therapist to decide how best to intervene, and may also limit the potential effectiveness of the work.

Why therapy?

The literature on bereavement and children's reactions to loss and to traumatic events suggests that preventative early interventions can help avoid long-lasting harmful effects. Morgan (1985), Worden (1991), Ward (1992), Yule (1992) and Yule and Gold (1993) all recommend that schools should have contingency plans for such events, and that in particular clear information should be given to children to help them cope with loss. Emotional and behavioural difficulties associated with children's experience of death and with coping with bereavement were systematically studied by Rutter (1966), who was struck by the fact that children attending a psychiatric clinic had often previously experienced the loss of a parent. Anti-social behaviour, depression and various phobias turned out to be associated with the loss of a close relative or parent in the recent past.

For a child, the experience of loss of a classmate, although very different from the loss of a parent or relative, may also be a traumatic event that can evoke distress, anger and guilt, and bring to life previous traumas such as abuse or witnessing a fatality. Indeed, the sudden death of a child in school is likely to have a traumatic effect that reverberates through the entire system and affects all its members. Sometimes bereavement can cause harmful effects in the longer term. The risk factors associated with the experience of loss are well researched in adults who have lost a spouse (Parkes, 1986), but are less clear with children who have lost a relative or friend (Sood and Weller, 1992; Fristad *et al.*, 1993). Black's (1993a) recent summary of the literature of children and bereavement describes how pre-verbal children express their grief in somatic responses like bed-wetting or disturbed sleep, whereas older children may exhibit psychosomatic symptoms or learning difficulties or school refusal (Weller *et al.*, 1992). Adolescents might show indifference or lack of feelings, which can be bewildering to adults in their vicinity. Often they show similar bereavement patterns to adults, becoming depressed and experiencing sleep and appetite disturbance. Long-term effects are often the result of factors such as poverty and social deprivation where death is just one of the contributory factors.

Some of the difficulties and disabilities experienced by the bereaved can undoubtedly be prevented by early sensitive interventions, such as early 'debriefing' in which children are able to talk about and work through the trauma (Black, 1993a, b). Bereavement counselling, which traditionally addresses the feelings of the bereft and allows space for grieving, can also be helpful (Leick and Davidson-Nielson, 1991). The sharing of experiences in peer group counselling can also be of use, and alleviates feelings of isolation while enhancing self-esteem (Pennells *et al.*, 1992; Boyd Webb, 1993; Pennells and Smith, 1995). Play therapy also offers ways of working through traumatic experiences. This method includes attending, observing and listening to the child's play, but also facilitates initiating, personalising and responding to the child's reactions – so it is both responsive and facilitative. Play therapy was initially described by Axline (1950) and used in the context of bereavement work with children by Le Vieux (1993), offering through play a non-directive way of expressing and exploring feelings.

Therapy needs to take into account the fact that responses to death vary over time. The literature of bereavement theory differentiates three phases of reactions to loss. The first phase often involves a state of shock or disbelief, a sense of being numb, lost, bereft or helpless.

The next phase is that of despair, characterised by realisation that loss has occurred and feelings of grief. The final phase is described as the phase of resolution, in which people come to terms with the reality and find some reconciliation (Weiner, 1985). In cases where the reaction to loss results in processes of numbness and inability to think about what happened, the bereaved will show a prolonged inhibition of the usual responses to loss, and will suffer unduly. Similar detrimental effects occur when the bereaved directs his/her attention away from painful thoughts and memories towards neutral or pleasant ones. The third observed process is that the bereaved person maintains a belief that the loss is temporary and that a reunion is still possible (Parkes, 1986).

Approaches to change

The traditional way of helping children and adults to cope with grief is by individual counselling which encourages expression of the various stages of grief over time. The systemic approach, in contrast, addresses the wider impact of the loss on the structure of the system, for example the family or organisation. Therapeutic work in school would thus take place at the interpersonal level rather than at the individual, intrapsychic level. While working at the interpersonal level the therapist should be aware of the impact of systems intervention on individual members, who mutually influence one another.

The present work shows how systemic consultation as developed by family therapists has been applied to schools. The emphasis is on treating the impact of the death on the school's organisation as a whole and on developing ways of helping teachers and pupils to come to terms with the fatality. One way of approaching this is by looking at the structure of the organisation following Minuchin (1974); structure means the invisible net of functional demands that organises the family interactions, or the transactional patterns within the organisation such as a school. The constraints put upon the transactional patterns are the universal rules governing the organisation: power hierarchy and mutual expectations in particular organisations' implicit or explicit contracts that persist out of habit, mutual accommodation, and functional effectiveness.

People's reactions to tragic events show in their patterns of behaviour. These behaviour patterns may require adjustment in order to enable those concerned to continue to function in their professional and personal roles as a teacher or a pupil. Their usual

repertoire of responses may be inadequate, or difficult to implement
in the context of the demands of the crisis caused by death. The
death of a schoolgirl/boy will create a gap in the position she/he held
in the group of her/his friends in class. This may destabilise the
group and may require the renegotiation of positions within peer
relations. Friendship patterns may be affected. The teachers may
also need to adjust to the absent member and his or her function.
Tasks and responsibilities may need to be evaluated and reallocated
in the light of the death of a pupil. Parents, governors and the
Education Authority may put the school's general functioning
under scrutiny. Death in school can be destabilising at various levels
within the organisation.

Systemic consultations provide a method of helping an organisation (such as a school) to adjust to the death and loss of one of its
members by conceptualising the organisation as a whole whose
members are interrelated. The whole is more than the sum of its parts
and is governed by the same rules that organise biological systems
based on circular causality. The main basis of the consultation offered
to schools as presented in the following pages is structural family
therapy (Minuchin, 1974; Stanton, 1980; Aponte and van Deusen
1981; Reay, 1988; Treacher, 1988). This approach conceptualises
families as hierarchical organisations, which are differentiated by
explicit and/or implicit rules that set out the power given to various
family members in different areas of family life.

Examination of how family members interact with each other will
reveal boundaries that are defined by the rules laying down who
participates in the decision-making process and on whose terms. In a
well-functioning system, boundaries are clear, with a capacity to
adjust to developmental life-stage events. The quality of boundaries
can vary from over-involvement (enmeshment) to disengagement,
and may be rigid, diffuse, permeable, close or distant. The therapist
will need to detect transactional patterns through which people relate
and communicate, and to understand the functional purposes these
serve for the family and its members. The various alignments of
family members, for example who is supporting whom against
whom, or who works together with or in opposition to one or more
participants, will tell the therapist about the family's functioning and
influence her interventions. The usefulness of this approach is that it
considers interpersonal relationships in terms of mutual causality
within the functional hierarchy of the family.

Like a family, the school is a hierarchical organisation, consisting of various subsystems which are delineated by boundaries. The school organisation thus operates on similar lines to a family, with the head teacher, deputy, senior management, teacher and pupils forming various subsystems with boundaries and alignments that lend themselves to systemic consultations (Skynner, 1974; Steinberg and Yule, 1985; Steinberg, 1989; Dare et al., 1990). Families and schools are both social institutions providing care and education for children. Both are systems: 'a family is a system that operates through transactional patterns of how, when, and to whom to relate, and these patterns underpin the system' (Minuchin, 1974, p. 51, 1981 edition); the school is 'an open system in constant dynamic interaction with the environment that it serves' (Burden, 1981, p. 35). Taylor defines school in terms of general systems theory and says that one can 'identify recurring cycles of input, throughput (or transformation) and output, kept in dynamic equilibrium by means of feedback or information exchanges with a changing environment across a permeable boundary, so that these processes act as corrective devices or regulators' (Taylor, 1985, p. 156).

It has been persuasively argued (Fisher, 1986) that the principles and systemic concepts applicable to family therapy can be useful in working with schools. This has been illustrated by Skynner (1974), Burden (1981), Campion (1985), Dowling (1985), Fisher (1986), and Plas (1986). Systems thinking has also proved useful in addressing issues at the interface between systems such as family/school (Aponte, 1976; Dowling, 1985; Dowling and Taylor, 1989). Systemic consultations offer a method of helping an organisation such as a school to adjust to changed circumstances which arise out of the experience of a pupil's death; see Campbell and Draper (1983), Fisher (1986), Imber-Black (1986), Campbell et al. (1989). The method concentrates on the process of interpersonal relationships within the organisation by exploring different perspectives, beliefs and meanings attributed to the pupil's death (Palazzoli et al., 1980). Consultation is carried out by the therapist 'on the basis of feedback from the family in response to the information he solicits about relationships and therefore, about differences and change' (Palazzoli et al., 1980, p. 8).

The importance of working with differences in perceptions among people derives from Bateson's (1972) notion that change and new ideas develop from the differences that makes a difference. This approach developed circular questions as a means of facilitating change. The term 'circular question' derives from the recursive relationships between participants in a system. 'To understand a system is to understand the coherence in its circular organisation. Thus it is the circular connectedness of ideas, feelings, actions, persons, relationships, groups, events, traditions etc. that is of interest... The questions are circular in that they attempt to elucidate these organisational connections' (Tomm, 1988). The purpose of circular questioning, use of feedback, reframing, punctuation and exploration of differences is to elicit the patterns that connect people, beliefs and actions (Campbell *et al.*, 1989).To ask a teacher what he thinks a colleague might need in order to be able to console bereft parents is circular in that it connects people while eliciting further information about their interdependence and relationship.

Structural family therapy, as described by Minuchin (1974) and Minuchin and Fishman (1981), focuses on transactional patterns and communication processes within the organisation. Structural and strategic systems therapy focuses on the transactional process in the here and now, and considers the content of the transaction as secondary, monitoring carefully, instead, who communicates what to whom. It also looks for alignments, alliances and hierarchy, and seeks to understand the functional demands made by group members upon each other.

Assessment

Familiarity with the structure of the organisation before a calamity assists the therapist to assess a school's strengths and its capability to respond to the sudden death of a pupil and the longer-term effects of this. A well-functioning school with clear communication lines between and across professional boundaries will be more likely to cope effectively with such a death than a less well-organised school. A well-functioning school can be characterised by a clear structural hierarchy, with boundaries between subsystems (head teacher, deputy, teacher, pupil, parent and so on) where boundaries are flexible and transactions carried out smoothly. A well-functioning organisation aims at maintaining its balance (similar to homeostasis in thermodynamic terms). According to the status, gender and function of the deceased member of the school, his/her loss or death may upset the equilibrium of the functioning of the organisation, and this will require re-organisation. A school with a well-functioning caring system and good morale will cope more easily with the crisis and be less likely to suffer from adverse effects such as losing parental support.

Systemic thinking, focusing on the transactional patterns within the school and understanding the process as circular in its causality, proved a useful way of conceptualising the impact of a sudden death. Family therapy, which is based on working with dysfunctional families, where the sick member is presented for treatment, conceptualises symptomatic behaviour as expressing the system's attempt to cope with stress. Similarly, the effect of stress on a school causes shock and disbelief, challenges the existing transactional patterns of its members, stresses the organisation and may cause dysfunction. In systemic terms, the pre-existing stability of the organisation is shattered by the removal of one of its members. The degree of disturbance that follows will depend on a number of factors, such as the importance of the lost member within the system and how the outside world responds to the event. Each member of the school will experience the death of a pupil differently and may attribute different meanings to its effect on others within the group. The way teachers interact with each other and with their pupils depends on a variety of factors such as their status, gender, and the power attributed to them by their colleagues and by pupils. There is also a clear differentiation between the rights and privileges of pupils as distinct to that of their teachers. The teachers are also differentiated by various grades and the topics they teach. All these have a bearing on the transactional and communication patterns that provide the main focus for systemic interventions.

The understanding of the grieving process as an internal, individual struggle between the avoidance of the realities of loss and the pull of wanting to continue with normal life (approach/avoidance conflict) is useful in assessing an individual's emotional state and readiness for change. Even if systemic consultation concentrates its main intervention on the process of interpersonal relationships, it is therapeutically helpful to incorporate feelings and the meaning of loss at an individual level in order to accelerate the healing process. Implicitly, feelings are always evoked by any intervention, even though they are not addressed directly.

Theory and the practical task

The members of the school community are likely to react in their own ways to the news of the death and this will affect the way they behave, and the expectations that they will have of colleagues or peers. The therapist must understand the various starting points of different members of the community so as to be able to help them interact with each other in a respectful and supportive way. Systems theory can help a therapist to conceptualise the complexity of the process needed to help the school community to accommodate to the death of a pupil and to facilitate the appropriate actions.

Crises may pull people together or set them apart, especially if criticisms are made against the head teacher or governors, who may be unprepared to cope. Such crises challenge the competence of the organisation and especially its leaders. Routine interactions between members of the school may be affected and show signs of stress. It is times of stress that may threaten relationships and challenge the way people behave towards each other within this community. It is important to establish clear boundaries and protect the well-established functioning of the organisation. It may be helpful if the therapist tries to keep members of the school community in touch by holding small group meetings in which each member can be listened to and have his/her needs acknowledged. Facilitating communication among group members builds on the strengths of the group sharing the loss of one of its members.

Attachment and strength within the system

So far, the emphasis of this chapter has been on relationships within the organisation as a whole, in keeping with the systems approach. It is, however, also important for the therapist to be aware of members of the system as individuals, because a child's earlier experiences within its family may affect how it reacts to stresses within the wider system. The literature of systemic thinking, as applied in family therapy and systems consultation, offers a means of combining ideas from individual child development and the general understanding of the impact of sudden death with its effect on the transactional pattern of groups of people who are dependent on each other, as they are in an institution such as a family or school.

Bowlby's (1980) theory of attachment and loss explains reactions to loss in terms of early experiences which determine the ability of bereaved people to cope with loss. He suggests that personality development is rooted in children's earliest experiences of interpersonal relationships in their families. These early experiences form the emotional base which supports an individual's self-understanding and relationship to the outside world. Children with a good self-image and a good understanding about interpersonal relationships will be capable of coping with stress and loss and will be less likely to suffer from prolonged grieving. The experience of parental love and approval teaches the child to feel good about him/herself and confident in relationships with others. Starting from a secure base of this kind, the individual is better equipped to cope with threatening events such as the sudden death of a friend.

Bowlby believed that most bereavement processes can be resolved without causing any long-term pathological effects. He argued that a process which recognises loss and acknowledges the feelings associated with the deceased provides for a healthy process of adjustment through mourning. Milgram and Palti (1993) showed that, in children, resilience to stress and the ability to cope are affected by the degree to which they have developed support-seeking and support-attracting attitudes that assist them in securing social support. This can then result in avoiding the detrimental effects of reactions to loss. Another variable affecting how an individual reacts to loss is the emotional equilibrium of the group to which the individual belongs, whether family or school. Bowen (1976) describes the impact of loss on a family as follows:

> The equilibrium of the unit is disturbed by either the addition of a new member or the loss of a member. The intensity of the emotional reaction is governed by the functioning level of emotional integration in the family at the time or by the functional importance of the one who is added to the family or lost to the family. (p. 82)

Bowen goes on to state that

> A well integrated family might adjust and adapt more quickly to loss than a less well integrated family, which initially might show little reaction at the time of death and later respond with symptoms of physical illness, emotional illness or social misbehaviour. (p. 83)

The intensity of reactions following the death of a family member may well depend on the importance and centrality of the deceased in the emotional life and stability of the family. The religious views of the family, if any, will also affect how its members react to death.

The effect on a child of the loss of a friend is less well understood than the effect of the loss of a family member (Dyregrov, 1991, 1994). Nevertheless, such a loss can clearly be traumatic. Adolescents in particular may identify more closely with their friends and experience the guilt of the survivor, the wish to change places with the dead friend, and a feeling of isolation in their grief (Pennells et al., 1992;

Pennells and Smith, 1995). Death as a result of having undertaken a forbidden thing (like taking drugs) may cause anxiety and confusion. Children may require assistance in learning to understand that carrying out prohibited acts does not deserve the disproportionate punishment of having to die.

A general background to our understanding of loss and change is provided by Marris (1991, 1993), who pointed to research into bereavement, depression and the effects of unemployment (ultimately also taking its toll on the children), which suggests that the nature of events themselves and the social context in which they occur affect people's resilience in coming to terms with loss and adjusting to change. The intensity of the emotional response to loss – grief – may be understood as being driven by two different mechanisms operating at the same time; one is to avoid facing loss, the other is to approach novelty. These two incompatible forces may contribute to initial grief reactions of numbness and denial. They may also result in an emotional tug-of-war between preserving the past and simultaneously trying to create a meaningful pattern of relationships in which the loss is accepted.

From theory to practice

It was on these theoretical foundations that the planning of the interventions and consultation to be described in the remaining pages of this chapter was based. Above all, the starting point is an understanding of child development, interpersonal relationships and transactional patterns of behaviour in reaction to loss. Facing loss presents a complex emotional, cognitive and organisational challenge. It requires an adjustment to sudden change which in the two presented cases occurred quite unexpectedly.

Where the educational psychologist has decided to take on the role of bereavement therapist, the first practical task is to assess the situation in the context of the pupil's death in the school. It can be helpful to analyse the organisation and its functioning by considering the following questions:

- What is the effect of the event on the school as a whole?
- What are the immediate needs as perceived by the Local Education Authority, the school's governors, head teacher, teachers, pupils and parents?
- Who perceives whom as needing what?

- What are the solutions desired by those suffering most from the impact?
- Who is frightened of what?
- How can the group help itself and its members to support each other?
- What resources are available to manage the present stress?

The therapist will need to assess the stresses on the system and intervene to promote the school's recovery, enabling it to continue to carry out its primary task of educating children rather than prolonging the process of coping with loss.

A preliminary exploration of the various subsystems within the school's community assists in identifying its structure, weaknesses and strengths. A bereavement therapist who is familiar with a particular school can readily draw on this knowledge, whereas the therapist who does not have that knowledge may find it helpful to construct an organisational map. This information can be obtained by informal observation as well as by interviewing. After a fatal accident, teachers in the staff room are likely to talk about the tragedy, which will allow the therapist informally to note who is sharing experiences with whom and how. This will provide an initial picture of the kind of difficulties that a school is likely to confront when coping with the crisis. Further understanding of how the school operates will emerge from looking at how responsibilities are negotiated and how problems are jointly solved. Who is deciding what should be done and who tells whom what to do among staff? Alliances among staff may be openly declared or remain covert, as will tensions and distance.

Observations of these relationships help the therapist to understand how the staff – teachers, head teacher or year heads – normally interact and how they communicate. Dysfunctional transactional patterns as well as weak communication systems will need to be detected as these may impede the coping process and may need to be addressed by the therapist. The repair and establishment of communication systems and the creation of flexible boundaries between subsystems may need to become the focus of the therapeutic work. Group meetings, where members listen to each other and are made aware of each other's needs, can help by allowing all concerned time to think together about how these needs can best be met. Staff may need to be encouraged to think 'what does my colleague think that I could do differently for him/her to feel more supported in the present situation?' Such circular questions bring to light the colourful dynamics of interpersonal transactions and draw out the functional demands made upon its members.

A therapist may also be asked to work with children within the school. In order to work effectively with the group the therapist will need to understand the structure of the group and its functional dynamics. Children form their own subsystems within the school, and within these there will be differences of status according to the popularity and power of individuals within the peer group. The therapist will need to observe the interactions within the group. Who tells whom what to do within the peer group? What implications does this have for the way that the group responds to the death of one of its members? What was the position of the dead pupil within the peer group? These questions are useful when preparing sessions with pupils, in order to address every child's need, not only those of the dominant characters.

When working with parents similar questions need to be asked about their relationship with the school, the nature of their involvement and influence and the support they can offer. When preparing for meetings or therapy sessions with any of these groups in the organisation it is useful to have these questions in mind. This will help the therapist to remain focused on boundaries and processes between members of the group in a way that will facilitate coping and adaptation within the group.

Death is both a very personal experience and a public event. Those involved may well be coping with overwhelming feelings aroused by loss at the same time as trying to make sense of the challenge presented by it, while also attending to more mundane but burdensome tasks such as arranging the funeral. This can affect members of the school community as well as members of the family of the deceased. For teachers death can evoke such strong reactions that they often feel unable to care for their pupils adequately (Dyregrov, 1991). The teachers' feelings and need for support will need to be recognised if they are to feel competent and strong enough to share sad news with the children in their class. For the therapist the bereavement work may reawaken overwhelmingly sad feelings associated with personal loss. The therapist needs to be aware of this before engaging in bereavement work. Stress on all concerned can be increased considerably by the intrusive interest of the press, especially if the death occurs within the context of the school. Children need to be shielded from media attention in order to prevent their grief from being exploited and artificially prolonged.

The therapist will need to be empathetic in order to engage with those seeking support, by being receptive to the emotional demands, bearing in mind the conflict individuals experience. The therapist should also try to help them comprehend and adjust to the new situation created by loss while still preserving the memory of the deceased, yet at the same time trying to leave the past behind. The therapist needs to bear the complexity of people's feelings in mind while mapping the system according to the various functional demands made upon each other before and after the death. What functions were carried out by whom? What was the position of the deceased within the system?

Case study 1: The death of a primary school pupil

Steven was murdered during the school holidays and the news was widely available in the local and national papers and on television. Because the death had occurred outside term time, the Education Authority was able to concentrate on the school's needs, given that the school could not be blamed or held responsible for what happened in any way. The educational psychologist was requested by the Education Authority to advise and support the teachers of the school. The school's head teacher felt that staff might require guidance in how to cope with the responses of pupils and parents to the news of Steven's death. He was keen for the educational psychologist to provide some help and it was agreed that the educational psychologist would offer some consultation sessions to the staff group.

First step

On the first day after the summer break, without sufficient time available for any joint preparatory consultation, all staff were assembled in the staff room to share the distressing news. They were absolutely silent. The consultant knew the school well and saw her immediate task as breaking the silence by inviting staff to share their initial reactions openly in the group. They were asked how they had learned about Steven's death and what they knew. Members of the group in the room were encouraged to share with each other what impact the news had upon them. The discussion covered areas of general grief, anger, disbelief and guilt feelings. They said how comforting it was to be able to share their overwhelming feelings of sadness at Steven's death and their horror at his brutal murder. Their shock initially made it difficult to think about what needed to be done. Once this had been discussed and time had been given for sharing feelings and reactions it was easier to identify the tasks which needed to be faced.

Second step

The next problem was how to present the facts to the pupils who were returning the next day. The consultant encouraged all the staff to consider various options, connoting each one positively. Positive feedback enhanced group cohesion and mutual support. It also encouraged more withdrawn staff to participate. Discussion focused on whether the class teacher should convey the news or whether the head teacher would announce Steven's death during the assembly. The consultant stimulated a rich debate, creating space for ideas, ensuring respect for all, and keeping the transactional process alive by circular questioning. In discussing the roles of different staff members it was acknowledged that Steven's class teacher had a special role. She agreed with this and with the group's decision that she should be the one to tell her class what had happened. The group decided that the head teacher should also make an announcement later in the day during the assembly of the whole school. The teachers were very supportive of each other, helping the class teacher by making positive suggestions on how she might phrase things and how she would talk to the pupils. The group then explored how the class teacher might expect the children to react and how they would respond, for instance, to expressions of anger and sadness. The importance of the way in which the class teacher would give the news to her pupils was discussed at length, and the use of factual, informative language rather than emotive descriptions was strongly recommended, using words such as 'death', instead of 'murder'. The discussion led the class teacher to feel quite confident in her ability to break the news to the class.

The group then decided to think about the pragmatics of talking to pupils and parents about the issue of children's safety. The session now developed into a task-oriented discussion on how to protect children. It was acknowledged that the murder happened outside school hours and that the teachers could protect the children only to the extent of teaching them about safety. Lengthy discussions took place about the questions parents might ask and how teachers could answer them. This was achieved by the consultant asking each member of the group how they would react, how they would respond and how they think their colleague might best phrase certain messages. Questions like 'Should the teachers have protected Steven more by making him more aware of dangerous situations?' were also discussed, leading to the realisation that he had received all the help possible from school. The consultant made a clear demarcation of professional boundaries concerning the role of teachers as distinct from that of parents. This helped teachers to recognise the limit of their duties and responsibilities.

The discussion led to consideration of how children who asked questions should be handled. Should they be talked to on their own or as a group? If parents did not let their children go home during the lunch hour any more, what should be done? The teachers were able to work out answers to these questions for themselves, and they decided that it was better to deal with individual children rather than address them as a group, except in the initial class assembly, so that the teachers could concentrate on individual questions and on the particular children whom they knew best.

As already mentioned above, in the next school assembly the head teacher spoke of Steven's death and how much he would be missed. He encouraged everyone to think of all their good memories of Steven. A number of children spoke about what they remembered about him, and some of his work was displayed. In the weeks after Steven's murder the anxiety and excitement slowly diminished. The school eventually decided to plant a tree in his memory.

Last step

The main worries of the parents concerned the safety of their own children. The head teacher discussed these issues with the consultant. The identity of the murderer was still unknown and was the subject of investigation by the police. The school could make no comments on this. There was no further involvement by the police or the press at school. The press can have a detrimental effect on a school's recovery from traumatic events by invading privacy and adding to the general stress. Education authorities normally hand this task to their heads of public relations and instruct staff not to talk to the press without briefing. In this case the absence of reporters helped the school to come to terms with events. On the whole the teachers managed extremely well in comforting the children and also in remembering Steven. His class teacher had a particular role to play. All teachers were given easy access to the consultant in case they wanted to discuss further issues relating to the death or the reactions of pupils or themselves.

There was no need for any longer-term intervention. Staff felt supported by the fact that the consultant attended Steven's funeral, which was also covered at length in the local press. The class did not attend but a few pupils came with their parents. The teachers were interviewed individually several months afterwards and asked how they had coped and what had been helpful. They said that they had felt very supported by the authority's acknowledgement of their needs and had been helped by the input of the consultant.

Case study 2: Death in a girl's secondary school

Shareen, a twelve-year-old girl, took malaria tablets from her family's first-aid cabinet, and brought them to school. During an art lesson she swallowed most of the tablets. She collapsed and was rushed to hospital, where she was pronounced dead. Shareen's death led to more extensive work in the school – a large secondary school for girls.

Because Shareen died during term time and on school premises, the Education Authority responded very differently from the way it had reacted in the previous case study. The school's inspector was called in and the head teacher was confronted immediately with public concern, including involvement of the police and the press. The head teacher found the media attention particularly stressful as it was difficult for her to attend to the needs of the school and to respond to reporters requesting interviews. The education welfare officer comforted Shareen's parents. The educational psychologist was asked to offer therapeutic help to two groups of girls and one individual girl. Her brief also included talking with three of the teachers who were most involved. The head teacher and the deputy head teacher made this request, believing that these particular groups needed extra support. In spite of some misgivings the educational psychologist accepted her brief. How useful could she hope to be while working within such restrictions? It might arguably have been more useful to work with parents or with teachers and pupils jointly, or with the whole school.

Planning the work

A contract was made with the deputy head teacher that the psychologist would offer one session to the teachers, if necessary more, and some ongoing therapy with the two groups of girls. One girl was seen individually at the request of the deputy head teacher because she was known to be a 'stirrer' in school and had a reputation of being a bully.

She was, however, not a member of the dead girl's class. As in most crises, there was little time to negotiate these arrangements. The deputy agreed to provide a quiet room and gather the group for each meeting.

The school was not known previously to the educational psychologist, but talking to teachers, senior staff and the girls, she formed the impression that in general the school was a caring organisation which provided a good service to its pupils. However, the school was clearly under stress and in crisis. Therapeutic intervention would need to focus on preventing long-term effects resulting from this traumatic experience and promoting adjustment to the loss. As Dyregrov (1991) points out, the death of a friend is often not recognised as bereavement. There is no social status given to friends during arrangements following death. They are frequently excluded from rituals which could support their emotional needs to come to terms with the loss. Furthermore, they may not be able to share their grief with family at home. This can make it more difficult to come to terms with what has happened.

Group sessions

Group 1

The first session with six of the dead girl's friends took place in the head teacher's office. This location gave the meeting a sense of special importance. The deputy introduced the therapist briefly to the group and disappeared. Sitting in a circle, the girls all appeared to be talking at once, mainly venting their anger about how the school had handled the whole incident. They were furious that they were forbidden to attend the funeral (an expressed wish of the parents of Shareen, the deceased girl). It felt like being in the lion's den with these excited girls. After a considerable while they noticed that their 'special counsellor' had not yet said anything, allowing the therapist briefly to assess the interactional process before taking charge of the group. This was deliberate, in order to allow the girls to express themselves and calm down before addressing particular issues. This gave the therapist a unique opportunity to observe their interactions for a few minutes, and allowed some mapping of the structure of the group. Some pupils were more assertive and were listened to, whereas others spoke simultaneously and were ignored by the group. They quietened down after a time and gave each other space to report facts, share feelings and complain.

After establishing rules of confidentiality with the group, the therapist encouraged the girls to take it in turns to speak. Each comment was acknowledged by the therapist, who expressed appreciation of each girl's contribution, making each one feel respected and valued. Some felt guilty because they explained the accident as an act of attention-seeking and they wished they had given the girl the attention she needed. Some thought that because the girl was a 'show off' they had tended to ignore her. If only they had spent more time with her she would not have had to seek attention by taking an overdose of tablets. It seemed important to lift the burden of guilt and responsibility from their shoulders and help them to reach a more balanced perspective. The therapist challenged guilt and blame by praising the girls' sensitivity and understanding of their friend's needs. She encouraged the group to work together to understand Shareen's actions and to modify their views. Gradually it emerged that they saw Shareen as quite self-confident, often cheeky, gregarious and good fun, and perhaps less vulnerable than they had initially feared. It also became clear that the members of the group had no part in their friend's unusual behaviour of bringing tablets from home to school. They believed that Shareen had been showing off how daring she was, and that she did not realise how dangerous the drugs were.

The next therapeutic task was to relieve the girls further of the burden of guilt and responsibility by thinking who else might carry responsibility for the care of youngsters. The group explored who should have the primary role of taking care of a child's needs, and they agreed that 'looking after a child' is not the sole function of a friend. Clear boundaries were recognised of what a friend should do in relation to what parents or teachers are doing. With the guidance of the therapist the group tried to differentiate between the responsibilities of a friend, a parent and a teacher, thus setting clear boundaries round each function and constructing a 'hierarchy of care'.

The secure atmosphere created by the therapist permitted the group to discuss their individual views and relationships to Shareen and what they missed most, or what they thought their friend might be missing most. This kind of circular questioning encouraged them to share their feelings and to become aware that Shareen's death both bound them together and enabled them to comfort each other. They also discussed who else could comfort them and identified a number of adults, including a parent, a relative, or even a teacher who might help them when they were distressed or overwhelmed. The setting of clear boundaries opened to the girls a wider perspective of the situation and made them less confused. Gradually they began to organise themselves better, becoming more able to focus on their own needs, each other's and the group's.

Sudden death commonly leaves unfinished business between people. The girls were asked whether there was anything that they would have liked to sort out with Shareen before her death. Some girls were very distressed because they felt guilty over minor unresolved quarrels. The group was encouraged to look at the meaning of the quarrels in relation to their overall friendship patterns. It emerged that Shareen may have contributed to quarrels within the group, and that this was a mutual affair rather than just one person having caused the disharmony or the problem. The therapist developed a picture of the deceased as a lively, controversial, popular girl with a mind of her own. The group confirmed that picture and again regretted having lost such a colourful friend.

Reframing the facts

The first half of the session alleviated feelings of guilt by putting them into a different perspective (reframing). It continued with a discussion of what had taken place. This led to a clear understanding that Shareen's death was accidental rather than planned. The therapist suggested an alternative word 'accident' to 'suicide' which most of the girls used in the session. It seemed appropriate to try to reduce the anxiety and excitement associated with the idea of suicide. It is easier to cope with an accident than a suicide. And in any case, the inquest was still pending. The death was reframed, in that, without changing the facts, it was given a different meaning. The tablets were taken to 'show off' rather than to end a life. The fatal consequence was not intended. Although Shareen had intentionally taken the tablets from the family's medical chest at home, her tragic end was an accident. The girls engaged in a lively discussion, teasing out the difference between the initial act and the end result. Each girl contributed constructively to the session and to trying to understand both her own reactions and the implications for the group.

Initially, the girls felt devastated by the loss of their friend. Once the death and its meaning had been discussed, they felt able to air other issues, such as the fact that they felt totally excluded from being allowed to help. They felt that the school, especially their teachers, had totally misunderstood their involvement. They blamed the school for misjudging their pain. When Shareen had appeared to faint in the art room, some girls had thought she was faking. Shareen had used such tricks in the past to gain attention. Those who thought that the fall had been a pretence were particularly upset when they discovered the truth. The teacher's attempt to shield Shareen from the rest of the class after the fall was perceived by most members of the group as a rejection. They felt that they had been left out of the helping process. Some time was allowed so that every girl could give her view of what had happened. They listened with interest to each other's views and condemned the teachers for not allowing the class to go with the ambulance or to help Shareen.

The therapist encouraged the girls to consider why the teachers might have acted the way they did. She also reframed the teachers' reactions as trying to protect the girls and onlookers from a distressing event. The disappointment over the teacher's actions created a strong bond between the girls. The therapist knew that the girls would need to find some outlet for their anger, and it seemed more appropriately directed towards teachers rather than towards themselves. However, in order to allow the school's life to continue it was important for the girls to be able to understand that the teachers had tried to help and protect everybody, while doing their best for Shareen. Undoubtedly the teachers would have been preoccupied with getting her to hospital as fast as possible, thus seeing the classmates as obstacles instead of helping friends. The girls felt that they had been prevented from providing the comfort and help which it was their right and their privilege as friends to offer. Clear boundaries had to be set between the function of the teachers and their responsibility, and that of friends and peers.

The next issue arose when the group's attention was drawn to one particular girl who felt extremely guilty because on their way to school she had seen Shareen with the tablets, about which she was bragging. She had even managed temporarily to take them from Shareen, only to have them grabbed off her again. To prevent the girl from continuing to believe that she was responsible for Shareen's death, the therapist gently challenged her account of events. The girls were encouraged to talk about their knowledge of drugs, their age, and the limits of their responsibility. This helped them realise that (a) none of them knew how lethal the tablets were, and that (b) they belonged to the dead girl's family. The group was questioned about the rights that the girl had to those tablets and whose responsibility it was to take them away from her. Issues arose around possessions and how to respect others; in fact the girl did tell Shareen not to take any tablets and that this would be very silly. It was also established that the girl who blamed herself for not having kept the tablets away from the owner was much weaker than Shareen and would not have been able to hang on to them without a major fight. After the mapping of the facts and setting some boundaries around the peer and teacher functions and the dead girl's family's function, general experiences of loss and death were briefly shared, reaching into the girls' past history to draw on their experiences of loss.

Anger and grief

The aim of the first session was to help the girls to express their feelings, share their experiences and enable them to feel less mixed-up and in conflict about what had happened. Outrage that life continues as normal is a common way of showing distress in the early stages of bereavement. In this case the girls were angry that life continued in and out of school 'as if nothing had happened'. Their loyalty to Shareen kept them in an almost frozen state of excitement, in which they tried to hang on to the immediacy of events surrounding her death, as if reluctant to allow it to pass, or to move away from the crisis. They wanted everyone to acknowledge that there had been a big change, creating a void in which it was difficult to function as normal. The girls themselves described finding it very difficult to concentrate and to follow their normal routine.

The family had asked that the class should not attend the funeral and this made it particularly hard for the girls to know how to 'say goodbye' to Shareen. A number of them tried to persuade the therapist to take them to the cemetery after the service. This created a dilemma about how to accommodate the girl's needs while also respecting the wishes of the family. The therapist pointed this out to the group, who showed very little readiness to appreciate the family's feelings. They felt that being a friend was at least as valuable as being a family member, and possibly more valuable. The therapist acknowledged the strong feelings of the girls but also emphasised that the family also had a right to strong emotions. She challenged the group's demand by asking the girls to consider how Shareen's mother might be feeling, how painful her death might be for other family members and how important it was to respect these feelings. Because of their own strong emotions the girls had great difficulty in accepting this. In a fashion very typical of girls of this age they argued that, since Shareen's parents were divorced, her friends were far closer to her than parents or relatives.

The therapist supported the girls' wish to visit the cemetery and agreed to negotiate this with the head teacher, provided that Shareen's parents and their own gave permission. This showed the girls that there is a hierarchy that has to be obeyed, that there are different roles, different functions and different executive power, and that it was not within the therapist's executive power to take the girls to the cemetery. This idea had a calming effect on the group; at last they would be given an opportunity to 'say goodbye'. Planning a visit focused the girls on action rather than reacting passively to the events.

Coping with the supernatural
Three girls in the group reported 'sightings' of Shareen in their favourite meeting place in the bushes in the playground. Another saw a chair move and Shareen appear. No witness was present but the moved chair was evidence enough. The phenomenon of people searching and seeing the deceased is quite common part of the mourning process, as is well documented in the literature by Pincus and Dare (1978), Gelcer (1983), Yates and Bannard (1988) and Dyregrov (1991). The therapist worked towards normalisation, affirming that some people have very strong feelings which make them believe that they hear voices or actually think that they may have seen the image of the dead person. This restored calm to the group and no further sightings occurred.

Reframing the ghost
In order to reduce their excitement, the girls were affirmed in the strengths of their feelings. Their loss must have been very strong, hence their ability to remember their friend so vividly that she appeared to them in their minds. The therapist assumed that the more normal the experience was perceived to be, the less exciting it would seem and the less likely that these apparitions would last. The girls felt that their love for their friend had caused something very beautiful and special to happen, but that this was by no means something unnatural or out of the ordinary. The apparition was prevented from spreading through the school by giving appropriate appreciation and meaning to it in the therapy group. The girls felt reassured that their experience was not an indication that ghosts exist.

Strategic/structural systemic thinking uses task setting as a means of promoting change. Setting the girls a task was used in this situation; it was felt to be most helpful for those girls who had been kept from doing something positively while their friend had fainted. The task was that each girl should ask their parents for consent to the visit to the cemetery. The therapist promised to negotiate with the head teacher to arrange the visit, and a further session was booked in a week's time. This allowed time to consolidate issues and feelings which were covered during the first therapeutic session.

At the next meeting all the girls had obtained parental permission to visit the cemetery. However, the therapist had not managed to gain the head teacher's approval. On the contrary, the head teacher was actually alarmed by the idea; everything was overwhelming, with the press still busy trying to make a story out of the event. The head teacher felt enormously stressed and could not allow the girls to visit the cemetery. Definitely in a 'one down' position, the therapist had to inform the group of the head teacher's reservation about the visit. This also clearly indicated the power structure of the school and showed the girls that there are certain rules that govern the school and have to be followed even by other adults. This is also part of the dilemma of crisis intervention which does not leave sufficient time for proper consultation. The head teacher was so preoccupied with dealing with the police, media and parents that she had little time to give to the girls' genuine need to 'say goodbye'; she had dispensed with this by handing the girls over to the therapist.

The girls were very disappointed by the head teacher's refusal. They very much needed a way to say goodbye to their friend and, having been unable to attend the funeral, they felt they had not had the opportunity to do this. The therapist now encouraged the group to think of ways of constructing a farewell in the absence of the permission to visit the cemetery. One girl reported that her mother had attended the funeral and gave a detailed description of the flowers, the beautiful dead body in the open coffin and the sadness of everybody attending. Some of the girls appeared less eager to go to the cemetery but were still upset. They cried bitterly during the session, comforting each other. A moment of silence developed into the singing of the Beatles song *Yesterday*. Two girls then felt that the lyric was not fully appropriate, so they hummed the tune. This session was in contrast to the first session where they had vented their anger and were quite excited and confused over many issues. Overall it was a calmer session and all welcomed the suggestion to write a song or a poem in memory of their friend for the next session, which happened to coincide with the last week of term.

At the following session each girl produced a poem. The therapist compiled these into a booklet, and sent a copy to each girl at home. It was agreed that, after having shared those poems in the group, the therapist would arrange for the poems to be printed and bound. Poems were also chosen to be read out in the school's assembly which was scheduled for the end of term. The group was seen for a further meeting in the autumn term following the summer break in order to make sure that the girls were coping better and were not suffering from traumatic stress or long-term effects. This turned out to be the case.

Group 2

The second group consisted of three girls who were in a class a year above and who, because of their close links with Shareen, required acknowledgement of their feelings of loss, sadness and guilt. The school thought that these three girls might be particularly vulnerable and less able to cope because of their temperament and previous personal history. Again, the referral was made by the senior deputy head teacher in charge of pastoral care. The parents had given permission for the girls to be seen and the initial meeting concentrated around how the girls felt. One of the girls was particularly vulnerable in the light of her own previous suicide attempt. Her home circumstances were particularly problematic (numerous confrontations with her mother's changing partners), she had a poor self-image and it was felt that she might have an adverse reaction to the death. The other girls had no previous history of mental illness or family difficulties. It was explored whether they could gain comfort from their parents in order to assess whether more than one session ought to be offered to this group. They all acknowledged their feelings and established the level of friendship to the deceased that had existed and their reaction to the event, and again they allowed each other space to share their experiences of guilt, anger and self-reproach. They seemed to be comforted by the session.

The main purpose of the session was to ascertain whether the group required bereavement work beyond one session. The assessment of the girls in the group suggested that they had some differences which led to physical and verbal confrontations that had been made worse by Shareen's death. There was some distress between two of the girls in this group, who could not stop fighting each other. This conflict already existed before the death of their joint friend, and the therapist asked the girls what each of them thought the other was doing that led to them feeling provoked. Ways were explored of respecting each other's needs and examining whether they could support each other by keeping the good memory of their deceased friend alive. They made up and tried to be more friendly to each other. While they felt that they would be able to cope with school life, they said that they wanted one more session in order to check whether they could manage the stress themselves with the help of their own friends in school.

The second group had been referred as a preventative measure so that the deputy head teacher could be reassured that there would be no undue distress which would be beyond the capacity of the school to handle. It was highlighted that the particularly vulnerable girl would require careful monitoring and possibly a re-referral to her previous therapist. While contained in the safe environment of her school this girl continued to cope quite well until the nearing of the summer break, when she stopped attending, then misbehaved and was excluded for some time. Outside school she then beat up her mother's partner and was taken into care, staying in a children's home, only to repeat taking an overdose. She was then seen later by a therapist but she remained very vulnerable and now receives home tuition. The mother only reluctantly agreed later for her to be seen by the therapist, and this case was not followed up as it was not referred to the educational psychologist but to a psychotherapist and psychiatrist. This was more appropriate given that she had started her treatment there long before Shareen's death.

Individual sessions

One girl in the first group suffered severe stress, fell physically ill and was seen individually for three more sessions until she felt in control of herself. The school and her mother thought she ought to receive help. As she was absent during the initial sessions with her peers, it was agreed that she would be seen for three more sessions so that she could mourn for her friend while developing different beliefs about herself in relation to her lost friend. It took her longer to accept that the friend she had known from the first day of school had died. She went through a phase where she would listen non-stop to her favourite music, at the expense of all other interests, which concerned her parents greatly. She gradually agreed to reduce the time spent listening to the tape and to keep it in a special place.

A joint meeting was arranged with her and her mother in order to include the family more actively in the process of recovery. In the family session with her mother it emerged that the child had always been considered to be highly strung and to have a vivid imagination, according to her mother. There was a strong bond between child and mother, and after this session the mother realised that she had to be more in charge of her daughter's life and that she might need to treat her like a younger child until she recovered from the loss of her friend. Two years later she was reported to be doing well in school and to have no emotional or behavioural problems.

Looking back, after the crisis has passed, it is possible to see that under different circumstances the work might have developed in a very different way and might have been much more extensive. However, in this case, with all the anxiety and media attention generated by the incident, the head teacher decided to restrict the scope of the intervention to pupils who required counselling, although work with the wider system might have provided teachers with more support than did pupil counselling. However, in the head teacher's view this was not an opportune moment to authorise interventions which might have brought to light weaknesses in the organisation, such as the functioning of the health and safety policy, style of management or the functioning of the school's communication system. The head teacher had to present a strong position of being in charge of the school and mistress of the crisis. She found personal comfort in the church and assistance in handling the media from the Education Authority.

Conclusion

This chapter describes two cases where systemic interventions facilitated the mourning process in cases of bereavement following the traumatic death of pupils. The therapeutic work described above illustrates two different ways of helping schools to adjust to the sudden death of a pupil by using a structural model of thinking about the impact of death on a school.

The first case study illustrated how working with the whole staff group of a school enabled teachers to cope more effectively with the impact of the pupil's death. Systemic interventions such as positive reframing and setting boundaries (professional versus parental responsibilities) empowered staff to face their pupils and their parents under tragic circumstances. Working with the whole staff group allowed for collective sharing and expression of grief while drawing strength from each other. The shock and sadness about Steven's violent death were openly shared. Working with the process in the here and now, for example by addressing the meaning of the loss of the pupil for the school, helped staff to overcome the initial 'paralysis' of shock and to begin to think together about how to meet the needs of their pupils and parents.

The second case study illustrated structural work with a subsystem of the school organisation. The dead girl's classmates felt guilty about her death and this made them accuse and blame each other. Their anger led to generalised blame of the organisation. The therapist addressed this by exploring how they met each others' needs, pointing out the reciprocal nature of friendship. Boundaries were clarified as the roles and responsibilities of friends, family and school community were explored. The anger against teachers was diffused by close examination of teacher/pupil responsibility. The pupils' genuine sadness about the loss was expressed personally by their individual poems, which were shared in a whole school assembly and which acknowledged their special relationship to the deceased in relation to the rest of the school's population.

The structural systemic approach to both cases offered a way of thinking in terms of process rather than content of interpersonal behaviour. Problems are perpetuated not by their content but by how people respond to each other. Even in the case of death and bereavement, in school it is more fruitful to focus on the way members of an organisation (family, school) interact with each other rather than concentrating on the content of individual messages. Challenging the demands people make upon each other (structure of the system) opens new ways of working with schools affected by traumas and bereavements. Bereavement work in school found concepts from systemic theory most effective in regulating the mourning process. Concepts like structure (functional demands made by participants of a system upon each other), boundaries, hierarchy of responsibility, and reframing proved most useful in introducing challenges which shifted attitudes and behaviour. Working with groups allowed intervention at the interpersonal level by exploring their mutual transactions and connectedness and helping them to make sense of their personal experience of death. This approach facilitated adjustment to the tragic events by creating a different context (by reframing), which helped to clarify feelings and identify issues and tasks to be done. The impact of the death of a pupil on teachers and pupils was lessened by showing them that they could actively contribute to the healing process. This was achieved by refocusing attention from initial shock and dismay into the positive action of caring and protection within the school's community. The effect of the pupil's death was given a different meaning.

Teachers were shown what they could do instead of having to wait for time to heal the wounds or wait for expert advice. They felt empowered after one session to assist in the aftermath of the traumatic event. Clarification of issues and establishing existing boundaries according to their functions within the hierarchy of the school organisation helped manage teachers' and pupils' reactions to the two deaths more effectively. The therapist deliberately took up an empathetic position, but took no particular stance over issues related to the school, focusing instead on the interactional process and thus facilitating a different interpretation of the effects of the death. Both groups were able to continue to function more constructively and to handle their own and others' feelings and anxieties associated with death.

References

Aponte, H.J. (1976) The family-school interview: an ecostructual approach. *Family Process* **15**:303–13.

Aponte, H.J. and van Deusen, J.M. (1981) Structural family therapy. In Gurman, A.S. and Kniskern, D.P. (eds) *Handbook of Family Therapy*. New York: Brunner/Mazel.

Axline, V. (1950) Entering the Child's World via Play Experience. *Progressive Education* **27**:68–75.

Bateson, G. (1972) *Steps to an Ecology of Mind*. New York: Ballantine.

Black, D. (1993a) Children and bereavement. *Highlight No. 120*. London: National Children's Bureau.

Black, D. (1993b) Traumatic bereavement in children. *Highlight No. 121*. London: National Children's Bureau.

Bowen, M (1976) Family reaction to death. In Walsh, F. and McGoldrick, M. (eds) *Living Beyond Loss* (1991). New York: W.W. Norton.

Bowlby, J. (1980) *Attachment and Loss*. London: Hogarth Press.

Boyd Webb, N (1993) *Helping Bereaved Children*. New York/London: Guilford Press.

Burden, R. (1981) Systems theory and its relevance to schools. In Gilham, B. (ed.) *Problem Behaviour in the Secondary School*. London: Croom Helm.

Campbell, D. and Draper, R. (1983) *Applications of Systemic Family Therapy. The Milan Approach*, vol. 3. New York: Grune & Stratton.

Campbell, D., Draper, R. and Huffington, C. (1989) *A Systemic Approach to Consultation*. London: D.C. Associates.

Campion, J. (1985) *The Child in Context: Family Systems Theory in Educational Psychology*. London: Methuen.

Dare, J., Goldberg, D. and Walinets, R. (1990) What is the question you need to answer? How consultation can prevent professional systems immobilising families. *Journal of Family Therapy* **12**:355–69.

Dowling, E. (1985) Theoretical framework – a joint systems approach to educational problems with children. In Dowling, E. and Osborne, E. (eds) *The Family and the School· A Joint Systems Approach to Work with Children.* London: Routledge & Kegan Paul.

Dowling, E. and Taylor, D. (1989) The clinic goes to school – lessons learnt. *Maladjustment and Therapeutic Education* 7:24–9.

Dyregrov, A. (1991) *Grief in Children. A Handbook for Adults.* London: Jessica Kingsley.

Dyregov, A. (1994) Childhood bereavement: consequences and therapeutic approaches. *Association for Child Psychology and Psychiatry Review and Newsletter* 16(4): 173–81.

Fisher, L. (1986) Systems based consultations with schools. In Wynne, L. McDaniel. S. and Weber, T. (eds) *Systems Consultations, A New Perspective for Family Therapy.* New York/London: Guilford Press.

Fristad, M.A., Jedel R., Weller R.A. and Weller, E.B. (1993) Psychosocial functioning in children after the death of a parent. *American Journal of Psychiatry* 150:511–13.

Gelcer, E. (1983) Mourning is a family affair. *Family Process* 22(4): 501–16.

Imber-Black, E. (1986) The systemic consultant and human-service-provider systems. In Wynne, L., McDanield, S. and Weber, T. (eds) *Systems Consultation: A New Perspective for Family Therapy.* London/New York: Guilford Press.

Leick and Davidson-Nielsen (1991) *Healing Pain.* London: Tavistock/ Routledge.

Le Vieux (1993) Terminal illness and death of father, case of Céleste, age 5$\frac{1}{2}$. In Boyd Webb, N. (ed.) *Helping Bereaved Children.* New York/London: Guilford Press.

Marris, P. (1991) The social construction of uncertainty. In Parkes, C.M., Stevenson-Hinde, J. and Mauric, P. (eds) *Attachment Across the Life Cycle.* London/New York: Tavistock/Routledge.

Marris, (1993) *Loss and Change,* rev. edn. London/New York: Routledge.

Milgram, N.A. and Palti, G. (1993) Psychosocial characteristics of resilient children. *Journal of Research in Personality* 27:207–21.

Minuchin, S. (1974) *Families and Family Therapy.* London: Tavistock, reprinted 1981.

Minuchin, S. and Fishman, H. (1981) *Family Therapy Techniques.* Cambridge, MA: Harvard University Press.

Morgan, S.R. (1985) *Children in Crisis: A Team Approach in the Schools.* London: Taylor & Francis.

Palazzoli Selvini, M., Buscolo, L., Cecchin, G. and Prata, G. (1981) Hypothesizing–circularity–neutrality: three guidelines for the conductor of the session. *Family Process* 10(1): 3–12.

Parkes, C.M. (1986) *Bereavement Studies of Grief in Adult Life.* Harmondsworth: Penguin.

Pennells, M. and Smith, S. (1995) *The Forgotten Mourners. Guidelines for Working with Bereaved Children.* London: Jessica Kingsley.

Pennells, M., Smith S. and Poppleton R. (1992) Bereavement and adolescents: a group work approach. *Association for Child Psychology and Psychiatry Review and Newsletter.* **14**: 173–8.

Pincus, L. and Dare, C. (1978) *Secrets in the Family.* Boston/London: Faber & Faber.

Plas, J.M. (1986) *Systems Psychology in Schools.* New York: Pergamon.

Reay, R. (1988) Structural family therapy. In Street, E. and Dryden, W. (eds) *Family Therapy in Britain.* Milton Keynes: Open University Press.

Rutter, M. (1966) Bereaved children. In *Children of Sick Parents.* Maudsley Monograph XVI (pp. 66–75) Oxford University Press.

Skynner, R. (1974) An experiment in group consultation with staff of a comprehensive school. In Schlapobersky, J.R. (ed.) (1989) *Institutes and How To Survive Them.* Selected papers by Skynner, R. London: Methuen.

Sood, B. and Weller, E.B. (1992) Somatic complaints in grieving children. *Comprehensive Mental Health Care* **3**:17–21.

Stanton, M.D. (1980) An integrated structural/strategic approach to family therapy. *Journal of Marriage and Family Therapy* **7**:427–39.

Steinberg, D. (1989) *Interprofessional Consultation.* Oxford: Blackwell Scientific.

Steinberg, D. and Yule, W. (1985) Consultative work. In Rutter, M. and Hersov, L. (eds) *Child and Adolescent Psychiatry.* Oxford: Blackwell Scientific.

Stoker, R.P. (1987) Systems intervention in schools – the ripple effect. *Educational Psychology in Practice* **3**(1):44–50.

Taylor, D. (1985) School as a target for change: intervening in the school. In Dowling, E. and Osborne, E. (eds) *The Family in the School: a Joint Systems Approach to Work with Children.* London: Routledge & Kegan Paul.

Tomm, K. (1988) Interventive interviewing, part III: intending to ask lineal, circular, strategic and reflexive questions. *Family Process* **27**: 1–15.

Treacher, A. (1988) Family therapy: an integrated approach. In Street, E. and Dryden, W. (eds) *Family Therapy in Britain.* Milton Keynes: Open University Press.

Ward, B. (1992) *Good Grief 1 & 2.* London: Jessica Kingsley.

Weiner, H. (1985) The concept of stress in the light of studies on disasters, unemployment, and loss: a critical analysis. In Zales, M.R. (ed.) *Stress in Health and Disease.* New York: Brunner/Mazel.

Weller, R.A., Fristad, M. and Bowes, J.M. (1992) Somatic complaints in grieving children. *Comprehensive Mental Health Care* **2**:17–25.

Worden, J.W. (1991) *Grief Counselling and Grief Therapy,* 2nd edn. London: Routledge.

Yates, T. and Bannard, J. (1988) The haunted child: grief, hallucinations and family dynamics. *Journal of American Academy of Child and Adolescent Psychiatry* **27**(5): 573–81.

Yule, W. (1992) Post traumatic stress disorder in child survivors of shipping disasters: the sinking of the 'Jupiter'. *Journal of Psychotherapy Psychomatics* **57**:200–5.

Yule, W. and Gold, A. (1993) *Wise before the Event.* London: Calouste Gulbenkian Foundation.

CHAPTER 5

On the Brink – Managing Suicidal Teenagers

K. Eia Asen

This chapter outlines a systemic approach to assessing and treating suicidal adolescents and their families. Suicidal behaviour is looked at in a variety of contexts: individual, family, social and professional. A whole range of different stressors contribute to the suicidal preoccupations of teenagers. Awareness of these stressors informs early intervention strategies as well as preventative measures. Following the individual assessment of the suicidal teenager, the family is reunited and becomes actively involved in the management plan. Specific family intervention techniques help to reframe the teenager's symptoms and problem behaviours. Parallel work goes on identifying the significant influences in the teenager's peer group, in the family's cultural setting and in the professional network. The resulting multi-systems approach creates a powerful context for change.

Attempted suicide, the family and society

Suicide is now among the three leading causes of death for those aged between 15 and 34 years. Over the past 20 years there has been an increase in the (completed) suicide rate of males aged 15–19 years (McClure, 1994). It is known that less than half of those who die have tried to take their lives before. However, the vast majority of those attempting to kill themselves never do. Whilst this may seem somewhat reassuring on the one hand, it still leaves two daunting questions: which of those 75,000–100,000 patients admitted to hospital every year in the UK as a result of self-poisoning are likely to succeed in taking their own lives next time round? What can be done to prevent this from happening?

Epidemiological data provide some general answers. We know that up to one half of young suicide attempters carry on to repeat their suicidal behaviour during a follow-up period (Stanley and Barter, 1970). It is also known that suicidal thoughts and behaviours among adolescents are fairly common: in a sample of 'normal' high school students some 20 per cent anonymously admitted to suicidal behaviour over the previous year, with 75 per cent of these not having received any therapeutic intervention during that period (Rubenstein et al., 1989). One implication of these findings is that there are a significant number of unidentified – and untreated – teenagers. It is also known that many more female than male teenagers attempt to take their lives by self-poisoning; that there is a high suicide rate among certain ethnic immigrant groups; and that deliberate self-harm seems to be so much more frequent among the lower social classes.

Much research has confirmed what everyone must suspect, namely that self-harming adolescents have a much higher rate of disturbed family relationships than matched controls, with an increased presence of physical abuse and a marked absence of warmth and support inside the family (Taylor and Stansfield, 1984). Further research has shown (Rubenstein et al., 1989) that teenagers who described family life in terms of a high degree of mutual involvement, shared interests and emotional support were up to five times less likely to engage in suicidal behaviour than their peers from less cohesive families: high family cohesion seems to lower the risk of suicidal behaviour about as much as high life stress raises it.

Suicide is a big subject for contemporary society: politicians urge psychiatrists to reduce overall suicide rates and set 'targets' – for example, to reduce the suicide rate in England by some 15 per cent by the year 2000 (Secretary of State for Health, 1992). Implied in this is the idea that suicide is preventable and that the improved management of suicidal teenagers or adults would lead to a reduction of suicide rates. Untreated mental illness, especially depression, is an important cause of suicide which is potentially preventable.

This chapter outlines a systemic approach to assessing and treating suicidal teenagers and their families. The term 'systemic' requires some explanation: it refers to a biopsychosocial model which views the specific behaviours of an individual within the various 'systems' of which he or she is part – family, work setting, neighbourhood and so on. Symptoms are therefore not only seen as the expressions of some individual turmoil, but also as having some 'function' for the system, for example stabilising the family at a particular point of stress. The systemic approach holds that families, like other organisations, have their own specific characteristics and rules and establish, over time, some kind of equilibrium, adapting to internal and external pressures. The family is seen as an open system with the individual members being the elements interacting with one another, behaving according to a set of explicit or implicit rules. The family is an important context for the teenager – but not the only one. School, peers, neighbourhoods are other settings which influence young people and need to be addressed, both in terms of assessment as well as therapeutic intervention. Moreover, the specific settings in which teenagers find themselves as the result of self-harm, such as a casualty department or paediatric ward, are part of medical systems that interact with families. Working systemically here means taking into account the very specific requirements of the medical context and the 'treatment system'. In short, the term 'systemic' refers to a multi-positional, multi-level approach addressing the presenting problem, that is the suicidal behaviour, in a variety of contexts: individual, family, social and professional.

Adolescent stresses and suicidal preoccupations

The beginning of adolescence is usually signalled by a growth spurt, promoted and accompanied by hormonal surges and marked changes in physique. Personality changes include 'discovery' of sexuality with homo- and heterosexual experimentation. Emotionally there are many ups and downs, often referred to as 'inner turmoil' with feelings oscillating between self-deprecation, misery and grandiosity. Younger teenagers begin to form independent opinions, to test the limits of adult authority, and to question, where earlier they would have obeyed. It takes time for them to learn how to express their feelings and thoughts in words and to acquire the negotiating skills which are needed for resolving conflict peacefully. The teenager seems often confused and no longer appears to know what his or her 'real self' is, resulting in a series of identity crises that can prove very testing for family and friends. There are also cognitive changes: young people develop critical thinking and acquire the ability to make hypotheses, deductions and abstractions. As far as many parents are concerned this cognitive leap seems to have the unpleasant side effect of getting their teenager to question and criticise all their values, actions and suggestions. Unwilling or unable to accept these the parents of

adolescent children have the tendency to turn almost everything into
an argument, from hairstyles to music, from staying out late to not
going out at all. But family pressure is only one of the many different
stresses the young person has to put up with: there are also mounting
pressures from the outside. The young person often gets caught up
between home and outside which increasingly seem two very
different worlds: the values of the peer group rarely match those of
the family, the drugs offered outside the school gate are distinctly
different from father's gin or mother's Valium. Most teenagers
become part of mixed-sex peer groups, developing intense friendships
with secrets not shared with the family. Adolescence is a time of social
changes – starting with the transfer from primary to secondary school
with its increased demands, to competitive examinations, higher
education and the prospect of unemployment. With all these internal
and external stresses around, it is hardly surprising that many
teenagers feel from time to time that it is all getting too much and
that they wish for a way out!

What then are the most significant stressors contributing to
suicidal behaviour? Pressure to achieve, sexuality and intense experiences of loss are the most common trigger factors (Rubenstein *et al.*,
1989). Stress from family pressure to live up to certain standards and
perceived failure to do so increases the risk of self-destructive
behaviour. The developmental tasks of managing sexuality and
achievement pressure are particularly strenuous amongst middle-class
youngsters. Arguments with parents and the threatened break-up of a
love relationship are common causes of self-harm, as are disappointments such as failure in an exam, or loss of a job. The loss of a loved
person, be that a parent, another close family member or a friend, can
also lead to suicidal preoccupations and actions.

It is not uncommon to hear from relatives of an adolescent who has
tried to kill themselves that they were taken by surprise. Yet, when
talking to the young person, it often becomes clear that suicidal
preoccupations had been silently present in his or her mind for some
time. While suicidal actions in these circumstances can be
understood as catastrophic reactions to loss or abandonment, they
also need to be viewed in an individual developmental context: they
are '*always* preceded by [ideas] that have left the adolescent with the
feeling that there is no alternative but to destroy something that is
hated, something that, he believes, is now housed in his own body or
mind' (Laufer, 1996).

Suicidal behaviour as a communication

The most common reasons given by adolescents for attempting to take their lives are the following: sense of isolation; getting relief from a terrible state of mind; wanting to 'escape' from a bad situation; feeling angry with someone and making others understand how desperate one was feeling. Only few adolescents admit to their suicidal act having been a conscious 'cry for help'. Self-harm can be viewed as a method of communication characterized by risk and danger. It has been argued that overdosers put a 'message in the bottle' (Kingsbury, 1993) and that it is left to family and professionals to decipher it. Such messages are rarely straightforward, but tend to be directed at more than just one person and may be full of contradictions. When responding to these communications a complex interaction between young person, family and helping system evolves (Hollis, 1987). The risk-taking behaviour is often part of an escalating pattern of symptoms causing an increasing concern in the person's immediate environment. If the family's responses do not acknowledge the importance of the underlying distress, suicidal behaviour can spiral out of control. It could be argued that suicidal behaviour is at times a form of problem-solving because it allows the individual to communicate something that cannot be communicated in any other way. However, when those near and dear are selectively deaf, the solution quickly becomes the problem. Things can escalate to a dangerous point when nobody takes the young person seriously: without wishing to die the young person goes too far and risks accidentally killing herself.

Much suicidal behaviour occurs in a relational context of change and conflict (Aldridge, 1984) and teenagers often want the grown-ups to read between the lines. They may talk about wishing they could sleep for a long, long time – or simply not wake up again. The adult hearing this can choose to ignore it, get alarmed or feel manipulated. No response from the parent(s) may be further evidence to the young person that nobody understands and confirm their (true or false) belief that parents and other adults are stupid or useless. Moreover, many teenagers are highly ambivalent about handling their distress all by themselves or wanting to share it with members of their family. In this way suicidal teenagers are on the brink: it seems that they have to court danger to clarify things, for themselves and others, but by doing so can cause much harm and distress to themselves and others.

Few situations are more traumatic for families than the suicidal attempt of an adolescent child, particularly when it seems to come 'out of the blue'. Parents respond with a mixture of fright, anger and self-blame, feelings of disbelief and impotence. Why did their son or daughter do it? How could they have prevented it – or at least spotted the signs? The fact that there are rarely answers to these questions only increases the sense of helplessness and anxiety: when is he or she going to do it next? How can it be prevented from happening again? Apparent family harmony turns overnight into conflict, with different family members finding clashing explanations for what happened. Blame and self-blame unbalance things further and soon the family is in crisis. Suicidal attempts are among the most dramatic communications that young persons can make both to the family and the world at large. It is known that the way a family responds to the self-harming behaviour of one of its members directly affects the likelihood of further attempts. This alone is an important reason as to why the whole family needs to be involved in the management of its suicidal teenager.

The setting: casualty staff, psychiatrists and paediatricians

The assessment of suicidal teenagers needs to address the following areas: the young person's danger to self or others; the sense of perception of risk by family members; and the family's ability and willingness to mobilise their own personal and social resources for coping (Gutstein et al., 1988). This implies a focus both on internal (psychological and biological) as well as on external (environmental stress) causes. Traditionally psychiatrists and related clinicians assess current suicidal risk, *examining* the individual characteristics of the self-harmer and viewing these in relation to known profiles of 'dangerous' or vulnerable *patients* (Hawton and Catalan, 1987). The patient will be asked a whole range of questions, drawn from a long checklist of signs and symptoms (Beck et al., 1974) to determine whether it is 'safe' to discharge him or her from the care of the hospital, and to make a *treatment* plan. For young people under the age of 16, however, such an approach is, of course, quite unsuitable for a number of reasons. In particular, it does not take account of the needs and resources of the adults who are legally responsible for the care and safety of the youngster leaving hospital. Nor does it take adequate account of the social context in which the self-harm has occurred in a way that establishes relationships upon which future therapeutic work can grow.

Interactions with the care providers very much affect how adolescents and their families engage in assessment and therapeutic work

(Munson, 1986). Good interactions between emergency room staff and families do positively affect the family's expectations regarding help and therapy. Staff need to avoid blaming the adolescent or family for 'causing' the suicide attempt and overcome barriers created by language, custom and how one deals with strangers. Specific staff-training programmes can be put into place to influence attitudes and behaviours not only of doctors and nurses, but also of admitting clerks, security staff and helpers on the ward (Rotheram-Borus *et al.*, 1996). It is important to ensure that the young person and family have some privacy – not an easy task in busy accident and emergency departments or paediatric wards.

The general ethos prevailing in casualty departments and the attitudes adopted are of great importance: if mental health problems get trivialised then it is likely that some needy adolescents will be sent home if there is nothing 'medically' wrong with them. For example, it is not uncommon for a teenager who has 'only' taken six paracetamol tablets to be sent away, as the quantity seems to suggest to casualty staff that the overdose was not 'serious' – only to be readmitted a few hours or days later with ten times that dose. Similarly it is not entirely uncommon for an adolescent who has tried to cut himself on his wrists and arms to be told that the injuries were 'too minor to warrant medical attention' and to be asked to leave the hospital, in a tone conveying both sarcasm and irritation. In young people, the danger-ousness of the act of self-harm often belies the seriousness of suicidal intent. This is one of the reasons why most accident and emergency departments adopt a policy of referring every self-harmer for a psychiatric opinion. Evolving a more or less formal response system, based on a good and responsive liaison system between casualty staff, paediatricians and mental health workers is a necessary precondition for managing suicidal teenagers.

Many self-harming adolescents will be transferred from the casualty department to the paediatric ward, both for treatment and observation. In well-functioning paediatric settings the member of the child psychiatric team is usually informed within a few hours of admission. It seems better to be involved right from the start rather than being 'handed' the patient once she or he is regarded as 'physically well'. Achieving such instant involvement is often the result of long and arduous negotiations with senior nurses and consultant paediatricians. It is, however, not uncommon for there to be ambivalent feelings regarding psychiatric or psychotherapeutic work which can be acted out in all sorts of ways, for example by constantly interrupting an interview, by failing to provide privacy, by 'forgetting' that a family meeting had been scheduled and sending the adolescent to the X-ray department at the same time, or by prematurely discharging a young person without multidisciplinary discussion or consultation. Such acting out can be remedied or avoided by regular multidisciplinary staff discussions and teaching events in which the work of mental health professionals is explained.

Increased understanding does help, because self-harming adolescents on paediatric wards may otherwise be regarded as a 'nuisance' being, as far as the ward staff are concerned, amidst children who are 'really' ill. Some teenagers, because of their apparent state of misery, evoke strong parental responses in nurses. It is a well-known phenomenon that institutions can mirror family dynamics, reflecting, for example, a split between the parental couple in a professional disagreement between, say, a senior nurse, paediatrician or mental health worker. At times this can lead to 'crisis buffering' when a powerful 'helping' network takes the place of the kinship system in terminating the crisis (Gutstein *et al.*, 1988). For example, protecting a miserable teenager from her family by insisting on observing some rigid visiting hours or, indeed, prescribing 'no visitors', will tend to distance the family. A clinician who uses a systemic framework can help members of the paediatric team to avoid getting caught up in family dynamics and encourage family meetings, conducted by a family therapist, thereby addressing issues openly and giving young person and family the opportunity to work something out together. Similarly 'stroppy' teenagers who act out on the ward in the midst of much younger children can often be handled by involving their family in helping to modify the disruptive behaviour on the ward. Managing adolescent self-harmers on general paediatric wards can therefore be complex: powerful wishes to infantilise, reject and punish are in operation (Hollis, 1987). Giving in to these may be understandable but usually does little to address specific individual and family issues.

Medico-legal reasons partly dictate the involvement of a child psychiatrist or allied worker. In the case of a young person under the age of 18, the paediatric team will require the specialist opinion of a mental health professional before discharge. The purpose of this is to ensure that there has been a formal assessment of suicidal risk, and an agreement with the adults who are responsible for the young person that they are able to take responsibility for safety, and a plan for follow-up. In some cases specific child protection issues emerge and need to be attended to.

Assessing the teenager and the family

Once the clinician has been informed by the paediatric team that a suicidal teenager has been admitted, the first meeting should be arranged as quickly as possible. As the family is likely to be in a state of crisis this tends to be a good time for intervention: emotions run high and 'raw' family interactions can be observed. A day or two later a new equilibrium is found with denial of how serious things are or have been. Meeting with the teenager and family sooner presents the clinician with an acute picture: the self-harmer on a busy ward plugged into various machines and drips, with members of the family sitting around her, all in various degrees of shock, disbelief and shame. The main objectives of the first assessment are (Spender, 1996):

1. To determine whether or not the teenager is safe to go home. This involves the assessment of whether he or she is suicidal as well as an evaluation as to whether the parents are able to keep the young person safe.
2. To identify any conditions that need further or separate intervention, such as bullying, sexual abuse, or acute psychiatric disorder.
3. To prepare the ground for further therapeutic work with the young person and family, if necessary.

When it comes to deciding whom to see first – the teenager, family or parents – the clinician has a choice. There are quite different views among professionals about the sequence in which family and individual interviews should be combined. Some clinicians favour a family interview first (Reder *et al.*, 1991), whereas others always precede the family interview with an individual interview of at least half an hour (Spender, 1996). My own approach is to leave it to the family to negotiate who is going to be seen in what order. This makes it possible to get first glimpses of family interaction, for example the family's decision-making process, providing valuable information on who the spokesperson is and who agrees and disagrees with whom. It is also possible to gain some understanding as to whether the parent(s) wish to delegate responsibility to a professional and therefore immediately 'instruct' the clinician to take the young person away and 'sort her out'. Whatever the outcome of the family discussion, the clinician takes a stance of curiosity (Cecchin, 1987), inquiring how and why a particular decision was made. This can be done by asking a variety of questions such as: 'What would be the advantage of me seeing your daughter first? And what might be the disadvantages?' Or: 'What do you see as the advantage of us talking here all together about what happened? Are there any disadvantages you can think of ?' Such questioning hopefully stimulates reflection, allowing the different family members to think about the implications of each action.

Connecting with suicidal teenagers

If it is decided that the young person should be seen first on his or her own, then the main initial task for the clinician is to establish rapport. To achieve this it is important that the interview takes place in privacy, preferably in a side room on the ward. At the outset the clinician needs to think about confidentiality issues and address these openly with the young person, such as what aspects of the interview might or might not be discussed with the parents or other members of the family subsequently. Many teenagers are worried that whatever they say will be passed on to the rest of the family. They therefore need to be reassured that this is not going to be the case – otherwise they might not talk as freely and openly as necessary. It is therefore good practice for the clinician to state at the beginning of the interview that whatever is being discussed would remain completely confidential, but also to explain that, if the information given involves acts that are criminal or a threat to safety, it would be the clinician's responsibility to share this information with others. This protects the mental health professional from the difficulties that can arise when the limits of confidentiality have not been made clear, and it emerges that there are child protection issues which require attention. It also makes clear that a 'blanket' guarantee of confidentiality is not possible and avoids the possibility of breaking the young person's trust.

Suicidal teenagers show a variety of responses to these opening remarks: most feel reassured, some seem threatened, there are those who decide to remain mute and others appear indifferent. Whatever the response, it is the clinician's task to connect with the young person so that it becomes possible to understand what led to the suicidal behaviour, how long the preoccupation with dying had been present before the act of self-harm and what signs he or she had given to those near and dear. In trying to assess the seriousness of suicidal intent clinicians will want to establish whether the young person:

a) wanted to die;
b) did not mind whether she lived or died;
c) did not want to die.

Asking about the time-span between the idea of self-harm and the act is important, since this helps the clinician to form an opinion on whether the suicidal act was impulsive or seriously contemplated. In a recent study on self-poisoning (Hawton *et al.*, 1996) it was found that some 41 per cent of patients admitted had seriously contemplated taking the overdose for less than one hour beforehand, while a further 33 per cent had done so for between one and three hours. Six per cent had thought of overdosing for between 3 and 24 hours and the remaining 20 per cent for more than one day. The most frequent explanations for why suicide was attempted turned out to be: escaping from an intolerable situation or an unbearable state of mind, as well as a desire to make other people understand how desperate one was feeling (Hawton *et al.*, 1996).

Each assessment interview is also an opportunity for therapeutic intervention: stimulating the young person into self-reflection and getting him or her to consider the impact of self-harm on the immediate family and friends. This approach has been described as 'family therapy without the family' (Jenkins and Asen, 1992), as it constitutes individual work with some of the major ingredients of the systemic approach. In conducting the first individual interview with the suicidal teenager the clinician has to walk 'on the brink', on a knife's edge, trying to establish a trusting relationship with the young person on the one hand while at the same time avoiding being drawn into a collusive relationship which might make family work difficult if not impossible in the future. The interview can be structured in such a way that significant others, that is members of the family, come 'alive' – without actually having to be present. This is done by asking a series of speculative and hypothetical circular questions, first pioneered by the Milan team (Selvini Palazzoli *et al.*, 1980) and subsequently developed by some of its followers (Tomm, 1987). The young person can, for example, be asked how, in her opinion, father or mother viewed the overdose. Or, how certain family members might be affected by the act of self-harm. The frame can be further widened by asking how a third person would view the relationship between the teenager and the mother (or father) and how having taken the overdose might change that. Bit by bit the (imaginary) views and responses of significant others to the self-harming event are elicited and the different family members, almost like ghosts, come alive in the room with their imaginary thoughts and feelings, while the young person's own emotions and actions are explored and mapped in relation to this omnipresent family.

Further questions that help to throw some light on past and future suicidal ideation and intent are as follow: what happened at the time, what were the thoughts and feelings that led to thinking about ending it all? What did he or she feel about waking up alive: was it a relief or disappointment? What would have to happen for there to be less preoccupation with dying? What are the hopes and fears for the immediate and long-term future? What situation might make a new suicide attempt more likely? What could be done to stop it from happening? Who would the young person talk to? Who or what would then be most helpful? Who would notice first that he might have more suicidal thoughts?

These questions encourage the young person to reflect about his actions and to look at himself through the eyes of others, adding different and new perspectives from which to view his predicament. At the end of the interview the clinician will want to return to the issue of confidentiality, namely what the parents need to know and what they need not know. It is important to ask the teenager to explain why certain bits of information should be withheld from the parents. This can lead to an exploration of what his or her fears are about the parent(s) knowing – and whether this would make things better or worse.

Kate, aged 16 and recovering from a serious overdose, had talked freely on her own about issues in the family, such as her rivalry with her sister, her own distant relationship with her father and her intense feelings about grandmother. The clinician asked her at the end of the first interview what she would feel about her parents knowing about these thoughts and feelings. Her immediate response was: 'that would be terrible!'. The clinician then invited Kate to specify her fears by asking a series of questions: 'What would your father say if he knew...? What would be the advantages of him knowing – what would be the disadvantages? What would be the advantages of your mother not knowing?' As Kate began speculating about their (hypothetical) responses she became less and less anxious and then said: 'Maybe they should know... maybe things should be out in the open'. One hour later she asked her family to listen to what she had to say and this was the beginning of some very fruitful family work, initially anxiety provoking and painful, but over time resulting in increased openness and trust all round.

'Guided suicide trips'

Some self-harming teenagers are themselves quite puzzled about why they had wanted to take their lives. At times it is impossible to know whether they really do not know or just do not want to talk about it, answering every question with a monotone 'I don't know'. Under these circumstances and in order to understand the reasons for the suicidal behaviour, the clinician may think it right to take the young person on a 'guided suicide trip'. This hypothetical journey through life after one's death can explore the effects which the completed suicide might have had – or would have – on those left behind. In doing so many of the feelings and thoughts underlying suicidal behaviour can come to light. Identifying these is a first step to thinking about alternative ways of communicating them to all those around. Such a 'trip' can be done both individually as well as in the context of a family meeting.

John, 14, had tried to hang himself on the apple tree in his grandparents' garden. In the first individual interview with John the clinician had attempted to get some understanding of why John had wanted to kill himself. John had not been able to give any reason whatsoever for his actions. He simply stated that he could 'not remember'. It was at this point that the clinician asked: 'If you had succeeded in killing yourself, who do you think would now be most upset?' John thought for a moment and then replied: 'My cat'. The clinician did not give up:

Clinician: And who next?
John: My sister.
Clinician: And then?
John: Well, my granny.
Clinician: And who do you think would have been least upset?
John: My mum… she just can't be bothered.
Clinician: If you had succeeded in killing yourself, who would have found your body?
John: My grandma.
Clinician: And what do you think would she have felt?
John: She'd be terrified of my mother… and she'd be very, very sad.
Clinician: How does that make you feel… your grandmother being terrified and sad?

John: I don't want her to be sad... I love her... she is the only one who has ever loved me.
Clinician: If you had managed to kill yourself – who would come to the funeral?
John: My mum wouldn't come... she's always angry with me... she'd feel relieved.
Clinician: And, supposing a year had gone by since you died... who would miss you most a year later?

John was silent for a few minutes. Then he broke down and cried: 'My mum... she'd miss me... but only if I'm dead... it's not fair'. This issue was taken up, at John's request, in the subsequent family meeting. Three months – and six family sessions – later the relationship between John and his mother was transformed. He felt she noticed him for the good things he was doing and she confirmed that her 'eyes have been opened'.

Some teenagers are initially a bit baffled by such a line of questioning. However, gradually they become interested in speculating about what might happen after their death. Together with the clinician the (real or imaginary) family response system is mapped out, helping to assess family relations, giving valuable information about, for example, the quality of attachments or the conflictual nature of certain relationships. The young person is invited to reflect on the impact of his or her (self)destructive actions: this process creates guilt, remorse and also lays opens covert anger and feelings of being let down. It could be argued that turning death, the great unknown, into some kind of reality and becoming preoccupied with one's relatives' grief helps the young person to think differently about current relationships. It also helps with identifying possibilities for change in the present rather than altering family relationships once and for all through death.

Working with the family

The first family interview needs to address a number of issues: the precipitants of the suicidal attempt and events surrounding it; its actual impact on the various family members; past and present family relationship problems; the attempts that have been made to solve these problems and the outcomes; and what help might be needed immediately and in the future (Reder *et al.*, 1991). One of the major tasks of clinicians is to establish whether or not it is safe to send the suicidal teenager back into the care of the family. This involves negotiating whether and how long the teenager should stay in hospital, getting the parent(s) to agree on what level of supervision is necessary once the young person returns home and determining what action should be taken should the suicidal preoccupation return. Most clinicians working with a systemic model will want to involve the parents centrally in enabling them to take responsibility for the management of their suicidal teenager. In particular, the decision about discharge from hospital should be made by the legally responsible parent(s) and the clinician's task is to highlight any aspects of the interaction which are impeding the decision-making process (Reder *et al.*, 1991). If parents are unwilling or unable to take responsibility for the safety of their teenager then the clinician will have to reach a decision with the parents about who else might need to be involved. If child protection issues are raised, the clinician may need to inform the parents of his obligation to seek help for the family from social services.

Clarifying these issues of responsibility is one major part of the family assessment, especially where teenagers are under the age of 16. Another involves assessment of the communication and interaction patterns between the various family members (Aggett, 1992). The clinician will want to understand the relative closeness and distance between teenager and others, see how much of a 'voice' he or she is given in the family, understanding in the 'here and now' of the family session to what extent the young person can be listened to. In this and subsequent family sessions the teenager is encouraged to talk with words rather than through (suicidal) actions. The clinician will draw attention to or even actively block interactions that result in the young person being silenced when it comes to talking about important feelings or ideas. Similarly the parents are asked to consider how they can be helpfully protective towards their son or daughter.

It is not uncommon for the youngster who has self-harmed to appear to be 'on the brink', half in and half out of the family. This tends to enrage the parents who perceive their offspring wanting to have the maximum of autonomy and the minimum of responsibility. From the parents' point of view their offspring wants to be left alone and be intensely cared for at the same time. In such situations clinicians can frame suicidal behaviour as the young person's ultimate statement that he or she can be in charge of life – and take it if or when he or she wants to. In this sense suicide is not a private matter, even if the young person angrily claims: 'it's my life... it's got nothing to do with you'. It faces parents with the limitations of their own power and responsibility; should they respect their son's or daughter's wishes and disconnect, or should they take over, for instance by instituting a 24-hour 'duty rota' at home? In family sessions the question is raised whether the issues of autonomy, power and dependence cannot be transferred on to safer ground, for example the familiar adolescent battleground of lockable rooms, coming home times or desirable and undesirable friends. Of course, the responsibilities and needs of parents and teenagers respectively differ greatly, depending on the age and maturity of the young person. The clinician may find it helpful to explore these developmental issues with the family.

It has been argued that the crisis created by the life-threatening behaviour of the adolescent can serve as an opportunity for family members to strengthen ties or repair family relationships that have disintegrated over past feuds or imagined injustices (Gutstein *et al.*, 1988). Suicidal behaviour can then be seen as a systemic move to keep a family together at a time of change and in a context of escalating conflict (Aldridge and Dallos, 1986). The threat that the family is at risk of breaking up, with one person about to leave, often appears to precede a teenage suicide attempt, which becomes a 'strategy' to maintain relationships at a time of threatened breakdown. This seems to be particularly the case with families where physical and/or psychological symptoms are used to manage conflict. When such 'distress management' keeps a family together, suicidal behaviour occurs at the threat of separation (Aldridge and Dallos, 1986).

Adolescent self-harmers tend to occupy powerful positions in the (emotional) hierarchy of the family because of their capacity of risk-taking by which other family members feel controlled (Hollis, 1987). Self-harm is not only the consequence of an 'incongruent hierarchy' (Haley, 1980), but also tends to reinforce dysfunctional family structures. Following an act of self-harm the parents may present with a mixture of shame, guilt and anger which is met by tearful or angry withdrawal of the teenager. To avoid further distress the various parties involved enter into a collusive denial of any problems, with the hope that everyone, particularly the young person, 'have learned a lesson' (Hollis, 1987). Once teenager and parents have formed such a collusive alliance, the anxieties about the young person's state of mind are transferred on to the clinician. The family unites and behaves as if the clinician were persecuting them all, rubbishing any intervention made. Follow-up appointments are missed with less and less plausible excuses and it is only a question of time until the clinician is finally dismissed. Clinicians who are aware of this common process can avoid being manoeuvred into this oppositional role. They will also need to be prepared to 'restructure' the incongruent hierarchy and facilitate more effective problem-solving in order to enable the parents to take responsibility appropriately.

Family intervention is helpful when it results in family members being closer, more open, more independent or honest. The clinician acts as a catalyst, enabling different family members to negotiate with one another how to make things between them better so that further self-destructive behaviours can be avoided. Further family work often needs to take place once the young person has been discharged, with the focus likely to shift from the intense preoccupations around the suicidal attempt to adolescent issues that families traditionally struggle with. However, if suicidal preoccupations persist then it may be useful to get the family to identify an early warning and response system that could be put into operation if needed.

Assessing the social and cultural network

Suicidal adolescents report significantly less satisfaction with their relationships with friends and more ambivalence and conflict. Generally the availability of an intimate confiding relationship plays a key role in lessening the likelihood of suicide in adults. Yet, for adolescents the situation appears to be different: being accepted by and well-integrated into a group of friends that is approved of by parents seems to be the key protective factor (Hirshfeld and Blumenthal, 1986). Peer pressure cannot be underestimated and as bullying in school is becoming a less taboo subject, more and more information is emerging on how consistent bullying can result in serious suicidal behaviour (MacLeod and Morris, 1996). Attempts have been made to teach teenagers the facts of life and death by means of suicide prevention programmes in schools (Ross, 1985) or even 'postvention' strategies designed to stop imitative suicidal behaviour in schools where a series of actual suicides have occurred (Hazell, 1991).

Can suicide be infectious? It is reported that Goethe's famous novel *Werther*, with its suicidal preoccupations, led to many copycat suicides among young people when the book was first published. More recently there has been considerable interest in the 'Werther effect' (Schmidtke and Hafner, 1988) and how media representation of suicidal behaviour influences suicide rates. The fictional death of the hero in a TV soap opera can seem as real to teenagers as the death of a relative. Emotions get stirred up that seem to connect with the young person's preoccupations and may lead to or reinforce existing suicidal ideas. There have been various reports (for example, Platt, 1987) of copycat suicide attempts following the screening of documentaries and fictionalised dramas. The most recent example occurred after the UK showing of a popular TV hospital drama series in which a teenage girl took an overdose of paracetamol tablets (*Casualty*, January 1993); there was a sudden nation-wide increase of paracetamol overdoses (Collins, 1993). Child mental health professionals assessing young self-poisoners in hospital settings all over the country reported how a significant number of teenage girls had watched the programme and how this had given them the 'idea' to do the same. It also emerged that some had discussed with their friends the programme and even 'dared' one another to do the same. While it is difficult if not impossible to prove scientifically a causal link between the screening of specific TV programmes and an increased rate of suicidal behaviour (Simkin *et al.*, 1995), at a clinical level there is little doubt that cult movies, TV programmes or other media events can help to create a context within which people are affected and become part of a mass phenomenon. At a practical clinical level it is important to explore possible media influences when assessing self-harming adolescents in terms of trying to provide answers to the crucial 'why now?' question.

It is possible to map the young person's world with a variety of techniques. The family life space can be visually represented through symbolic drawings (Geddes and Medway, 1977) in which the whole family can participate, highlighting the different perceptions each family member has of the relative distance and closeness of various relationships inside the family. This can be extended by asking the young person to draw a map of his or her relationships with significant others outside the family and then combine both maps to illustrate the complex interplay between home and outside world. It is possible to detail the picture further by inserting bullies, 'enemies', danger points and other pressure contexts, thus allowing a more detailed exploration and dialogue to take place. In the course of this the clinician may discover that the teenager has been subjected to intense long-term bullying. It might emerge how ashamed the youngster is of having these problems which they believe they should sort out alone. Almost inevitably a boy in this situation will see himself as a failure, a 'wimp' or 'chicken', who should be tougher and be able to stop the bullying (MacLeod and Morris, 1996).

Adolescents are very susceptible to peer pressures and these can be heightened through specific cultural and religious factors. While adolescent suicidal acts can and do happen in any culture, the meanings attached to such acts can vary. For example, cultures that believe in reincarnation tend not to treat suicide as a taboo subject and it consequently does not carry connotations of shame. In some Hindu cultures suicide appears to be sanctioned in religious scriptures and is seen not only as a legitimate way out but also as a pathway to the next world which, hopefully, is better than this. For some, the act of suicide can carry the meaning of a 'quest for a better life' or a longing to be reunited with a deceased beloved. Such longings contrast sharply with the beliefs of the Catholic church which, until fairly recently, taught that suicide was so sinful that it precludes admission to heaven. The teachings of Islam forbid the taking of one's own life.

Apart from the different *meanings* different cultures attach to suicidal behaviour, there are also different *reasons* for suicide, to do with specific cultural traditions or expectations. In Japan, for example, suicide is an accepted way of dealing with social disgrace.

Similarly, in Korea academic stress is closely associated with suicidal behaviours particularly in male pupils and students (Juon *et al.*, 1994). This can in part be explained by the great importance Korean society puts on academic performance, no doubt related to the socially sanctioned desirability of economic independence. As a result particular pressures operate on males rather than females, generating stress, substance abuse and suicidal acts.

There is also a strong cultural pattern to the *methods* used to attempt suicide. In Western cultures most attempted suicides in teenage girls present as self-poisoning, with paracetamol being by far the most likely drug used. However, in less industrialised, predominantly rural cultures, pesticides are much more available and more frequently used. Other forms of suicide are more common outside Europe and North America. For example, while suicide by burning is relatively common in some cultures in Asia and the Middle East, accounting for up to 20 per cent of suicides in India (Venkoba Rao, 1983), it is fairly rare in European cultures. Nevertheless, in a study of suicide by self-burning in England and Wales, Asian-born women were over-represented (Prosser, 1996). This is a reminder that the form of a suicidal attempt does not necessarily say anything about the degree of disturbance or seriousness of intent: there may be culture specific aspects that can explain both method of and reason for wishing to end one's life.

Suicidal behaviour may carry yet another meaning for immigrant families living in Western cultures. Issues of adjustment to a different society with very different values can lead to social isolation and despair. Acculturative stress can also manifest itself in conflicts between parents and their adolescents that may in part explain the higher incidence of self-harm amongst Dominican and Puerto Rican families in New York City (Shaffer and Piacentini, 1994). Some of these conflicts are related to the parents' over-reliance on their oldest child, particularly when the support of the extended family has been severed through immigration (Zayas and Dyche, 1995). Moreover, many ethnic minority families are subject to discrimination and racism and it has been argued that this could in part account for higher rates of self-harming among some of this population. Self-poisoning is more common among young females in the Asian community in the UK than among their 'white' peer group (Glover *et al.*, 1989). Attempted suicide is more frequent in the Asian and West Indian communities in the UK than in their respective countries of origin. How can this be explained? When ethnic minority families feel under threat from the outside this can have the effect of strengthening the family boundaries. However, increased parental concern can be perceived by the adolescent as intrusive. As she strives for more autonomy and differentiation, her parents become more protective. Cross-generational family conflict can emerge and may lead the teenager to take an overdose (Goldberg and Hodes, 1992).

It has been argued that there is a link between racism and overdosing. Being subjected to constant discrimination and racism contributes to low self-esteem and depression (Fernando, 1988). There may come a time when the victim may 'agree' with the racist about her worthlessness and the adolescent girl, poisoned by racism, poisons herself with paracetamol, thus acting out the views of the dominant group. Racism is an attack on the person that is reproduced by overdosing – as an attack on the self (Goldberg and Hodes, 1992). The act of overdosing can be understood as an attempt to take control and to communicate something that is too difficult to talk about (Hodes, 1990).

What then are the clinical implications? Clinicians need to have an awareness of how cultural diversity affects methods, meanings and reasons for suicidal behaviours. This awareness needs to be translated into eliciting the young person's and his or her family's view of the act of self-harm. This will hopefully lead to joint understanding of the responses of the family and the immediate social network, enabling the clinician to work with young person and the larger family in a culture-sensitive way.

Conclusion

The initial request for the involvement of mental health professionals is usually to undertake a risk assessment. To systemic practitioners the notion of 'assessment' cannot simply imply some kind of 'objective' stance, but it is part of an interaction between the paediatric team, the suicidal teenager, the family – and the clinician. Where assessment ends and treatment starts is impossible to disentangle: each assessment is an intervention in its own right as it is impossible for the young person and family not to be affected by the assessment process. Managing suicidal teenagers requires simultaneous interventions at the individual, family and socio-cultural levels. In what order these interventions take place very much depends on the specific context within which the clinician works: what is important is to combine an individual with a family approach flexibly (Zimmerman and La Sorsa, 1995). Some of the techniques described in this chapter, in particular 'interventive' circular questions, induce self-questioning and self-reflection, both for the individual as well as for the different family members. Given that the management of suicidal behaviour often starts in a hospital setting, this form of intervention tends to be more acceptable in medical contexts where traditionally the doctor asks questions and the patient is expected to answer these.

Systemic work with suicidal adolescents goes through a number of different phases: the intense crisis work in the casualty department and on the paediatric ward is followed by a few sessions, closely spaced together, either in the home or a clinic context shortly after discharge from the medical ward, with follow-up sessions spaced out in weekly to monthly intervals. It is not uncommon that a few months later the focus has totally shifted – from the young person's suicidal attempt(s) to other issues in the family. It is at this point that young person, family and clinician can walk again on safer ground.

References

Aggett, P. (1992) Putting the person in charge: a systemic approach to persons who self-poison. ACT dissertation (unpubl.). London: Institute of Family Therapy.

Aldridge, D. (1984) Suicidal behaviour and family interaction: a brief review. *Journal of Family Therapy* **6**:309–22.

Aldridge, D. and Dallos, R. (1986) Distinguishing families where suicidal behaviour is present from families where suicidal behaviour is absent. *Journal of Family Therapy* **8**:243–52.

Beck, A.T., Schuyler, D. and Herman, I. (1974) Development of suicidal intent scales. In Beck, A.T., Resnick, H. and Lettieri, D. (eds) *The Prediction of Suicide*. Philadelphia: Charles Press, pp. 45–56.

Cecchin, G. (1987) Hypothesising, circularity and neutrality revisited: an invitation to curiosity. *Family Process* **26**:405–13.

Collins, S. (1993) Health prevention messages may have paradoxical effect. *British Medical Journal* **306**:926.

Fernando, S. (1988) *Race and Culture in Psychiatry*. London: Croom Helm.

Geddes, M. and Medway, J. (1977) The symbolic drawing of the family life space. *Family Process* **16**:219–28.

Glover, G., Markes, F. and Nowers, M. (1989) Parasuicide in young Asian women. *British Journal of Psychiatry* **154**:271–2.

Goldberg, D. and Hodes, M. (1992) The poison of racism and the self-poisoning of adolescents. *Journal of Family Therapy* **14**:51–67.

Gutstein, S., Rudd, M.D., Graham, J.C. and Rayha, L.L. (1988) Systemic crisis intervention as a response to adolescent crises: an outcome study. *Family Process* **27**:201–11.

Hawton, K. and Catalan, J. (1987) *Attempted Suicide: A Practical Guide to its Nature and Management*, 2nd edn. Oxford: Oxford University Press.

Hawton, K., Ware, C., Mistry, H. *et al.* (1996) Paracetamol self-poisoning. Characteristics, prevention and harm reduction. *British Journal of Psychiatry* **168**:43–8.

Haley, J. (1980) *Leaving Home. The Therapy of Disturbed Young People*. New York, London: McGraw-Hill.

Hazell, P. (1991) Postvention after teenage suicide: an Australian experience. *Journal of Adolescence* **14**:335–42.

Hirshfeld, R. and Blumenthal, S. (1986) Personality, life events and other psychosocial factors in adolescent depression and suicide. In Klerman, G. (ed.) *Suicide and Depression Among Adolescents and Young Adults*. Washington DC: American Psychiatric Press.

Hodes, M. (1990) Overdosing as communication: a cultural perspective. *British Journal of Medical Psychology* **63**:319–33.

Hollis, P. (1987) The management of adolescent overdose – a systems approach. *Journal of Family Therapy* **9**:161–75.

Jenkins, H. and Asen, K. (1992) Family therapy without the family: a framework for systemic practice. *Journal of Family Therapy* **14**:1–14.

Juon, H.-S., Nam, J.J. and Ensminger, M.E. (1994) Epidemiology of suicidal behaviour among Korean adolescents. *Journal of Child Psychology and Psychiatry* **35**:663–76.

Kingsbury, S. (1993) Parasuicide in adolescence: a message in a bottle. *Association for Child Psychology and Psychiatry Review and Newsletter* **15**:253–9.

Laufer, M. (1996) Understanding suicide: does it have a special meaning in adolescence? In Laufer, M. (ed.) *The Suicidal Adolescent*. London: Karnac.

MacLeod, M. and Morris, S. (1996) *Why Me? Children Talking to ChildLine About Bullying*. London: ChildLine Publications.

McClure, G.M.G. (1994) Suicide in children and adolescents in England and Wales, 1960–1990. *British Journal of Psychiatry* **165**:510–14.

Munson, S. (1986) Family-oriented consultation in paediatrics. In Wynne, L., McDaniel, S. and Weber, T. (eds) *Systems Consultation*. New York: Guilford Press.

Platt, S. (1987) The aftermath of Angie's overdose. Is soap (opera) damaging to your health? *British Medical Journal* **294**:954–7.

Prosser, D. (1996) Suicides by burning in England and Wales. *British Journal of Psychiatry* **168**:175–82.

Reder, P., Lucey, C. and Fredman, G. (1991) The challenge of deliberate self-harm by young adolescents. *Journal of Adolescence* **14**:135–48.

Ross, C. (1985) Teaching children the facts of life and death: suicide prevention in the schools. In Peck, M., Farberow, N. and Litman, R. (eds) *Youth Suicide*. New York: Springer

Rotheram-Borus, M.J., Piacentini, J., Miller, S. *et al.* (1996). Toward improving treatment adherence among adolescent suicide attempters. *Clinical Child Psychology and Psychiatry* **1**:99–108.

Rubenstein, J.L., Heeren, T., Housman, D. *et al.* (1989) Suicidal behaviour in 'normal' adolescents: risk and protective factors. *American Journal of Orthopsychiatry* **59**(1):59–71.

Schmidtke, A. and Hafner, H. (1988) The Werther effect after television films: new evidence for an old hypothesis. *Psychological Medicine* **18**:665–76.

Secretary of State for Health (1992) *The Health of the Nation: A Strategy for Health in England*. London: HMSO.

Selvini Palazzoli, M., Boscolo, L., Cecchin, G. and Prata, G. (1980). Hypothe-sizing, circularity, neutrality: three guidelines for the conductor of the session. *Family Process* **19**:3–12.

Shaffer, D. and Piacentini, J. (1994) Suicide and attempted suicide. In Rutter, M., Taylor, E. and Hersov, L. (eds) *Child and Adolescent Psychiatry: Modern Approaches*, 3rd edn. Oxford: Blackwell Scientific, pp. 407–27.

Simkin, S., Hawton, K., Whitehead, L. *et al.* (1995) Media influence on parasui-cide. A study of the effects of a television drama portrayal of paracetamol self-poisoning. *British Journal of Psychiatry* **167**:754–9.

Spender, Q. (1996) A systemic approach to the treatment of teenage self-harm: integration with other models. ACT dissertation (unpubl.). London: Institute of Family Therapy.

Stanley, E.J. and Barter, J.T. (1970) Adolescent suicidal behaviour. *American Journal of Orthopsychiatry* **40**:87–96.

Taylor, E.A. and Stansfield, S.A. (1984) Children who poison themselves. *British Journal of Psychiatry* **145**:127–35.

Tomm, K. (1987) Interventive interviewing: Part II. Reflexive questioning as a means to self-healing. *Family Process* **26**:167–83.

Venkoba Rao, A. (1983) India. In Headley, L.A. (ed.) *Suicide in Asia and the Near East*. California: University of California Press, pp. 210–37.

Zayas, L.H. and Dyche, L.A. (1995) Suicide attempts in Puerto Rican adolescent females: a sociocultural perspective and family treatment approach. In Zimmerman, J.K. and Asnis, G.M. (eds) *Treatment Approaches with Suicidal Adolescents*. New York: John Wiley & Sons, pp. 203–18.

Zimmerman, J.K. and La Sorsa, V.A. (1995) Being the family's therapist: an integra-tive approach. In Zimmerman, J.K. and Asnis, G.M. (eds) *Treatment Approaches with Suicidal Adolescents*. New York: John Wiley & Sons, pp. 174–88.

CHAPTER 6

A 'Dysfunctional Triangle' or Love in All the Right Places

Social context in the therapy of a family living with AIDS

Lawrence Levner

This chapter presents an alternative to the perspective of the 'dysfunctional family' in the conceptualisation of treatment and intervention with a gay couple, both HIV positive, and the children and ex-spouse of one of the partners. The author will discuss:

1. *Social context, particularly the definition of 'family', as it constructs belief systems and informs clinical practice through the internalisation of dominant social themes by both therapist and client.*
2. *Development of a different cognitive and emotional frame of reference grounded in context rather than dysfunction. That is, what maintains patterns of interaction as opposed to what causes them.*
3. *Reading and intervening in family process as a methodology for attaching the new frame of reference to the client's experience.*
4. *Framing process in terms of competency as opposed to causation.*

The author will present a theoretical and conceptual basis for therapy, followed by a case study of a family (two male partners, female ex-spouse, and grown children of one of the men) over five years from the time the husband and father openly identified himself as gay, through the couple's divorce while continuing a close relationship, his testing HIV positive, finding a gay partner (also HIV positive), both men's deteriorating health, and ultimately the family's struggle to stay together and to take care of one another as the men are dying.

Introduction

As a family member dies, particularly when death is premature or circumstances are exceptional, people whose roles have been familiar, clear and defined, experience a forced transition to an unfamiliar life stage in which they feel de-skilled in their relationships; no longer quite sure how to function, how to manage, how to make a difference, how to feel relevant.

Empowerment, previously derived from experiences of validation – from celebration, accomplishment, intimacy, ritual, occupation, avocation, affection, friendship, sexuality, and resolution of conflict – becomes increasingly restricted to the ability to cope with the physical effects of illness, and the management of medical systems. Ultimately, when a sick person is physically, intellectually, or socially incapacitated, someone will have the 'power of attorney' to make legal, financial, parental, and even moral decisions. It is not surprising that family members fight over who is to have this last position of relevance as the role of the person needing care is reduced to that of a 'patient' whose capacity to reciprocate is diminished along with the expectations of family, friends, and co-workers. Functional identities – mother, father, son, daughter, brother, sister, partner, lover, friend – are constricted, while status within the family is undermined as those who are struggling to redefine themselves, experience the conflict, stress, and misunderstandings that accompany this uncertainty about role and function.

Although it is popular to understand these problems in terms of individual and intrafamilial inadequacy and maladjustment, these dynamics do not occur in a social vacuum. Rather, they are constructed by social context. Gender, sexual preference, economic status, culture, and age, all contextualise dying. The individual experience of this life stage is differential, not only because each of us has a different personal story (parental relationships, birth order, childhood experiences, family of origin, religion, education, developmental stages) but because behaviour, affect, role definition, and self-esteem vary with social status and social rules that monitor access to power. Thus, a therapy that defines problems and change exclusively internal to the family system, even if effective and clinically expedient, will reinforce existing roles and power relationships.

The family therapy term for 'inadequacy and maladjustment' is dysfunction. Superficially, this appears to be a minimally toxic, unblaming way of understanding and intervening in troubled relationships. Unfortunately, family or individual therapy that is organised around understanding and interrupting dysfunction, establishes and reinforces the very social context that creates disempowerment. To the degree that the theoretical basis for therapeutic intervention has evolved from the dominant social reality, therapy, as a powerful social institution, often cannot help but convey the notion that human problems derive exclusively from individual and family failings and shortcomings, and cannot help but to reinforce the blame and self-blame that already characterises family interaction. A therapy that challenges social reality by encouraging non-traditional roles and equal power in relationships, offers families the opportunity to experience their competency and capacity as it inhibits their internalisation and incorporation of prejudicial social beliefs and attitudes.

Social context, belief systems, and clinical practice

Families living with AIDS face the horror of extraordinary physical deterioration and death compounded by the homophobia and alienation that contextualize their lives (Walker, 1988, p. 29). Death from AIDS-related illness is culturally associated with a socially unacceptable lifestyle; often to the degree that there is a differential response to men who are believed to have been infected by AIDS through homosexual contact and others who acquired the disease via blood transfusions or even through intravenous drug use (which to some people is more acceptable than homosexuality).

'Family', as traditionally defined, may not even include its gay members and certainly not the gay couples who until recently were the primary victims of this disease. One consequence of this narrow definition of family is that people with AIDS may live and die in the closet until the disease has become so debilitating that it can no longer be hidden. This fosters isolation, alienation and damage to self-esteem at a time when people most need supportive relationships and personal strength. They often do not speak about the illness, even to their closest relatives, in the belief that their homosexuality would be unacceptable, that they would be ostracized, and isolated from primary support systems. Some live a lie in order to maintain a degree of attachment to their families. Services and supports, health insurance, social security, veterans benefits, employee assistance programmes, daycare and so on, available to traditional families are often not accessible to families whose context for dying is a sexual preference or a family constellation that is considered to be socially and morally unacceptable (Walters *et al.*, 1988, p. 253).

Because both therapists and families have internalised these socially dominant beliefs about sexual preference and self-esteem, the therapeutic discourse tends to be played out within such traditional belief systems, replicating existing patterns while limiting opportunities to develop new perspectives. Therapeutic intervention that is informed by social context challenges traditional frames of reference and belief systems that circumscribe family members' self-esteem and sense of competence (Walters, 1981, p. 53). Social context refers to the social systems that define access to power. Gender, race, ethnicity, class, age and, certainly, sexual preference, craft the human experience both in terms of perceived social advantages/disadvantages and the corresponding relevance, and also with respect to the esteem experienced differentially in relationships. Therapy, in that it reflects traditional values, is a powerful conduit of these values, via interventions and strategies, in constructing belief systems, frames of reference and patterns of response that fit traditional socialisation. This is called adjustment. Adjustment is a social concept, not just a personal one. It implies acceptable standards of behaviour and relationship that all too often designate non-traditional families and individuals as dysfunctional. We see this pointedly in terms of the traditional definition of 'family', in that single-parent mothers, gay and lesbian couples, extended families, or communities, are generally viewed not as family and as inappropriate to fill familial and parental roles.

Participants in non-traditional relationships internalise the same traditional, dominant belief systems by which they are defined as dysfunctional. As the various models of therapy (including family and systems therapy) concentrate on etiology, history, psychology, and dysfunction of the individual and the family system, they do not challenge the social structures and their internalisation which pathologise non-traditional roles and relationships. Themes of dysfunction in therapy confirm family members' already internalised feelings of unacceptability, social exclusion and self-hatred, even as the intent of these themes is to facilitate problem resolution and adjustment. Thus, therapy that follows such themes is liable to validate the very experience of diminished competence that brings families into therapy to begin with. The focus on dysfunction, on deciding what is dysfunctional and what to do about it, is not merely 'technique' but carries meaning far beyond the efficacy of treatment. That is, the focus on individual and family pathology and dysfunction achieves therapeutic results, problem resolution and improved cooperation, often at the expense of encouraging patterns of interaction that diminish self-esteem of the least powerful family members.

A therapist, informed by social context, knows that it is impossible for a 'self' or a 'system' to exist unaffected by accessibility to power and that social disapproval and the accompanying internalized self-hatred experienced by non-traditional families effect both self-esteem and relationship (Walters, 1990, p. 25). Such a therapist considers a counter proposition (different frame of reference) to the perspective of dysfunction before choosing interventions. She appreciates process in terms of the socially assigned roles and behavioural styles in which people manage their lives and experience empowerment by searching for the competent function of behaviour as opposed to pathologising intentions and interactions.

Interventions contextualised by the ideology of dysfunction are likely to achieve results at the expense of reinforcing roles, patterns, and stereotypes that ultimately diminish self-esteem and maintain existing power relationships (Walters et al., 1988, p. 25). In family therapy theory, the term, 'dysfunctional triangle,' describes a repetitive transactional pattern that functions to detour the conflict of a dyad through a third person. This is considered most dysfunctional when either generational or subsystem (parental, spousal, sibling) boundaries are crossed, again reinforcing the idea that traditional arrangements in families are to be valued and implying that 'counterculture' relationships, particularly those that include non-related persons in caring roles, or larger caring systems, are somehow not as functional as the traditional family model of relationship. As this pattern is understood to cause relationship difficulties, it can lead to therapeutic interventions to block or interrupt 'deflected communication' and to exclude the 'triangulated' participant from the helping system. This conceptualisation can be problematic, particularly in emotionally charged situations, where people already feel failed in attempts to manage complex experiences in socially prescribed and patterned ways. It proffers the idea that one person should not be involved in facilitating the interaction of others. It discourages participants in therapy from looking for emotional support and guidance, while devaluing those whose competence is invested in their capacity to provide caring and nurture. In this way, it reflects the belief that emotional well-being and self-actualization are manifested in one's capacity for self-reliance, and that it is only after this has been firmly established that one can expect to participate in a healthy relationship. The therapeutic intent of the strategy and sometime goal to interrupt triangulated communication is to enhance effective communication. Often it does so at the cost of constructing a reality where care-taking and facilitation of relationship are socially and psychologically less valuable than the capacity for autonomy and independent decision-making. Because women are socially identified with the capacity for care-giving and nurturance, while men have learned fewer of these skills, the ideology and practice of working with triangulation cannot help but to pathologise women and expect too little of men (Mason and Mason, 1990, p. 210).

Often, in families where someone is dying, family members get stuck in repetitive sequences of interaction that are identified with and limited by their internalised social roles (for example gender) and their position in the family (mother, father, child) that result neither in empowerment, problem resolution, nor productive communica-tion. To the extent that both the family and the therapist adhere to dominant beliefs about social adjustment, the stage is set for therapy to be organised around interrupting dysfunction within family members' existing repertoire, as opposed to encouraging role differ-entiation and renegotiation (Bograd, 1990, p. 81).

As an alternative, the understanding that social realities influence intimate lives creates a frame of reference, not located in dysfunction, from which to challenge interpersonal dynamics and require family members to take responsibility to change. For example, the social reality that a woman derives personal and economic status from marriage, directly affects her assertiveness, expectations, willingness to be subservient to her husband and her inclination to be emotion-ally protective when she experiences him as vulnerable. It limits her participation to roles that maintain the marriage and limits her options for self-expression within the marriage to nurturing and care-giving. Concurrently, the man, whose social status is independent of the marriage, has not had to learn the skills of attachment and relationship because his personal and economic status is socially assumed. As he expects his spouse to fulfill her prescribed role of maintaining the relationship, she might feel conflicted as the reality of this position limits her sense of personal power and privilege.

In terms of dysfunction, this conflict would be seen as manifested in the depressed, angry, controlling, or intrusive behaviours that are symptoms of low self-esteem. A therapist might work in this frame of reference to discover their cause as rooted in the woman's past or to interrupt these behaviours as they are manifested in family process. In terms of social reality, a therapist would see the woman's communica-tion style and behaviour as reflective of her fear of losing her self to the relationship, while understanding the man as being unsure about his ability to stay attached and to keep her connected to him. This therapist would validate the wife's relational capacity, understand her behaviour as functioning to engage her husband and create emotional intensity, challenge her to expect and believe in his capacity to attach, while challenging him to be emotionally competent.

An understanding of the gendered construction of power and responsibility in relationships is of particular importance to intervening in the patterns and role definitions in a family where there is critical illness and premature or exceptional dying, as it offers the therapist the opportunity to offer a competency based perspective, depathologise family process and encourage role differentiation and interdependence.

The family

The family members in this case study are a gay couple, Edward (age 43) and Bob (32), Edward's ex-spouse, Susan (43), their children, James (18), a college freshman, and Julian (16), a high school student. Edward initially sought family therapy when, after 26 years of marriage, he told Susan that he was homosexual and asked for a divorce. He wanted help in maintaining close family relationships as he began to explore a gay lifestyle (Ahrons, 1995, Chapter 1).

Edward, Susan and their sons were the epitome of a traditional, white, Protestant, middle-class family. Edward and Susan were childhood sweethearts. Both were raised in families with traditional values and fundamentalist Christian beliefs. He served in the army, completed a masters degree and ultimately was quite successful in a federal administrative job. She had some college credits, was a full-time mother when the children were young, and eventually took a full-time government job in which her relational and organisational skills earned promotions and a good salary. She continued to find satisfaction in being a mother; rushing home from work to have dinner on the table, staying involved with the boys, monitoring their school work, coordinating their activities and making sure that they had a good relationship with their father who often seemed busy, preoccupied and otherwise engaged with work, exercise, and other interests.

Throughout the marriage, Susan's desire to be cared for by Edward conflicted with feelings of guilt for this 'neediness'. She rarely questioned his routines and requirements, not out of fear but because she felt fortunate to have him as a partner and at times felt undeserving. She withheld her opinions and preferences and anticipated the family's emotional needs. She expressed little resentment that her availability was taken for granted. She did not question Edward's whereabouts and facilitated his spending time away by organising family life around his schedule. She was not fulfilled in their sexual relationship but he was her only partner and as long as he seemed satisfied she was content. Overall, she was happy during this period of her life although later began to wonder if she should have been.

Edward provided a comfortable lifestyle for the family and in this way felt competent as a husband and father. In retrospect, he knew that he was emotionally distant, although he would not have thought so at the time. He attributed his unavailability to the feelings of conflict about his sexual preference that he had experienced since he was an adolescent. After four years of marriage, Edward began to seek anonymous homosexual encounters whenever and wherever possible, at baths, clubs, hotels and truckstops. This behaviour became routine and he found that much of his energy was going to planning and consummating these encounters. In Susan, he had an accepting and unquestioning partner who believed his fabrications about staying late at work or joining friends to run and exercise. He continued this 'double life' as he began regular business trips to Washington DC, where he joined an active and open gay community, developing friendships and enduring sexual relationships while using an alias to protect his anonymity. For the first time in his life he began to accept his sexual identity. This, together with the frustration, depression and anxiety from 15 years of self-denial, brought him to the decision to 'come out', end their marriage and move to Washington DC to lead a gay lifestyle.

He transferred jobs, moved in with Fred (his partner before Bob), joined a gay church and began psychotherapy. Susan loved Edward, despite the fact that her life was turned upside down. She wanted to stay with him and wanted Julian to finish growing up with his father (James was away at college). She followed Edward to Washington making every effort to stay involved. Edward encouraged her. She tried to become familiar with the gay community; she went to Edward's (gay) church, invited his gay friends to her home, visited clubs and coffee houses and joined a support group for women trying to maintain relationships with their gay spouses. However, Susan's involvement threatened Fred and he moved out.

Almost immediately upon meeting each other, Edward and Bob identified themselves as a couple. Bob, 11 years younger than Edward, had been openly gay for all of his adult life and was more comfortable with his sexuality than was Edward. His mother had died when he was an infant and his father had abused and abandoned him. He had been abused by men into his young adulthood. There was a class difference: Edward was educated and white collar while Bob had a high school diploma and was working class. Despite Susan's ongoing attempts to befriend him as a way of staying connected to Edward, Bob was jealous of their ongoing relationship as they continued to parent, celebrate rituals, and attend family events as they always had. He felt that Edward never had really divorced Susan and that he (Bob) would always be second to her in every way except sexually (Patten, 1996, p. 23).

When he moved in with Bob, Edward's connection to Susan created conflict for the two men. Bob felt jealous, excluded and victimised by Edward's continued involvement with Susan. He did not have a large friendship network and was exclusively focused on the relationship with Edward for most of his personal satisfaction. He never felt that Edward totally committed to their partnership and manifested these feelings in hostility, withdrawal and passivity. Susan, the consummate care-giver, protected everyone. Bob's feelings were exacerbated when both men tested positive for HIV and Susan's involvement in their lives increased dramatically.

Initially, Julian and James were not told the reason for the divorce or about the illness. Even as he chose a gay lifestyle, Edward continued investing in maintaining the image of a traditional family. He also feared that the boys would disapprove of his sexual preference. Susan supported Edward in this deception both to protect her family emotionally and as a way of maintaining her attachment to Edward.

Their extended families did not accept Edward's homosexuality and refused to acknowledge the divorce. Susan and Edward, in many ways, presented themselves to their families as they always had – a heterosexual marriage. Bob's parents were dead and he was not in touch with his only brother.

The structure of therapy

This chapter will discuss an alternative to 'dysfunctional' family therapy that:

1. is informed by social context and is organised around challenging existing belief systems;

2. understands and intervenes in process in terms of what maintains sequences of interaction and patterns of behaviour;
3. encourages different patterns of interaction and attachment, linking these to new belief systems.

In this case, the redefinition and renegotiation begins with the choice to include all of the available family members, sometimes as a unit, sometimes in different groupings. It validates a non-traditional definition of family composition and thus presents a counter perspective – that they are a functional family unit, despite social disapproval and their own doubts.

The inclusion of a father's gay partner (Bob) along with his ex-wife (Susan) in parental discussions, both expands the definition of family and underlines the significance of the men's relationship. Susan's involvement in planning, supporting and ultimately caring for both men as their health deteriorated, validates the men's relationship and enhances the self-esteem derived from her emotional capacity.

On the other hand, the choice to see each family member individually might reinforce a cultural affinity for independence and the belief that strength and competence are primarily vested in autonomy, not in relationship. It might reflect the belief that each of the men should deal with his sexuality as an individual psychological concern, without the benefit of the rituals, ceremonies and events that represent attachment in family life. It would construct a therapeutic system that plays out each man's isolation from support networks, precluding interdependence and reliance on other family members. Finally it would implicitly convey the idea that sexual preference is mostly personal and not to be dealt with in a social or relational context.

The choice to see only the couple might reflect the notion that the only relevant social structure is the dyad and that involvement of someone outside this relationship is intrusive. Organising the therapy this way could construct a reality that gay men should only turn to each other, or that divorce means that people who have a long history of involvement can no longer support and care for one another. Including only the biological mother and father in discussions about the adjustment problems of their sons, or about the effect of their father's illness, might reflect the belief that their father's partner should not be involved, either because he is a step-parent or because he is gay. His absence from therapy may well construct a response that would exclude him from a parental role.

As the family members begin to present the story of their difficulties, the therapist looks for their belief systems and begins to construct a challenge (Walters, 1981, p. 58). In the following sequence when the therapist asks Edward why he thinks that Bob doesn't know how much he (Edward) loves him, Edward's response that 'In all of his (Bob's) years, he has never had anyone who has given him love; his mother died when he was a baby, he was raised in a poor family and he was rejected, used and abused by a lot of different people', reflects the belief that Bob's dysfunctional upbringing is the defining factor of his experience and behaviour, and therefore of their problems together. In other words, he believes that Bob's difficulties are constructed by past deprivation. Edward feels irrelevant and incompetent to make a difference in terms of Bob's history, while Bob's sense of victimization and rejection seems all too familiar in his relationship with Edward. Susan feels responsible 'to make it all right' for everyone.

The therapist selects the 'importance of managing to stay together' as the point of intervention, as an alternative to conceptualizing the relationships as a dysfunctional triangle. Organising the therapy around this focus constructs a belief system that validates the functionality, relevance, and significance of the men's relationship, while challenging the belief that their difficulties are rooted in individual, idiosyncratic history. This frame of reference ultimately signifies the need for attachment and makes it possible for Edward to experience his emotional and relational competence with Bob.

Note that the therapist does not join the family's self-blaming and pathologised perspective by locating the problem in the individuals or the system, viewing each family member as maladjusted: Edward as an inadequate partner and father who is looking for mothering from Susan; Bob as a victim; and Susan as perpetuating their difficulties by her neediness and intrusiveness. Nor does he see the system as triangulated – Edward and Bob unable to communicate without Susan in the middle, and Susan needing this role to feel good about herself. Therapy was not organised around understanding the cause and effect of dysfunction on the content of their lives: What causes Edward to maintain two 'intimate' relationships? Is he exploiting both Susan and Bob? What role does being HIV positive play in his eagerness to stay involved with her? What has happened to Susan that she is so needy as to want to continue a relationship with someone who lied to her for 20 years? Where is her anger? Why does Bob tolerate Edward's involvement with her? Why does he have such low self-esteem that he cannot insist on Edward's attention and commitment?

Bob: He just got a new life insurance policy and I felt for sure that I would be the beneficiary, but nooo... [pointing to Susan] it's her! He is so afraid to leave me anything... I shouldn't be saying this, I didn't want to bring this up because I don't want Susan and the boys to be hurt and to be mad at me but that's the way it is and it hurts... it tore me apart. Whatever is mine is his but what he has with the boys and Susan is not mine. We've been together for three years and the way I see it, their life together should have ended, as a couple, not as friends, but as a couple.

Therapist: [to Edward] Do you agree with this?

Edward: No. He doesn't change, he won't accept that I care about...

Bob: [interjects] He won't commit himself...

Edward: This is why going to therapy is very important for us... to help us to manage to stay together.

Therapist: Why is it so important for you to manage to stay together?

Edward: Because I love him. I love him very much.

Therapist: Why do you think he doesn't know that? Why do you think that he doesn't feel the behaviour that would make him trust the love?

Edward: [thoughtfully] Because in all of his years, he's never had anyone to give him the kind of love that I give him. His mother died when he was a year old, he was raised in a real poor family, he's been used and abused in his life by lots of different people, and so he has no trust factor.

Bob: So where is the love there?

Therapist: You mean that you don't experience it?

Bob: Well, every once in a while. The only time that I experience it is when we're in bed by ourselves. These are the only times that I feel that he's mine.

Susan: This has to be very difficult for you [Edward] because we never had this kind of interaction. I was always so passive and if we had an issue, you could always talk me into it. [to Bob] Your standing your ground has got to be really new for him to have to deal with it.

Bob: [defiantly] When I got AIDS, I promised that I wouldn't let anyone run over me ever again.

Susan: I really feel bad right this minute that I'm causing the problem here.

Therapist: I'm not sure it's you causing the problem, Susan... maybe it's that Bob doesn't experience Edward's love because

Edward is so sure that he [Bob] is damaged from his own past that he [Edward] doesn't try hard enough to get Bob to hear his way of loving.

In the following sequence, Susan describes her guilt for feeling entitled to be taken care of at a time when Edward's and Bob's medical conditions are worsening and her son, Julian, needs her. Julian quit his job and left his friends to return home to help his parents. The therapist does not think of Julian as enmeshed or as a parentified child, but instead frames his return in terms of his capacity and calls his return a wonderful and important experience. The therapist understands Susan's guilt as socially constructed: that having internalised the socially prescribed role of 'care-taker,' she doesn't feel entitled to feel 'important'! In constructing this belief system, the therapist validates Susan's need in terms of her being a good care-taker, not instead of or in opposition to her socialised role. Informed by gender socialisation (that women are assigned the role of facilitating relationships), the therapist does not diagnose Susan as being in denial, needy, repressed, dependent or co-dependent, over-involved, or unable to care for herself, and does not intervene accordingly by encouraging her to be assertive, independent and to disengage (Walters *et al.*, 1988, pp. 28–9).

Susan: When I realise that there is a me, I feel like I'm just not there for them. I get very depressed about it. I want to do for them but I feel like I'm not getting the same back from anybody else. It's like I give, give, give and not much is coming back, so then I get on a guilt trip about that. I feel like I shouldn't think that way. All of a sudden I find that I'm thinking that I'm important too but that this is really bad timing because there are other issues that are more important... and I have a battle with that.

Therapist: Have you ever questioned your significance to all of these people?

Susan: No... no; and I know they care, but I feel like I'm being taken for granted. Nobody really wants to say, 'hey thanks', or 'I needed that', or 'I'll be here if you need me'. That's where I come into this guilt thing. All of a sudden, I'm wanting it from people but yet I feel like I shouldn't, not now.

Therapist: Well Susan, you should. You should want people to let you know how much it matters. I think that for people who are really superb care-takers, like yourself, other people don't know how much you also need and, in fact, you lose sight of it yourself. They take it for granted because you're so good at it.

Susan: [smiling modestly] I agree, I really do. As much as I want to care and take care of him [Edward], I don't want to interfere in this relationship here [pointing to Edward and Bob]. I worry about Bob having to take care of Edward because you always worry about the person who has a problem, but what about the people who take care of him? It's a mixed thing because I don't want to cause a problem... but it's a lot for Bob. It's not just Edward's sickness, but Bob has to tolerate that and he has his own illness too. It's like the care-takers get forgotten and the reason that I feel that for him [Bob] is that I know what that feels like. You're just expected to do it.

Therapist: You said that you don't want it to get in the way. How would it get in the way for Bob?

Susan: If Bob's jealous of this relationship. He's told us, [to Bob] we just had this discussion the other day in the hospital...

Bob: Um hmm. [nods]

Susan: It's difficult to want to care for them and yet not interfere with the relationship that they have. It's the same with Julian. He needs me now that his father is sick... he has his life... he shouldn't have to...

Therapist: But it's wonderful for him that he came home to help you... that he can help you.

As the session continues, Susan describes the classic dysfunctional triangle when she addresses her conflict about whether to intrude into the men's relationship in order to take care of them. The therapist again validates Susan's care-taking role while simultaneously challenging her and the others to not lose sight of 'how much she also needs'. This sets the stage for the following sequence where the therapist expands the challenge to the men – that they have the capacity and responsibility to provide caring as well as to receive it. It is significant that the therapist does not pursue Susan's feelings of guilt and conflict at being triangulated in Edward and Bob's relationship.

Therapist: Have you talked with your sons about any of this?

Susan: No, he [looking at Edward, who laughs] came out and I went in! I have a lot of issues with his sickness and his relationship with Bob. I have not shared any of this. A lot of it has been habit because from the beginning, this whole topic has been mine to bear.

Therapist: Do you now feel that the boys are beginning to understand how much you need people to be there for you?

Susan: I don't think they know to what degree, no.

Therapist: [To Edward] Would you agree that they don't know?

Edward: I guess...

Susan: [interrupting] For instance, Julian knows I'm on Prozac for depression but he doesn't take the time to ask 'what depresses you Mom?'

Therapist: And is Edward asking you now how you're doing?

Susan: No, he asks if I'm on one or two day [everyone laughs] but not 'Why do you feel like you need it, or why are you taking it'. No-one has asked me [in an angry voice]. I get very angry with myself because I do try to protect them so much. This is something new for me to have that feeling [anger].

Therapist: The thing about it is, Susan, that when you got angry with Edward about why he didn't ask you about the Prozac and why you were taking it, I think you feel guilty about that, that you begin to think oh, 'I'm being an unpleasant person'.

Susan: [interjects] Oh, I do.

Therapist: That's so wonderful for you... to do it [get angry]... I think Edward needs to hear that... I think your son needs to hear it... I think even Bob needs to hear it sometimes. They can help you. You worry about them... they can worry about you. [to Bob] You need to worry about her some. She's in a tough place too and you know how to worry about people, you take care of a lot of people.

To this point, the men have offered Susan very little. In the following sequence, Edward, and to a lesser degree, Bob, offer emotional support. Susan feels guilty and has difficulty accepting it, even though she has been angry about not receiving it. Urging Susan to accept the emotion and caring from Edward, the therapist constructs the experience that he has the capacity to expand his role.

Edward: [emotion in his voice] I don't think Susan has acknowledged or recognized how much James and Julian have become very close to her and taking care...

Susan: [interjecting] Julian only just came back home and James has only in the last couple of months, it has been just about a month, he didn't...

Bob: [interjecting to Susan] I think it's so hard for you to see.

Therapist: Susan, there is another thing you need to hear with Edward; that this is very meaningful for him. He's very choked up with feeling about it. He cares that his sons care about you. [Edward nods his head]

Susan: It's definitely different. I'm not saying it hasn't always been there; it's just that in the last couple of months I've told them [James and Julian] that I do have issues that I'm dealing with, that I do get upset, that things aren't great. I can't deal with this all of the time with a smile on my face. They've had to face that reality.

Therapist: But you're so unused to hearing Edward be so emotional about you. You have to be able to accept it. It tears him up, and that's wonderful because it's tearing him up about you. He cares so much that you and your sons have this relationship. But you immediately moved away from it.

Susan: I have a hard time dealing with people wanting to give to me.

Therapist: No kidding! Who would have guessed...

The therapist has offered a counter-proposition to the family's belief system – that Edward is incapable of nurturing while all of the emotional capacity is invested in Susan – by emphasising the sense of competence, meaning and esteem that Susan derives from care-giving, while urging Edward to reciprocate even as he begins to deteriorate physically. This highlights her competence while enhancing his relevance and functionality, even as he is dying. It encourages Susan to experience her relevance in ways other than care-taking of Edward, while not defining her care-taking as dysfunctional. The challenge to Bob, by including him in the family process and enjoining him to take care of Susan, was to redefine his traditional ideology of family by countering his belief that he had to compete with Susan for Edward's attention and affection. This proposition ran counter to Bob's lifelong experience of isolation and exclusion.

Such socially contextualised challenges to the family's belief system at a time of an increased sense of futility and helplessness begin to create the basis for working with their process to construct new pathways and patterns of esteem and relevance.

Working with process

Process refers to the repetitive, patterned, ways in which relationships are organised (Walters, 1981, pp. 54–5). The concept evolved in structural therapy as an alternative to linear, cause and effect thinking. Process is a conceptual link between context and content; between belief systems and behaviour. Process reflects socially prescribed rules for empowerment, self-esteem and the behaviours which ultimately define the content. In the previous discussion, the role of emotional care-taker, socially assigned to women, plays out in this family's process as Susan facilitates communication, protects vulnerable family members and diffuses conflict. In this way she feels competent and empowered. Process structures life events in terms of repetitive patterns of interaction that define the content of relationships. So Susan, the penultimate caregiver, feeling guilty for wanting to be taken care of, repetitively refuses support from Edward, Bob, and her sons. She protects them from feelings of uncertainty about their capacity to care for her, maintaining them in comfortable and familiar roles. The men stay somewhat distant and disengaged in terms of Susan's problems, while she ministers to their medical and emotional needs, maintaining her in the caregiving position, one that is comfortable and familiar, albeit increasingly discomforting.

As families describe their difficulties, it is the content of the statement of the problem that represents their experience of dysfunction and inadequacy. Although it is tempting to address this content or to problem-solve, these pursuits invariably elicit linear constructs, cause and effect thinking, statements of failure and experiences of diminished control and manageability, that replicate the family's experience. This has the effect of joining existing belief systems and limits opportunities for change.

Working with process – focusing on repetitive patterns, their function in terms of social rules and opportunities – and developing an understanding of what maintains problematic family dynamics, offers a different level of knowing that moves families beyond familiar patterns of experience. Working with process generates a focus on adaptivity and competency. When Susan describes her anger at the loss of her marriage and her life with Edward, we see the family's process. Edward manages by laughing, staying neutral, looking alternately at Susan and Bob. Bob is stiff and withdrawn. Susan tries to make it all right by attending to both men. The therapist has the opportunity to frame and challenge each interpersonal transaction: Susan's care-taking is capacity; Edward's neutrality is love for both Susan and Bob; Bob's withdrawal is concern about how to be effective. The therapist challenges them to add to their repertoires; to define their roles differently; to create possibilities and new choices. One caution: when process is considered to be the cause of symptoms and pathology within the family, it follows that the goal of therapy will be to block, interrupt, redirect, and change process as if it is exclusively a property of the family system and is unaffected by traditional power arrangements. This is unacceptable. For example, 'detriangulating' the system (changing the process by getting Susan out of the middle), may well improve communication while viewing her as to blame for the dysfunctional interaction. Alternatively, intervention in process identifies patterns of interaction, looks at what maintains these patterns, frames them as adaptive and offers alternatives.

> *Therapist:* [to Susan] You are a real care-taker, aren't you?
> *Susan:* Oh yes, oh yes.
> *Therapist:* You have that capacity to say 'It's alright, it's alright, it's alright', to everyone.
> *Susan:* Oh, I have anger.
> *Therapist:* You do? [Edward laughs, Bob is withdrawn]
> *Susan:* I haven't gotten rid of it. It's buried. I know it's still there.
> *Edward:* [still laughing, looks at Bob] It comes out every once in a while.
> *Susan:* I'm not saying that I'm proud of it but I'm not going to sit here and say that I don't have anger about any of this. It's there but it's buried. As long as I love him [touches Edward's arm] as much as I do, I will always be angry because our life isn't what I thought it could have been. But I don't want to interfere with their relationship. [looking at Bob who stares straight ahead]
> *Therapist:* You're angry at the loss, of course.
> *Susan:* He's just such a special person, you can't help but love him. It's hard to stay angry for very long.
> *Edward:* [touching Bob's hand. Bob looks rigid and stern] Bob wouldn't agree with that.

In the following sequence Susan identifies herself as 'still married' to Edward even though they are divorced. She has no other frame of reference for caring about him other than marriage. Bob also understands her commitment to Edward in terms of marriage, and he feels left out as there is an absence of an acceptable model for relationship in which he can experience esteem and relevance other than through the idea of marriage. The therapist frames the process of Bob's passivity and rigidity in his interaction with Edward and Susan as being an adaptation to managing his anger at feeling excluded from their relationship. This frees him to express himself more directly and open a dialogue with Edward about their relationship. As Susan continues to be involved in the men's dialogue, the therapist frames it as trying to make everyone feel better.

> *Susan:* As long as he's alive, right now, I don't want to be in a committed relationship with another man. He is very important to me and in a way, emotionally, I'm still married to him and that's the way I like it. His coming out to me and being gay is just another part of him. He's still the same person. [Bob tenses as Susan speaks]
>
> *Therapist:* But you're pretty extraordinary.
>
> *Edward:* [Looking at Bob, who remains tense] It's not just like you walk into something like this and it happens; there is a lot to deal with; him [Bob] dealing with her and me dealing with him and him dealing with the kids. It's complicated.
>
> *Therapist:* [to Bob] When Susan said that she still felt married to Edward, your cheeks became red and you managed it by not saying anything and holding back. Yet I know you had a reaction to it when Susan said she still felt married.
>
> *Bob:* My only reaction is that he's still married to her, 100 per cent. Nothing has changed between them.
>
> *Therapist:* But you weren't going to speak about it, were you?
>
> *Bob:* No. I have a lot of anger dealing with all this stuff and it's better for me not to bring it up...
>
> *Therapist:* So that is how you manage it.
>
> *Bob:* Yes!
>
> *Therapist:* And did you think that Edward and Susan didn't know that you felt angry?
>
> *Susan:* I knew but I didn't do it to make him angry.
>
> *Therapist:* [to Susan] You protect him very nicely.
>
> *Bob:* I told Edward before we were even together a year that she still felt married to him. I said she would never get married to another man and he doesn't believe me.
>
> *Edward:* But I'm on a different wavelength, I don't see it that way.
>
> *Bob:* She told you she still felt married!
>
> *Edward:* She told me the wavelength she was on...
>
> *Susan:* [interjects] He doesn't see it the same way as I do.
>
> *Edward:* I don't see it the same way as she does.
>
> *Bob:* You've got a blind spot. I can see things that you don't see. [to Susan] He doesn't see that with you, he sees what he wants to see. I knew right from the beginning when we were together that he was still married to you and you were married to him.

Susan: Well maybe marriage isn't the right word.

Bob: Let's put it this way, he would probably move in with Susan and marry her again... have a gay relationship on the side...

Susan: I don't think so. To begin with, I wouldn't do it. Not that I couldn't deal with it but he wouldn't be happy with that.

Therapist: I think what Bob is saying is that there is an emotional attachment between the two of you, call it marriage if you like, that in some ways makes him feel left out.

Bob: I already told myself that he's still married to her. He always will be, and I'm just somebody he sleeps with... Let's get off this issue!

Susan: Oh no, you shouldn't feel that way. You have to know him enough to know that that is not true.

Therapist: This is what you do, Susan, you try to make everybody feel better.

Bob: [to Susan] It's not your fault what Edward is doing, it's his fault. [to therapist] My anger isn't toward Susan, it's towards him.

Therapist: Yeah... or maybe it's about marriage being a more powerful union than a relationship based solely on choice... maybe that makes you angry...

Linking new patterns to belief systems

Change occurs when the new patterns of interaction (process) that have evolved in therapy are linked by the therapist to new belief systems and perspectives; integrating experience and understanding. The therapist creates these links through:

1. constructing an experience of capacity and possibility in therapy;
2. developing ideas about what maintains process;
3. understanding the process of the family and the presenting problem in terms of social context.

Constructing an experience of capacity and possibility in therapy

When Bob describes his estrangement in visiting Edward's family of origin with Susan and the boys, Edward, whose mother, brother, and extended family have not accepted his homosexuality (they continue to view Edward and Susan as a married couple), acknowledges his own alienation and inability to help himself and Bob to feel accepted. The therapist challenges Edward to help Bob, creating an experience of capacity and possibility in the therapy.

Bob: When we go to his family, our relationship doesn't exist. When I went home with my ex [previous partner], his family knew that we were together, that I was his partner. We were considered a couple. Now when all of us go to his [Edward's] family, they still see Susan and Edward as a couple. [to Edward] Don't shake your head no!

Edward: I don't think they do.

Susan: I think Bob's right. It's a big pretence. When you sit down at the dinner table where you've always sat in the same chairs for 25 years [pause] ... The divorce has never been discussed. If we go to his mother's house now, to spend the night, we would be expected to sleep in the same bed in the same room we've always slept in. They should know better. It shouldn't be this way. They know we're divorced; they know about Bob; they know that I know about Bob...

Therapist: But Bob feels invisible there.

Edward: I feel invisible there too. The last couple of times I've been around my Mom, she's spent about five minutes talking to me ...

Susan: She likes to spend time with me.

Edward: If anything comes up about AIDS, she'll change the subject or get away. I have a hard time being around her now.

Therapist: So you don't think you can help Bob because it is difficult for you there?

Edward: I want Bob to be there with me because if we weren't there then it would be total denial. I told Bob at Christmas, 'I really need you there!'

Therapist: And what does Bob need when he's there?

Edward: [sighs deeply and hangs his head followed by a long silence].

Developing ideas about what maintains process

After Edward finally identifies a way to meet Bob's needs, the therapist enjoins him to consider what maintains him in the position of not doing what he knows he should do, namely, make a commitment to Bob. Edward identifies his own internalised homophobia as the obstacle. This is a very different answer to his earlier response that it was Bob's personal history of deprivation that interfered with their relationship – an idea that left them blaming each other, feeling powerless and frustrated in attempts to change their relationship. It also gives Edward the opportunity to reconsider his history of self-denial that maintained him 'in the closet' and inhibited his self-acceptance.

Therapist: So just answer that one simple question. What does Bob need when you are with your family?

Edward: He would need for me to show that he's part of my life.

Therapist: So what do you think keeps you from doing what you really know to do with this man... your partner... who is saying that he thinks he doesn't have your commitment?

Edward: [long silence] I guess... I wonder... [suddenly sitting back, looking shocked] It's my own internal homophobia [looks at Bob]... It just amazes me how slow it is to grow out of that homophobia and I try to think through where in the hell could I have gotten that hard a case of self-denial and hate because of my sexuality. I can't answer that but I guess the longer I think about it this way the more I'll be able to get out of it and be able to love myself and love Bob. AIDS, I think, is an asset, not a liability, because living with AIDS you realize that your tomorrows are limited, you face your own mortality so you have to do a lot. It's been a push for me to go through my own homophobia. When you asked that real hard question about when I'm around the family how can I help Bob. It made me think.

Understanding the process of the family and the presenting problem in terms of social context

The therapist sees the issues of Edward's maintaining a central relationship with Susan as opposed to prioritising his relationship with Bob, in terms of a broader social perspective – the absence of social approval of a gay relationship relative to a heterosexual one. This depathologises the process and creates possibilities for empowerment and attachment that do not exist when the problems are understood to be caused or maintained by dysfunction. The perspective that it is internalised homophobia and not a dysfunctional triangle (nor Edward's narcissism at wanting to stay central, nor Susan's neediness, nor Bob's history of neglect) that has inhibited the men's relationship, creates a context of empowerment through challenging traditional social rules, personally as well as socially and politically.

Therapist: Well Edward... I think you've hit on something. I think that's partly what keeps you... not just in relation to your family, but in general, from knowing and accepting that this... you and Bob... is a central relationship. It's because a homosexual relationship simply doesn't have the approval that a heterosexual one does. So it's very hard for you to think of your relationship to Bob as

primary. What remains for you in many ways a primary relationship, intellectually, is your relationship with Susan.
Bob: Thank God that I'm not the only one who sees this!

A wedding and two funerals

The conceptualisation and interventions introduced in this session are
the foundation for a continuing challenge to the family's perspective
and for the integration of experiences of empowerment that is the
essence of this therapy. The content of family life as Edward's and Bob's
health deteriorated and the dominant social context of disapproval for
their family form and sexuality made it difficult for family members to
feel relevant in terms of familiar life events and tasks.

James' wedding was representative of just such an event. Having
continued over 14 months to work on signifying their relationship, both
in therapy and in becoming involved in AIDS activism (and after much
conflict and discussion, not dissimilar to that of the session above),
Edward and Bob attended the wedding as a couple. Edward referred to
it as his 'coming out party' for which he 'paid a price' of increased
estrangement and alienation from his mother and brother. He felt that
by 'dancing with Bob at James' wedding', he had made a choice about
his own dying – that he would die without his mother. In this context,
the relationship with Bob became increasingly conflictual, even though
it had become primary, and the focus of therapy was again to work with
the process as a reflection of homophobia as opposed to dysfunction.

Their health had deteriorated and Edward in particular was weak
and in and out of the hospital with opportunistic infections. The men
could no longer physically care for one another; they couldn't drive
and their activities were increasingly limited. Their sexual relationship, which had been central to their attachment, was non-existent.
Susan and the boys had been caring for both men emotionally and by
getting them to medical appointments, discussing economic plans,
shopping and cooking.

Edward felt hurt and angry at his mother's rejection and rarely
called her. When she inquired about his health he was short and in a
hurry to end the conversations. Susan facilitated their relationship.
During one hospitalisation, the therapist met with Edward, Susan,
and Edward's mother, who came to see him despite her fear of being
rejected and sent away. Even as Edward's mother had difficulty
accepting her son's sexuality, Edward maintained her in this position
by his inability to represent himself as a gay man in his relationship

with her. Out of his fear of rejection he had never discussed Bob and their life together. In this context he was willing to try, and talked with his mother about a trip he and Bob had taken to Hawaii, a place she knew he had always wanted to visit. In his words, 'he pushed through his homophobia to get close to his mother'.

Bob died first. He had been less symptomatic than Edward but he contracted pneumonia, was hospitalised and died within five days. The family (Edward, Susan, Julian and James and his wife) was together for the funeral. Edward's mother sent flowers.

Edward's health took a downturn. His family, including his mother and brother, kept vigil at the hospital along with his friends. He died five weeks after Bob. The funeral service was at Edward and Bob's church. His mother and brother were there.

Conclusion

The notion that the process of therapy is defined by, representative of, and constructed by social reality – rules, status, access to power, tradition, and role definition – poses a two-part challenge for the therapist:

1. How to create change and empowerment in ways that do not reinforce the personal and familial internalisation of dominant social themes by incorporating them into therapeutic ideas of dysfunction.
2. How to create interventions that go counter to these themes and that represent alternative perspectives and possibilities for self-esteem and empowerment. This does not mean that therapy should consist of social/political education (although social action is often quite empowering). Rather, it means that, to the degree that therapists are socially and politically educated, their therapeutic conceptualisations will be informed by awareness of and sensitivity to the fact that people relate to one another, understand themselves, and find their value and relevance, in ways that are socially prescribed. It also means that we need to create interventions that lead to alternatives and challenges both to family process and also to the social framework that contextualises it.

In this case, homophobia constructed both the individuals' experiences and the family process. It influenced not only the definition of family roles at a time of great stress, but also the extent to which a gay man could identify his homosexual relationship as primary while at the same time maintaining his connection to his children and ex-wife. This was at an especially significant time in their lives when relationships, connections and support systems were of paramount importance because the men were dying of AIDS. When challenged to see their relationships in this context – that their difficulties had to do with homophobia rather than personal and familial dysfunction – they were able to adopt an expanded, non-traditional meaning of what it means to be a family.

References

Ahrons, C. (1995) *The Good Divorce*. New York: Harper Perennial.

Bograd, M. (1990) Scapegoating mothers: conceptual errors in systems formulations. In Mirkin, M. (ed.) *The Social and Political Contexts of Family Therapy*. Boston: Allyn & Bacon.

Mason B. and Mason E. (1990) Masculinity and family work. In Perelberg, R. and Miller, A. (eds) (1990) *Gender and Power in Families*. London: Routledge.

Patten, J.T. (1996) Married with children (a case study with commentary). In *The Family:* January. Takoma Park: Maryland.

Walker, G. (1988) An AIDS journal: confronting the specter of a modern plague. *The Family Therapy Networker*. Jan/Feb. Washington DC.

Walters, M. (1981) The elements of structure in therapy. In Tolson, E.R. and Reid, W. (eds) *Models of Family Treatment*. New York: Columbia Press.

Walters, M. (1990) A feminist perspective in family therapy. In Perelberg, R. and Miller, A. (eds) *Gender and Power in Families*. London: Routledge.

Walters, M., Carter, B., Papp, P. and Silverstein, O. (1988) *The Invisible Web: Gender Patterns in Family Relationships*. New York: Guilford Press.

Further reading

Benkov, L. (1994) *Reinventing the Family: The Emerging Story of Lesbian and Gay Parents*. New York: Crown Books.

Bruner, J. (1976) *The Process of Education*. Cambridge MA: Harvard University Press.

Mirkin, M. (1990) *The Social and Political Contexts of Family Therapy*. Boston: Allyn & Bacon.

Weston, K. (1991) *Families We Choose: Lesbians, Gays, and Kinship*. New York: Columbia University Press.

CHAPTER 7

Working Systemically with Older People and their Families who have 'Come to Grief'

Alison Roper-Hall

People in later life have a wealth of experiences that includes an increasing possibility of losses. These may be construed as positive, negative, or with a mixture of significance. Older people who have 'come to grief' may seek help from professionals. Ageist attitudes can impede referral for psychological therapy, or concerns may be seen as more physical or medical. When referral is made for psychotherapeutic work, engagement can be difficult if the contextual influences of these beliefs are not explored.

A systemic approach invites multiple perspectives, considering the importance of a loss for each family member, and for the family as an evolving system, however many or few of the family come to therapy. Case stories illustrate how systemic approaches can offer opportunities for positive change. They show the recursion between therapy and theory, being explicit about therapist intent. The examples reflect important issues of later life, and some particular developments arising from systemic work with older people. The frameworks and ideas are equally useful with other client groups.

Introduction

Later life brings with it a double-sided coin of a cumulative wealth of experience, and a cumulative possibility of loss. The range and variety of loss that can be experienced is as diverse as the rich tapestry of life. This chapter draws on my experiences working in a psychology service for people aged over 65 years. It contemplates different kinds of losses older people and their families can face or fear with advancing years. In particular the focus is on those circumstances when older people or their families may 'come to grief' and seek help through therapy. Consideration is also given to factors which diminish the likelihood of older people coming for therapy, such as ageism in the referral system, cultural expectation and family influences.

The therapist working with people in later life will be relatively unseasoned, being younger than their identified clients. The therapist's experience of later life is vicarious, because they have not reached that perspective in their own life cycle. This can take a therapist into challenging and uncharted waters. In relation to bereavement, therapeutic conversation may move towards an earthly practical plane, a spiritual domain about beliefs of life after death, a philosophical plane in life review of the meanings of life. Ways of connecting these domains with presenting difficulties are suggested with case examples.

Working systemically can enable understandings to emerge of how grief, though personally felt, is experienced directly and indirectly with others grieving in a tangle of emotional and social relationships. Most of the literature on bereavement takes an intrapsychic perspective for understanding grief and mourning which can be useful, informing work with individuals. Less consideration is given in the literature to how each grieving person operates within this tangled web of others in the grieving system. Loss can be punctuated from a number of different positions in a system of human relationships. Any loss in a social system is likely to influence a number of people who tread a balance between attending to their own grief and supporting other family members in theirs.

Every loss through death resonates with all previously experienced deaths and those anticipated in the future. The ways in which responses to death are approached and ritualised have implicative influences on future episodes for all family members. An ageist response to older people's bereavement may be more likely when an older person is seen alone. Decisions about how to respond to an older person's grief may be premised with the idea that losses are 'to be expected' and therefore easier to deal with, and that in later life there is inherently less of a future for an individual. These attitudes would make referral for help in bereavement unlikely. A systemic perspective creates a different view, showing the importance for each member of the family and for the family as an evolving system.

Exploring these many influences between relationships, ideas and beliefs can offer new ways forward. This chapter aims to show how this can be helpful whether working with members of a grieving system conjointly or on their own.

Using a systemic approach, each therapeutic relationship is uniquely co-constructed rather than using a 'recipe' or prescription in therapy to lead people through their grief. The chapter offers ideas circulating through the recursions between theory and practice, which could be used as guidelines for systemic work with older people and their families in relation to loss. These ideas are portrayed through case stories; practice examples are given to enliven theory; my intent as therapist is included in the story of therapeutic relationships to clarify for others when and how different ideas may be useful.

Possible losses in later life

It is probably possible to lose anything you have in life. The older you get, the more likely it is that you will lose something or someone significant to you. There is also the increasing chance of significant losses being cumulative. Meanings attributed to loss may be positive, negative or a mixture of positive and negative. The same loss is likely to vary in significance for different members of the system affected.

> Frank, a man in his eighties with a seven-year history of strokes that led to increasing physical, emotional and cognitive difficulties, eventually died. His wife Mary had devoted her life to him, including caring for him at the expense of her own health. His adult children and grandchildren had been more distant from the caring positions adopted by their mother/grandmother. Frank's death is viewed by Mary as an overall negative loss of her lifelong intimate partner. The younger relatives, though saddened, more easily construct his death positively as a relief and may underestimate Mary's grief.

Any loss, as a change in a system, is accompanied by apparently opposing positive and negative elements. When the overall significance is considered negative, then experiencing some of the potential personal advantages (for example, relief, emancipation, freedom from undesirable tasks) can be confusing and intensifies the negative aspects with further guilt. This may decrease the likelihood of these positives being discussed easily among close relatives and friends, complicating communication patterns.

> A year or so after Joan's caring and protective husband Len died, she began to experience an emancipation never known in her life before. At the age of 71 she learned to drive, which Len had said she could never achieve. Her pleasure at this achievement made her feel unfaithful and guilty that she could ever feel happy without him, which pulled her back into grief. Grief appeared as a message to herself and others about how much she loved Len.

When the apparent overall significance of a loss is considered positive, then any negative sequelae (for example unfamiliarity, disruption, new demands) may be viewed as 'resistance', and again may be difficult to voice, understand and feel understood.

> In a bid to overcome loneliness and isolation, Edie moved out of her small terraced house into a purpose-built single person's flat. This was in a warden supervised complex for older people with 30 other residents. It was six years since her husband had died and all of her friendly neighbours had died or moved away. She was moving closer to friends from work with whom she had kept in touch since retiring ten years previously. Everyone had thought this was a good idea but the depression remained. Edie was struggling with unfamiliarity, loss of the marital home, acquiring the label of being an older person, and the sudden apparent requirement to join in with social activities. The paradox of her experienced depression with the move to a supposed better way of life was difficult for her and those around her to understand.

The dilemmas like those above which may emerge through therapy, can be constructed in the vocabulary of Cronen and Pearce (1985) as strange loops (see Figures 7.1A, B). Engaging in conversations with clients to identify these processes can bring a clarity from confusion, enabling them to understand and act differently in their situation and towards one another.

Common losses generally considered to be predominantly negative in later life can be distinguished as: death; loss of mobility; loss of cognitive function; and loss of valued social status (which may be separate from or related to one of the previous kinds of loss). These are the losses most likely to be associated with precipitating relational and emotional difficulty, leading to seeking help from outside agencies. The case stories presented reflect some of the issues, dilemmas and practices when working with people referred who have experienced losses such as these.

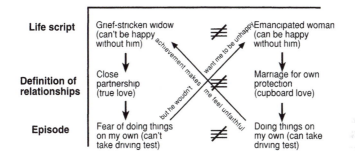

FIGURE 7.1A   Joan's grief depicted in a strange loop

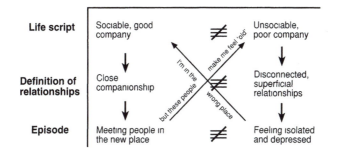

FIGURE 7.1B   Edie's loneliness depicted in a strange loop

Each of these kinds of losses can have many different configurations, and the possibility of a cascade of contingent or subsequent changes. Difficulties for some people may not be associated with a single episode of loss. The first case story is about the O'Reilly family. Mrs O'Reilly's help-seeking symptoms were coincident with her retirement, which seemed to echo other difficult earlier transitions including the death of her mother. The second case story is about Mrs Hayes who came for therapy, diagnosed as depressed by her family doctor, presenting with a dilemma over where she should live.

Her story was one of multiple and unconnected deaths of close family members over a period of about a year.

Deaths in the family

Case Story No 1

A physician referred Mrs O'Reilly with predominantly physical symptoms that had no medical explanation. These had begun with abdominal pain about two months after retiring, aged 65, from a lifetime job as a classroom assistant in a local Catholic primary school. She later developed a shuffling gait and complained of coldness and numbness in her lower legs. This had followed a stay in hospital for observation and investigation when she had been alongside patients with Parkinson's disease. No disease process was diagnosed to explain her condition and she was discharged to the care of her family doctor. A repetitive cycle ensued of escalating physical complaints which Mrs O'Reilly took to her family doctor; he referred to specialists; they found no medical condition and they referred back to her family doctor.

> This observed pattern of a problematic, escalating spiral of repeating sequences of behaviours in a system has been described in several ways from early on in the systemic literature. Wynne (1971) describes recurrent interaction patterns in which people can get caught without realising. He recommends that therapists be aware of them and avoid repeating the pattern unhelpfully in the therapeutic relationship. Watzlawick *et al.* (1974) devote a whole chapter to a repeating pattern they describe as 'more of the same', when the attempted solution (for example seeking medical help) becomes a problem. From research into conjoint enactment, Pearce (1989) refers to 'unwanted repetitive patterns' as an experience that seems quite common and noted repetitive sequences in predictable situations where people seem to inevitably act in certain ways even though this is undesirable.

Four years later (!) Mrs O'Reilly was referred for psychological therapy. By then Mr O'Reilly had given up work outside the home in order to take on work inside the home which Mrs O'Reilly was no longer doing. Mr and Mrs O'Reilly were invited to come with any other members of their family they chose to include.

This is a convening strategy I often use, particularly when there is not enough information in the referral about family structure for me to invite anyone else (see Roper-Hall, 1993).

The O'Reillys came as a couple to the first meeting. I was working with a therapy partner, using Milan systemic ideas (informed, for example, by the works of Selvini Palazzoli *et al.*, 1980; Burnham, 1986; Cecchin, 1987; Boscolo *et al.*, 1987). With so little information about the family structure I decided to draw a genogram with them. This was partly to map out other important relationships, and also to focus on the potential connection of the onset of symptoms with Mrs O'Reilly's retirement. The genogram that was built up and subsequently built on is shown in Figure 7.2.

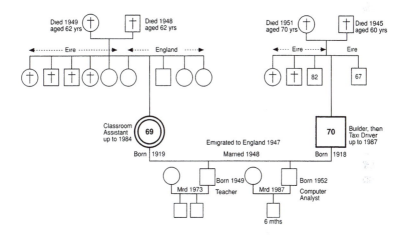

FIGURE 7.2   The O'Reillys' genogram, mapped in 1988 with a four-year history of difficulty

Genograms can be used to map relationships and provide a useful technique to shift thinking for both therapists and clients from an individual focus to interactional patterns and a broader contextual view. The display graphically shows complex inter-generational family patterns. This provides a rich source for hypotheses connecting a problem with the family context and shows the evolution of both problem and context over time. Genograms also provide an efficient clinical summary so that a practitioner unfamiliar with the situation can quickly grasp a large amount of information. A written summary tends to guide the reader into the story the writer constructed about a family's situation. A graphical representation leaves the observer more free to construct their own view. A fresh look at a genogram can allow new connections and ideas to be constructed; this is useful both for clients and for therapists. McGoldrick and Gersen (1985) offer an instructive and entertaining text which shows how using genograms can provide a way of organising therapy. They outline principles for exploring, constructing and interpreting family systems, and distinguish several clinical uses of genograms.

Completing the O'Reilly genogram was informative in a number of ways. At the level of content there are a striking number of potentially significant transitions over a five-year period (1947–52). In sequence these include: emigration from Eire, death of Mrs O'Reilly's father, marriage, birth of first child, death of Mrs O'Reilly's mother, death of Mr O'Reilly's mother (herself recently widowed), birth of second child. There would seem barely time to recover from one event before the next was thrust upon them, hardly time to enjoy or grieve before the next major life event. Five of these major transitions had occurred within two years.

At the level of therapeutic process, the mapping did indeed draw out the connection of retirement with onset of difficulty, although this was not received as news to the couple. Another significant pattern revealed was the sequence of deaths, first in their parental generation, then amongst their siblings, with only one or two siblings apparently cushioning them from being next in line. Such a pattern is not uncommon for people of this age, but the revelation of this with them in the room was stunning and discomforting. Although the information was tactfully elicited and drawn, the experience was disengaging and therefore not therapeutically productive. This disquieting experience has led me to be more cautious in the use of genograms with clients. I use them now, at least initially, to assist in mapping patterns of relationships out of the therapeutic interview.

The cluster of transitions that we observed in the genogram, particularly in the two-year period 1947–9, seemed important. Our observation of this led us to one hypothesis that Mrs O'Reilly's retirement had not been the primary trigger, but had created a context and time when these earlier events could be allowed to resurface. We thought that the conflicting life-cycle tasks of bereavement of parents and attachment to newly born children could have left some unresolved issues. These perhaps could not be addressed at the time, nor subsequently in the busyness of adult life, and now, so long after the events, could not be expressed and communicated overtly.

Walsh (1991) refers to research she carried out with McGoldrick on conflicting life-cycle tasks. In particular they investigated the situation of concurrent death of a parent with the birth of a child. They noted the inherent stress of juxtaposed conflicting demands on the daughter/mother, the requirement for incompatible tasks, and thus the potential for failure to mourn. McGoldrick (1991) talks of the vulnerability of families to difficulty when mourning is delayed or avoided.

These ideas (among other hypotheses) were central in our thinking about the O'Reilly's situation. I gradually explored them with the couple as sufficient rapport was developed. By the third session the couple had elaborated some of the details of the cluster of transitions between leaving Eire and the birth of their second son. Mrs O'Reilly's recollection of this time was very vivid; many of the decisions and circumstances she recounted as difficult still seemed raw with emotion. She remembered the arrival of their first son as a mixed blessing. She had been pleased with the birth of their first child, happy that he had arrived in time for her mother to see him, sad that she could not spend more time with her mother, thwarted that she had not been able to care for her mother through her illness, and clearly upset that she had not been the daughter chosen by her mother to care for her.

Any attempts through questions and interventive statements to contextualise or otherwise relate Mrs O'Reilly's current difficulties to these past turbulent times seemed not to make an acceptable fit for her. She said she preferred to think of these events as past and forgotten but, paradoxically, declined to return as she had found the session too upsetting. Mr O'Reilly came alone to what became the last session.

Engagement had been difficult for a number of reasons with this couple. Mapping the genogram with them had been counterproductive to engagement, and rapport had been slow to develop. They may have been stepping outside their cultural boundaries by coming to us for help. There were indications that their family cultural script allowed them to be physically ill but not to be in need of psychological help.

Older people as a cohort tend to have a heightened fear of psychiatric illness and psychological problems preferring to construe problems as physical. This is associated with the cultural norms and attitudes about madness and senility that prevailed earlier in their lives, when services and service ethos were different. I have generally found people referred by physicians more difficult to engage than those who come from family doctors or psychiatrists. I now spend more time initially considering people's expectations and talking about these issues if people indicate they think the referral was a mistake.

The feedback in the last session from Mr O'Reilly created additional concerns for us:

- Had we 'fallen in love with the hypothesis', (Boscolo *et al.*, 1987) and, even when the clients saw no relevance of 'unresolved grief' to the current situation, we persisted with this idea?
- Had the timing or pacing of the questioning been a poor fit with the clients' readiness?
- Were there cultural issues influencing engagement with therapy that had been left unexplored?
- Might some of the other hypotheses explored have been more relevant and healing for the client?
- Was most of the clients' therapeutic work to be done outside of the sessions, with important connections having been made that the clients could now explore with their own self-healing?

On follow-up through contact with the medical care system, it seemed that the escalating spiral of physical symptoms identified before referral, had ceased. I found out that two years later Mrs O'Reilly, then aged 71, had died following a stroke. There had been no opportunity for feedback directly from the clients. It can only be hoped, therefore, that these last two years of her life yielded a better quality than had the previous four. The therapy may have been instrumental in changing the undesirable repetitive pattern of seeking medical help in the absence of a diagnosable complaint. Whether the therapy provided any helpful perturbation of the family's beliefs about bereavement remains uncertain. It may be that this episode of therapy was more interventive for the therapists! Reflecting and reflexing on episodes when things apparently have not gone well can be more informing for developing practice than therapies that might more readily be regarded as successful.

Case story No 2

Mrs Hayes was in her early seventies when she was referred. She had been to seek help from her family doctor, apparently in a deep suicidal depression. From the doctor's letter, the focus of help was to resolve the grief of three family deaths four years previously, and alleviate the associated depression. Mrs Hayes, however, presented her initial concern in therapy as the dilemma of where to live, as she could not settle in England, nor previously in Scotland. She chose to attend therapy on her own. This was partly a forced choice because she had become quite isolated from significant others. It was partly a conscious choice as she had close friends in England who were sensitive to her difficulties, but Mrs Hayes did not want them to be privy to some of the details of her story. I was working, as I do from time to time, as a solo therapist, still using a systemic approach. I constructed the genogram (Figure 7.3) using information from referral and from conversations with Mrs Hayes. It was drawn outside my therapy sessions with her (following the caution instilled by the previous case).

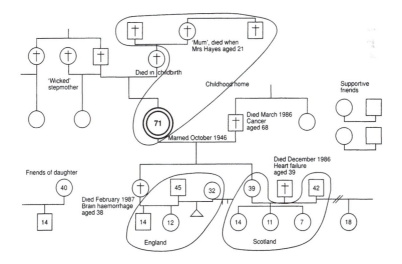

FIGURE 7.3   Mrs Hayes' genogram

Some of the important relationships and events mapped can be elaborated from Mrs Hayes' story. Her husband died in 1986 from cancer of the stomach after being cared for by Mrs Hayes, who previously had worked as a nursing auxiliary. They missed their ruby wedding anniversary by six months. In December the same year, a few days before Christmas, her 'favourite' son-in-law died suddenly from a heart attack. The following February her oldest daughter died unexpectedly and tragically from a brain haemorrhage. She was subsequently cut off from her two grandchildren by her 'rogue' son-in-law. On the advice of friends and police (feeling intimidated by her son-in-law), she gave up her family home two years after the deaths and moved to Scotland to be near her other daughter and three grandchildren. However, she felt she could not settle there and moved back to England after 18 months. It was six months later that she had sought help from her doctor.

During the first session Mrs Hayes decided to talk about the three deaths as part of the story to explain her dilemma. Although the story of each death appeared tragic in its own way, Mrs Hayes recounted them as if detached from them. She seemed unmoved by them emotionally but at the same time said that she felt there was something wrong, that she had not really grieved for any of them, and had not even cried over her daughter's death. I responded by opening a discourse of curiosity about different beliefs, theories and meanings of different behaviour during grief.

It was helpful to construct distinctions between her person, her perceived internal world and her external world. Connections between these constructions could then be patterned in a recursive way. That is, each distinction made could be seen to mutually influence the others; one distinction could be used to set the context for understanding another. For example, instead of asking her how she felt about not crying for her daughter, or seeking ways to help her do this, asking questions that contextualised and patterned the behaviour were more opening for her. For example:

'When was it that you realised that you had not cried for your daughter?'
'When you realised that you had not cried for your daughter, what effect do you think that had on you?'
'Do you imagine that others in the same situation would have been able to cry more easily?'

'What gives you that idea/where do you think that idea comes from?'
'How would you say others in your family were affected compared to how you have shown your grief?'
'How does that make you think about yourself/about your family's ideas about showing grief?'

> The pacing and timing of such contributions to therapeutic conversations are important. Early on questions might be useful to gather information towards a systemic understanding of the problem. Later in a therapeutic relationship they may help to embed a more positive view of self, others and circumstances. They can free someone from beliefs and explanations which if taken as truth can tie people to a particular way of being that is undesirable for them.

It became clear to Mrs Hayes that she was balancing uncomfortably between a number of messages/influences about how she should have grieved, and how she should have recovered.

> It may be helpful to use the gentle challenge of curiosity to facilitate change (Cecchin, 1987) if the clients' ideas seem restrictive, or in some way constraining to clients' abilities to move on. It might be useful to challenge the notion of conventional ideas about correct mourning and invite the client to consider other ideas from theory, literature or the therapist's clinical experience. A systemic approach to bereavement is similar to a systemic approach to other situations. There is a preference for using theory as guidelines rather than for prescriptive direction (Amundson et al., 1993). Ideas from bereavement theory could be introduced in therapeutic conversation as ideas that may or may not be useful. Explanations are generally left open, and possibilities for other explanations are opened out.

> This move away from working with normative theories, and a correct modus operandum, accompanies a movement in systemic approaches away from expertness, authority and 'wilfulness' in therapy (Atkinson and Heath, 1990). This is accompanied by a corresponding shift towards empowerment, partnership and an openness to a variety of solutions – in a position of 'not knowing the answers' (Anderson and Goolishian, 1992). Validity is given to the clients constructions of loss, bereavement, grief and mourning, and the therapy is co-constructed with these ideas.

Responding with such openness to Mrs Hayes' concerns (about whether she had been grieving correctly) had the intent and influence of freeing her to find her own path through grief. Paradoxically, recognising that she did not have to cry as part of 'the normal grieving process', enabled tears to flow on the next anniversary of her daughter's death. She said these were as much for her husband as for her daughter, the two episodes of loss intermingling in her grieving experience. I thought it was important to explore with her the significance and influence of this episode of grief. I asked her questions which connected this experience with her relationship to bereavement, and to how she thought other people might understand her behaviour. She had found the crying experience positive, though painful. It indicated to her that she was doing some of the things that were important to her. She thought that others would consider it appropriate that she had cried, and appropriate that it had been when she was alone. Deconstructing and reconstructing this episode in this way promoted her sense of well-being, movement and positive direction.

Adopting a framework informed by the Coordinated Management of Meaning (Cronen and Pearce, 1985) provides ways of thinking and enquiring about a range of connected distinctions about contextual influences. It enables a systemic therapist to focus more on patterns of relationships between people, events and ideas, and less on what happens intrapsychically to individuals. The framework is shown in Figure 7.4.

The framework proposes recursive relationships between levels, in which it is possible for each level to be understood in relation to the others, as well as giving meaning to the others. An activity at a 'higher' level can directly, contextually influence the activities described within more specific levels, giving meaning to them. An implicative influence from a more specific level of experience can give meaning to more general levels. Using this framework can enable enquiry about how contextual and implicative influences give meaning from one level to another. These influences can be considered introducing the dimension of time. Questioning which explores the reflexive connections between levels of context can open the possibility for new meanings to be generated. Tomm (1987) clarifies different kinds of reflexive questioning that can be used in this facilitative way to promote self-healing.

The following examples of reflexive questions (using Tomm's 1987 categories) may have been useful in facilitating change for Mrs Hayes:

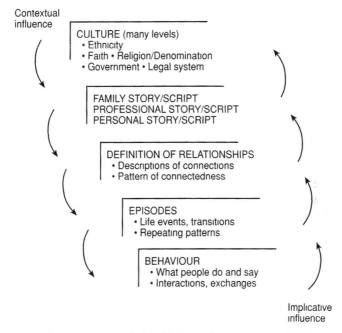

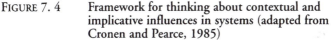

FIGURE 7. 4   Framework for thinking about contextual and
implicative influences in systems (adapted from
Cronen and Pearce, 1985)

Supposing you had done this four years ago, what differences do you
think that might have made to where you are now?' (*unexpected
context change*).

'Now that this has happened, what differences might your daughter
see in you?' (*observer perspective*).

'How do you imagine now how things could be for you in a year's
time?' (*future orientation*).

'What do you think might happen if you were to talk about these
things and perhaps even cry with your daughter next time you visit?'
(*embedded suggestion*).

'Supposing that you hadn't believed so strongly that this was
something that you had to do, do you think you could have felt like
this sooner?' (*introducing hypotheses*).

Questions may be asked relatively frequently if the client seems to find it hard to generate a narrative. At other times there may be long intervals between the questions as each question punctuates a client's flowing narrative. The language of the questions and answers would be socially constructed to be meaningful to client and therapist. Systemic interviewing emphasises interest in process and pattern, often in preference to emphasis on content and entities. Observer perspectives can promote this interactional view and can be particularly useful when working with a client alone. For example, asking about the hypothetical views of people who cannot be present, including the person who has died, can introduce different perspectives into the therapy (White, 1988).

None of Mrs Hayes' remaining family was available to come with her to therapy. She had no-one else with whom she could talk about the things that distressed her. Asking 'If I were to ask your daughter in Scotland what she thought your life was like here now, what do you think she would say?' generated new ways for Mrs Hayes to think about her situation. Questions like this seemed to open the possibility for Mrs Hayes to communicate more with her daughter. Asking 'If your daughter (who has died) were able to comment, what would she be likely to say about your decisions to live in England, near her children, or in Scotland near your other daughter and her family?' opened the possibility of other views suggesting alternative actions or solutions. For Mrs Hayes questions like this had the influence of confirming her decisions, and consequently enabling her to feel more settled.

One of the most significant aims in therapeutic conversation would be to broaden pre-existing views so as to look at contextual influences on connections brought forth. Contexts that are likely to be considered important are various societal influences and other cultural influences. I use an acronym of *social GRACES* to prompt thinking and questions about these potentially important influences in clients' lives and problems. This is depicted in Figure 7.5. Having this in mind can influence the therapist to be more prepared and responsive to comments their clients might make. Some examples of using this prompt in my own practice have been to enable me to enter discourse about clients' spiritual lives; to discuss clients appearing as victims of their own ageist attitudes; to explore discrimination clients may experience associated with their gender, ethnicity, sexuality; and to consider how these contexts relate to their reasons for being in therapy.

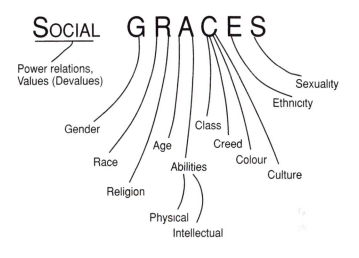

FIGURE 7.5   Acronym to prompt thinking about important
influences in clients' lives and problems

Lessons from Cases 1 and 2

Both of these clients presented an initial dilemma for the therapists in that the story of difficulty the clients portrayed seemed to the therapists to minimise the importance of the bereavements. The dilemma for the therapist in Case 1 was whether to explore with a hypothesis of covert grieving, or whether to work with the 'face value' presentation from the clients of restriction by physical problems. A way forward, illustrated in the second case, is to work both with ideas presented by clients and ideas generated by therapists, co-constructed in ways meaningful to client and therapist (Hoffman, 1992). In particular, using the 'discipline of curiosity' (Burnham, 1993), which counteracts a therapist's unhelpful attachment to a preferred hypothesis, can serve to maintain partnership in the therapeutic relationship.

Differences in my stance as therapist in relation to these two cases may have introduced different therapeutic possibilities. With the O'Reilly couple, the genogram drew connections with the past bereavements so strongly it had the tendency of stifling my curiosity and that of my therapy partner. The therapeutic tasks seemed to involve enabling the clients to see these connections and then, through revisiting the bereavements, their grief and current difficulties might be resolved. This is no longer a path I would tread without curiosity. By adopting a stance of curiosity in the second case of Mrs Hayes (although similarly ostensibly presenting with something other than the bereavements), I enabled the client to draw her own connections with her grief, and to free her (and myself) from presuming normative ideas of bereavement and mourning (see Stroebe, 1992/3). This had the influence of introducing a particular clarity, and from this new perspective the client was able to co-construct in therapy a way forward that she could activate in the recursion between life in therapy and life in her 'real' world.

Other issues raised in the work with Mrs Hayes show the relevance of this approach when working with individuals. Systemic therapy initially developed as a way of working with families and other social systems. Increasingly people using the approach have recognized that, when circumstances dictate, it can offer a valuable way of working with individuals. It can be useful when working with bereaved people who have become disconnected from their significant others, and for whom certain emotional experiences seem to be unduly interfering with their lives. There is less invitation of descriptions of intra-psychic events, and more emphasis on enquiring about how a person connects their perceived internal world with an observable world. Relationships, interactional patterns and connectedness are regarded as important emphases when working in this way, whether with a family, a large social network, or one person in the room. This can be especially important with older people who may feel cut off (through loss or geographically) from family and others. Sensitivity is an important aspect of the therapist's enquiry, as the sense of loss can be enhanced by the absence of those very people with whom the client might be wanting to share their story of recovery from grief.

Losses worse than death in the family

Case Story No 3: Loss of mobility

Mrs Humphreys was referred by her family doctor when she expressed suicidal ideas following the amputation of her right leg (associated with diabetes). A meeting was arranged at her home and the invitation was extended to any others that she might wish to invite. She chose to be seen alone, though the interview began with her giving reasons why it was either not appropriate or not possible for others to be present.

This technique of convening, mentioned before, both opens the possibility for significant others to be present when an individual is referred, and provides a relational focus at the beginning of the meeting, even when working with people on their own.

The genogram (Figure 7.6) shows some of the information which was gained early on in the first meeting. Mrs Humphreys was divorced from her husband 12 years previously, and now lives alone. Her son lives with his family 30 miles away, and occasionally makes contact. Her daughter emigrated with her family to Canada and occasionally writes. She seemed both resentful of and resigned to the very little contact with these and other members of her family. She sees a previous colleague from work regularly and has a friendly neighbour. Each of these friends may go with her on her many visits to hospital.

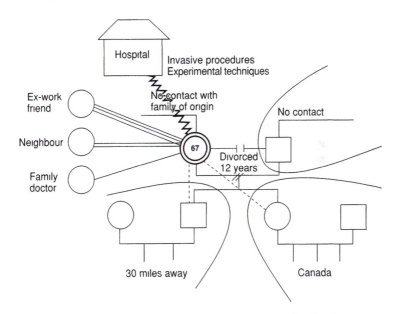

FIGURE 7.6   Mrs Humphreys' genogram at time of referral

Mrs Humphreys' main story was a long history of treatment for back pain, including experimental and invasive procedures carried out at a local teaching hospital. She angrily attributed her amputation not to diabetes, but to side effects of one of the experimental drugs she had received for her back pain. She was also angry that no-one had counselled her before the amputation, and she said she had no idea that they were going to cut off her leg. She certainly did not intend to give permission for this. She had been warned by the surgeon that she may not be 'in the clear' as far as her left leg was concerned. Her firm intention was not to undergo any further surgery and hoped that refusing a further amputation would hasten her death. She said she saw no point to life in the circumstances she faces. She saw death as a better option for her and thought others would too.

By exploring contextual influences (in similar ways to those described above) on this decision, and particularly around the possibility of her actively killing herself, it became clear that her intentions were more passive than active. She said she would refuse medical treatment which would then leave her with a life-threatening condition. She would not, however, deliberately do anything to kill herself. As a Roman Catholic, her religious beliefs precluded her from suicide and her faith was strong enough for this preclusion to hold meaning for her. Exploring the influence on family and friends of the death she wished for herself, had the effect of enabling her to re-acknowledge her significance as a family member, though she had previously described a picture of alienation.

> Talking about significant others who are absent, and their influence, in this way can serve to reconstruct the influence of relationships for a person who has little contact with their family.

This was an important intervention and perhaps contributed to Mrs Humphreys choosing to consent to the second amputation when the time came. Equally important was the intervention with the referring doctor. She was recently qualified and new to the practice. The thought of a patient in her care committing suicide had thrown her into controlled panic. The referral was not inappropriate, and my feedback to her that suicide was unlikely enabled her to refocus her efforts on the medical care for her patient.

Lessons from Case Story 3

This case highlights that bereavement/fear of death is not just for clients, patients and their families, but is also an issue for professionals and other significant relationships in the systems of which they are a part. Mapping relationships to include professional systems can be useful. Sometimes the significant relational systems of older people can be a complex mixture of family, friends, helpers and professionals from different agencies. Sociograms can be useful to map non-biological significant relational systems. I also use ecomaps (Hartman, 1979) to assist in broadening the contextual view and generate hypotheses about the referral which include related professional systems. Neidhardt and Allen (1993) have included in their book a useful description of the use of ecomaps when working with older people.

The work with Mrs Humphreys shows the importance of drawing out cultural and religious influences on meanings of death and suicide. Spiritual and religious dimensions are important contexts to be aware of in this enquiry. Talking about clients' beliefs about death, and life after death, will be crucial in the co-creation of pattern, questions and ideas in a therapeutic conversation. With some clients, talking about the influences of a person lost by physical death, in their death, through their life, and in their life after death, can redefine the importance of that person in life after their death. There may be recognition of a continuing relationship with aspects of the person that can always remain, and with that person through a religious or spiritual dimension.

Case Stories 4 and 5: Loss of cognitive function

Coincidentally within a few weeks of one another, two men were referred with their families following a diagnosis of probable Alzheimer's. The similarities and differences in these two cases draw some interesting comparisons.

Both men were in their early sixties but were referred to the service for older people because of the diagnosis. The referrals had been made in both cases because another health professional had perceived the couples as having particular difficulties adjusting to the diagnosis.

This can be a problem for most people, especially when the probable diagnosis has been made early on, with the prospect of living with Alzheimer's for several years. This kind of loss has been called 'ambiguous' for relatives of people living with dementia because they experience loss of the person they knew, even though the person remains present in their lives (Boss *et al.*, 1988). In early dementia the person experiencing cognitive changes will also experience anticipatory loss, both of their abilities and of their plans for the future.

These clients were invited to separate appointments with their wives, other family members and anyone else concerned in the situation. In response to the invitations both men came with their wives, and with Alzheimer's disease as a central feature of their concerns. As the men were in the early stages following diagnosis, there were issues of anticipated loss for themselves and their wives. Curiously both had a son in his 30s still living at home; and both couples described their son as disconnected from the events that had overtaken their lives. Despite invitations through the clients to their sons, neither ever came to a meeting. In the ways previously described, the sons' positions were included in the thinking about the situations, and in the therapeutic conversations.

A major difference between these two cases was the influence of the diagnosis in their lives. Mr and Mrs Baird had accepted the diagnosis, both fearfully and as some sort of relief, because it explained some of the disastrous mishaps that had been occurring over the last year or so, including the loss of £14,000 through cognitive error in accounting with the small business Mr Baird managed – a loss which had cost him his job. The influence of this new explanation (in the form of the diagnosis) was to draw the couple closer, and strengthen their Christian faith. The therapeutic relationship with this couple was short (two meetings). The main intent became embedding their own ideas about positive relational strengths between themselves and in their faith. It was also clear they were now in contact with their local professional team that supported people with this diagnosis.

In the other case, Mr Rushton had accepted the diagnosis to explain observed memory loss and had plunged into a deep depression, alienating him from his wife. At times he became suicidal, fearing what may lie ahead for him and his wife, and thinking that they would both be better off if he could die. His explanation was contextualised by having worked on the Community Health Council, in which part of his role had been to inspect services for people diagnosed with a dementia. Although his work and that of others had been to improve services for these people, he had constructed at the time his worst fear, namely of one day being in that position himself. Therapeutic work with Mr and Mrs Rushton has included exploring the interrelationships between themselves and 'Alzheimer's', depression, anxiety, humour, panics, achievement, therapy and reassurance.

This kind of work has led me to a new form of mapping best described as 'ideograms'. An ideogram graphically represents the connections between ideas as co-constructed in therapy. It relates theoretically to the ideas of narrative and externalising expounded by White (1988/89) and White and Epston (1990). In my work with families where stroke or dementia of some kind has been diagnosed, I have found it helpful to talk about the diagnosed problem as an 'entrance' in the family system, in the same way that people can be seen to enter or exit a family system during the family life cycle.

The next conceptual step was to put the diagnosis (or whatever other word the family uses to describe it) graphically on the map. This enables an interactive construction that shows the relationships between the problem, the people it influences, and the people who influence it. The next step was to include on the map other significant ideas which interrelate and have recursive influence with the people and the problem. As such, the ideogram is akin to a graphic systemic formulation or synthesis of the case. An ideogram of a view of the Rushtons case is shown in Figure 7.7. It is usually helpful to draw several ideograms of each case to represent different hypotheses, or conversations and changes over time.

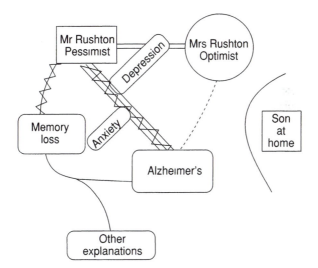

FIGURE 7.7   Ideogram showing a view of the Rushtons' situation

Though the initial intentions in my approach to the Baird and Rushton cases were similar, they elicited a marked difference in response from the two men. The first session for both couples included enquiry about the story of their coming to therapy, their expectations in therapy and what they hoped therapy could offer them. In both cases this led into enquiry about the influence of the diagnosis in their lives. It also led to using the gentle challenge of curiosity in exploring the diagnosis as an explanation of their problems, and in exploring their understanding of the diagnosis.

> The paper 'Return of the question "Why" (Furman and Ahola, 1988) shows how exploring with people their explanations for things can soften a rigid view and enable people to consider multiple ways of construing a situation. The 'return' finds the therapist not just asking 'why...', but 'why do you think...', and frees both clients and therapists from a discourse seeking truth in an objective world, to a discourse of ideas which might fit, in a pragmatic multi-verse (Mendez et al., 1988).

Despite similar intentions on my part, the contrast between the conversations with each couple was striking. Mr Baird had great difficulty keeping in the conversation. He seemed to lose the content of a sentence before he got to the end of it. My usual kind of questions seemed too long or complex for him, and he had difficulty following them and understanding what was being asked. It was easy to see how he could begin to become marginalised in conversations, either by deferring more and more to his wife, or by others assuming he could not manage a conversation. The therapeutic guideline of neutrality influences the therapist towards a validating approach such that the pace and content of the conversation adjusted to match Mr Baird's ability, thereby enabling him to continue taking part. It seemed that the effect of the diagnosis for this couple was much less important than the experiences they described. It seemed to make no difference to them what anybody else called it, except that the label of Alzheimer's disease had opened some doors for them to professional support for which they were very grateful. It may also have been helpful in the legal repercussions of their financial difficulties.

Mr Rushton on the other hand, talked about his perceived difficulties as fitting with the diagnosis, but he showed none of the difficulties he described. Indeed, when his wife could not recall the name of one of the professionals he had seen, it was he who remembered it. Whilst the experiences he described were troublesome, it was more the influence of the diagnosis that was devastating for Mr Rushton, namely the prospect of living his worst nightmare. Mrs Rushton appeared to be more strongly influenced by the depression Mr Rushton showed than by the memory difficulties he experienced, which she regarded as trivial. Opening a dialogue which viewed Alzheimer's as only one of a number of possible explanations for Mr Rushton's difficulties had a between-session influence which this couple found extremely freeing. Mr Rushton arrived at the next meeting with the news that the depression had completely lifted and he no longer thought that what he was experiencing would inevitably turn into his worst nightmare.

Lessons from Cases 4 and 5

Ostensibly these cases seemed very similar: men referred of similar ages, apparently with the same diagnosis and reasons for referral, and with similar family configurations. However the different belief structures contextualising the situations for each family invited very different work with each family. The contrast between the two cases highlights the lack of fit between what you may find yourself doing in therapy, and any guidance that referral information may give you! This questions myths about correspondence between family configuration, diagnosis, reasons for referral and indications for therapy.

Further issues highlighted in these cases include for the therapist whether, and how, to work with family members who may show cognitive or language impairment, which embarrass usual interviewing styles, (see Jeffery, 1987, and Roper-Hall, 1992, for discussion of some of these issues). You may wish to reflect on your position in relation to these issues, and consider how you might assess the influence of your own preferences and opinions, and those of others in the significant relational system, on the convening and interviewing processes.

These two cases show the importance of mapping the influence of loss whether it is ambiguous or distinct. I invite you to explore with the ideas earlier in this chapter, and generate questions you could use with people presenting you with similar issues.

Conclusion

This conclusion aims to summarise some of the main points raised when working with older people in the context of their families or other significant relational systems, in relation to grief. In work with older people it seems clear to me that grief and mourning are not simple processes, either for individuals or for interrelated social systems. It seems both difficult and perhaps not meaningful to focus therapy through a grief work hypothesis. Older people come with a long history representing a rich tapestry of significant events that have occurred in their lives. These multiple transitions can both obfuscate a clear focus in therapy and provide a rich source of contextualising information. Adopting an approach with therapeutic curiosity can enable the therapeutic relationship and task to be co-constructed.

Problem identification and the referral process

Factors including ageism in the referral process may diminish the likelihood of referral for therapy or increase the length of time between initial experience of difficulty and referral. In two of the cases presented here there was an interval of four years before a psychological approach was considered. Older people themselves, or those around them, may not construct loss as anything out of the ordinary in later life; nor may they see an older person's problems in psychological terms, or consider it appropriate for someone late in life to begin psychotherapy. Physical or medical symptoms may dominate the discourse with their family doctor, though referral for medical help may prove unfruitful.

The context from which people arrive in therapy will influence the ways they engage in therapy and influence the ways in which therapists seek to engage with their clients. Exploring expectations and beliefs about the referral can help to establish a therapeutic relationship. It can often be useful to establish a 'both/and' position (Bateson, 1980) in relation to medical symptoms and psychological problems (Griffith *et al.*, 1990), especially with older people who may worry that they may be seen as becoming 'senile'. Co-constructing with them a systemic picture of their grief can dispel the idea that they are wasting your time. Mapping the influence of the loss in the family system can create different perspectives, removing the stigma of an older person being a seen as a problem or burden to their family. Therapy may be viewed then as an opportunity to generate change beneficial to the family as a whole, for example by creating new narratives for the family around loss and bereavement.

Convening

Family therapy is still a relatively unconventional approach particularly for older people, who will usually be referred on their own for psychological therapy, or expect to come for therapy alone. The technique of convening described, namely inviting the person referred to define their relevant system, both opens the possibility for significant others to be present and begins the therapeutic relationship with a relational focus. If a person to be seen on their own finds transport difficult, it is important to work flexibly enough to visit them. If I had not been prepared to do this, I would not have seen half the people who have been referred. '

Some clients will choose not to come with others when there are bereavement issues, so as to keep some of their concerns and perhaps emotions private. Some clients will have become isolated geographically or socially from their family, or others they regard as significant to their bereavement. Indeed, the very person they would want to be there is the person they have lost. Working systemically with people on their own can enable important influences of relationships to be reconstructed for a person having little contact with their family. It is important though to be aware that the sense of loss may be enhanced by the absence of the people with whom the client might be wanting to share their story of recovery from grief. Including in the enquiry how absent members would perceive the changes occurring through therapy can restore the client's sense of connectedness, embed positively perceived changes, and open fresh possibilities for the future. It can also bring recognition of continuing relationships with aspects of people which can always remain, and with a person who has died, through religious or spiritual dimensions.

Mapping

Constructing genograms with older people can be useful in a number of ways. However, because the older we get the closer we get to the end of our lives, mapping genograms with people in later life can graphically display this as well as other information. If this is likely to be a sensitive issue for clients it may be preferable to proceed cautiously and either map outside the therapy session, or later on when more is known about the family and when the genogram is intended to be used for something more than simply gathering information.

The significant relational system for older people may not be a biologically related system. Using sociograms to map significant relationships between people may be more useful. Ecomaps can be helpful in shifting thinking to different contextual levels, to consider for example relationships between different helping agencies that an older person may be connected with. A next step for me has been developing 'ideograms', which can show connectedness between people, ideas, events, places and so on, akin to a graphic systemic formulation or synthesis of the case, representing different hypotheses, or conversations and changes over time.

Intervening

Working with older people either on their own, or as a couple may require adopting a particular approach in order for the changes they experience to influence the broader system. Reflexive questioning, described above, can influence the relationships people have in therapy with those unable to be present. Changes in clients' life scripts occurring in therapy reflexively influence relationships and behaviour in those relationships, introducing change in the family script and family story. Through this families may come to have different relationships with bereavement.

Nature of loss in later life

Common losses considered in this chapter which are likely to be associated with precipitating relational and emotional difficulty for older people and their families or significant others, can be distinguished as: death; loss of mobility; loss of cognitive function; and loss of valued social status. Some of these losses can be described as ambiguous because although the person is still physically present, the person they knew is not recognisable to them. Older people frequently also experience anticipatory loss, including their own death or that of their partner, even when no life-threatening conditions prevail.

Because of the nature of working with older people experiencing loss, professionals need to be prepared for the influence of these transitions, not just in clients' lives but also how they might relate to their own. Professionals may find it helpful to anticipate loss, including the possibility that clients may die.

Reflecting and reflexing on episodes of therapy can be interventive for the therapist, particularly those episodes when things apparently have not gone well. Therapy can be seen as an unfolding relationship between therapist and therapist experience. One of the areas in particular that has unfolded for me by working with bereaved older adults is in a spiritual dimension. Spiritual lives seem to become more relevant to people as they grow older, and I have become more sensitive to the doors which open to explore this domain with people in their grief, and in their hope. I hope I continue to learn from my clients.

References

Amundson, J., Stewart, K. and Valentine, L. (1993) Temptations of power and certainty. *Journal of Marital and Family Therapy* **19**(2): 111–23.

Anderson, H. and Goolishian, H. (1992) The client is the expert: a not-knowing approach to therapy. In McNamee, S. and Gergen, K.J. (eds) *Therapy as Social Construction*. London: Sage.

Atkinson, B. and Heath, A. (1990) Further thoughts on second-order family therapy – this time it's personal. *Family Process* **29**:145–55.

Bateson, G. (1980) *Mind and Nature: A Necessary Unity*. London: Fontana.

Boscolo, L., Cecchin, G., Hoffman, L. and Penn, P. (1987) *Milan Systemic Family Therapy: Conversations in Theory and Practice*. New York: Basic Books.

Boss, P., Caron, W. and Horbal, J. (1988) Alzheimer's disease and ambiguous loss. In Chilman, C., Cox, F. and Nunnally, A. (eds) *Families in Trouble*. Newbury Park, CA: Sage.

Burnham, J. (1986) *Family Therapy: First Steps Towards a Systemic Approach*. London: Routledge.

Burnham, J. (1993) Systemic supervision. *Human systems, The Journal of Systemic Consultation and Management* **4**(3–4): 349–81.

Cecchin, G. (1987) Hypothesizing, circularity, neutrality revisited: an invitation to curiosity. *Family Process* **26**:405–13.

Cronen, V. and Pearce, B. (1985) Toward an explanation of how the Milan method works: an invitation to a systemic epistemology and the evolution of family systems. In *Applications of Systemic Family Therapy*. London: Grune & Stratton.

Furman, B. and Ahola, T. (1988) Return of the question 'Why': Advantages of exploring pre-existing explanations. *Family Process* **27**:395–409.

Griffith, J.L., Griffith, M.E. and Slovik, L.S. (1990) Mind–body problems in family therapy: contrasting first and second order cybernetic approaches. *Family Process* **29**(1): 71–91.

Hartman, A. (1979) *Finding Families: An Ecological Approach to Family Assessment in Adoption*. Human Services Guide vol. 1. London: Sage.

Hoffman, L. (1992) A reflexive stance for family therapy. In McNamee, S. and Gergen, K.J. (eds) *Therapy as Social Construction*. London: Sage.

Jeffery, D. (1987) Should you involve an older person about whom there is an issue of cognitive competence in family meetings? *PSIGE* **24**(Oct):8–11.

McGoldrick, M. (1991) Echoes from the past: helping families mourn their losses. In Walsh, F. and McGoldrick, M. (eds) *Living Beyond Loss: Death in the Family*. New York: W.W. Norton.

McGoldrick, M. and Gersen, R. (1985) *Genograms in Family Assessment*. New York: W.W. Norton.

Mendez, C., Coddou, F. and Maturana, H. (1988) The bringing forth of pathology. *Irish Journal of Psychology*, special edn. **9**(1): 91–129.

Neidhardt, E.R. and Allen, J.A. (1993) *Family Therapy with the Elderly*. Human Services Series Vol. 22. Newbury Park, CA:Sage.

Pearce, W.B. (1989) *Communication and The Human Condition*. Carbondale, IL: Southern Illinois University Press.

Roper-Hall, A. (1992) Better late than never. *Clinical Psychology Forum* **48**:14–18.

Roper-Hall, A. (1993) Developing family therapy services with older adults. In Carpenter, J. and Treacher, A. (eds) *Using Family Therapy in the 90s*. Oxford: Blackwell.

Selvini Palazzoli, M., Boscolo, L., Cecchin, G. and Prata, G. (1980) Hypothesizing, circularity, neutrality: three guidelines for the conductor of the session. *Family Process* **19**:3–12.

Stroebe, M. (1992/3) Coping with bereavement: a review of the grief work hypothesis. *Omega, Journal of Death and Dying*. **26**:19–42.

Tomm, K. (1987) Interventive interviewing: Part II: Reflexive questioning as a means to enable self healing. *Family Process* **26**:167–83.

Walsh, F. (1991) Some personal reflections on loss. In Walsh, F. and McGoldrick, M. (eds) *Living Beyond Loss. Death in the Family*. New York: W.W. Norton.

Watzlawick, P., Weakland, J. and Fisch, R. (1974) *Change: Principles of Problem Formation and Problem Resolution*. New York: W.W. Norton.

White, M. (1988) Saying hullo again: the incorporation of the lost relationship in the resolution of grief. *Dulwich Centre Newsletter*, Spring.

White, M. (1988/9) The externalizing of the problem and the re-authoring of lives and relationships. *Dulwich Centre Newsletter*, Summer.

White, M. and Epston, D. (1990) *Narrative Means to Therapeutic Ends*. New York: W.W. Norton. Originally published as: White, M. and Epston, D. (1989) *Literate Means to Therapeutic Ends*. Dulwich Centre Publications.

Wynne, L.C. (1971) Some guidelines for exploratory conjoint family therapy. In Hayley, J. (ed) *Changing Families: A Family Therapy Reader*. New York: Grune & Stratton.

Further reading

Jones, M. (1988) *Secret Flowers*. London: Women's Press.

Sarton, M. (1973) *As We Are Now*. London: Women's Press.

Sarton, M. (1978) *A Reckoning*. London: Women's Press.

Sarton, M. (1988) *After the Stroke: A Journal*. London: Women's Press.

Index